TANDEM

Rage of Battle

This diary of a young soldier of sixteen in the
bitter cruelty of the Great War on the Western
Front is a chronicle of almost unbelievable
bravery and heroism mixed with anguish and
despair.

His diary covers only six months of that world-
shattering holocaust during which time he came
to know the full ruthlessness, horror and
brutality of war. Gripped by the almost daily
savagery of hand-to-hand fighting, he became
obsessed with the blood-lust of a dedicated killer
whose life was filled only with the moans of
dying men, the seemingly endless scream and
crash of the shells, the engulfing mud and
excrement of the battlefields, and the sickening
smell of poison gas.

This account proves that no one could have
survived unaffected by the experience of that
period of destruction from which the world has
never recovered, and from which mankind can
never be redeemed.

Rage of Battle

T. S. Hope

TANDEM
14 Gloucester Road, London SW7

First published in Great Britain by Putnam & Co. Ltd, as
The Winding Road Unfolds

Tandem edition 1965
Reprinted by Universal-Tandem Publishing Co. Ltd, 1972,
as *Rage of Battle*

Copyright © T. S. Hope

To
the volunteers
under military age
of all the
belligerent countries
who served
1914–1918

Made and printed in Great Britain by
Hunt Barnard Printing Ltd, Aylesbury, Bucks.

CONTENTS

FOREWORD

THE. lines in italics at the beginning of each chapter are copied from the diary that I kept in France in 1917.

It was written under peculiar circumstances in peculiar places on scraps of paper, or on anything that would take writing. During periods of rest out of the trenches and in hospital I wrote up these brief notes into the story practically as it now appears.

On account of military regulations, occasional gaps in the story were unavoidable, and these I have had to fill from memory, but I have tried not to introduce anything I did not think and feel at the time.

In the slight editing that has been necessary for publication I have altered most of the surnames, including my own; otherwise I have adhered strictly to facts. People tell me that some of the sentiments expressed are not those of a boy of sixteen, but I have not changed anything, because I know and believe that what I have written is correct.

T. S. H.

Edinburgh.
 January 1937.

Chapter One

YPRES

July 20th, 1917, Ypres. *Arrived at Ypres, the Mecca of all good soldiers.*

July 22nd, Ypres. *Still at the ramparts, Ypres, and thoroughly enjoying myself. Lucky to be with Mac and the boys. It's all so exciting. An Australian division next door to us.*

July 30th, Ypres. *Potidjhe dug-out. To-morrow is the "great day." Feeling fine and looking forward to going over.*

Weather very hot.

From the rear of the transport lorry the long winding road unfolds itself like a mysterious grey ribbon, revealing to my excited gaze the whole cavalcade of war. I am as happy as a schoolboy at his first picnic, revelling in this new life of guns, limbers, ammunition columns, parties of infantry, all going the same way—"up to the front."

For the last three nights I have watched this procession start at dusk, heard its rumble all through the hours of darkness, and at dawn have crept out of my bivouac tent and have seen the stragglers disappearing in the morning mist that enveloped the road.

And now I am one of them. The day for which I have waited so long has arrived. To-night I go up the line.

The lorry jolts its way over the uneven road, past shattered farm-houses and through the rubble heap of a one-time village, until we are in the area of gun-pits and shelling. Working parties, limbers and ammunition columns become more numerous. The activities of night at the front converge on this thoroughfare as darkness casts its mask over the eyes of the Boche across the way. The first Verey lights soar up into the sky as our lorry comes to a standstill and the driver informs us: "Get off here, boys, this is as far as we go."

We stumble out with our equipment and stand at the side of the road. There are twenty of us, but to me they are all strangers, mostly men who have been in the back areas undergoing special courses of training. Nobody pays any attention to me, and with many "Good lucks" and "Cheerios" they pair themselves off and disappear into the dusk. I have forgotten the map reading and the position name of the headquarters I was told to report to. I don't even know where I am or in which direction to go, so wander off the road a little as everybody else seems to have done and try to puzzle things out. Gun flashes seem to be everywhere, yet I am surprised at the loneliness of it, and begin to wonder if I'll stray into the Boche lines. If I do, I'll give them something to remember me by, so run my foolish thoughts. I stand and look around me and am exhilarated by the unfamiliar sounds and smells. It is all so very new and exciting.

Behind me lies the life of ordered things, comfort, security, peace and the hundred and one things that constitute the life I know. Before me—darkness, with gun flashes to right and left, and smaller flashes away in front in the Boche lines, the strange noise of shells going over my head like a canister of boiling water hurtling through space, and the heavy crump of bursting shells near at hand, a semicircle of sickly green Verey lights as far as the eye can see, and darkness—mostly darkness.

Ahead is the unknown—danger, hardship, wounds, perhaps death, but these possibilities leave me unmoved. I can only think of heroics, of battles won, of returning heroes, glorious deeds already enacted perhaps on this very ground, the newspaper war I have read so much about. What if I had missed all this, if I had been born too late; but why worry, I am here, proud and glad to be here, and that is all that really matters. This is my great adventure.

I find my way across some sort of canal with the aid of a rickety foot-bridge, and it is only then that I perceive any visible sign of life. The steep bank is honeycombed with dug-outs, and each entrance has its group of khaki. I walk along a planked pathway with a wooden railing on the canal side. The railing holds my interest; why, I can't tell, unless I think it is so unusual for the army to pay attention to these details. Without it I notice how simple it would be to slip down the bank and into the canal. Still, I am surprised at the army worrying about a drowned soldier or two, at least to the extent of putting up a railing to prevent it. I live and learn.

By dint of asking every few yards if anybody can tell me where the King's Liverpools are, I eventually come across one fellow who thinks they are out in reserve and billeted in the ramparts near the Menin Gate. Every twenty-four steps I make another enquiry until it seems the odds are ten to one that they actually are in the ramparts. There is a sort of sympathetic look in these fellows' eyes, which I can't understand, as they eye me up when I mention the word "ramparts," just as if I had borrowed a bottle of poison from them, then asked the way to the mortuary. I seriously begin to wonder what the word "ramparts" means. To my knowledge it is an old fortification or earth-work which our great-great-grandfathers built round their cities to keep the wild men out, but there is nothing in that to worry anyone. However, I'll enquire again.

"Yes, they're in the ramparts, mate, straight ahead, but I'd ditch it for a minute or two, Jerry has a barrage down."

H'm, here's something else I'm up against. "Ditch it"— now what the devil does that mean?—and "barrage." I've heard that word before, something to do with artillery if I remember right, but what, exactly, I don't know. One thing seems certain, I've got to get to the ramparts before I can find that battalion of mine, so it's straight ahead and the ramparts for me.

Eventually I come to the end of the planked path and go down a sloping embankment. The canal seems to disappear here, or perhaps it is just too dark to see it, then through some tangled undergrowth, while all the time that peculiar whistle of shells goes on overhead, and I seem to be walking in the direction of a terrific din of some kind.

Hello, here's a house of some kind, not much of one though; there's only half a gable wall left. There seems to be somebody moving about beside it. There he is shouting through a megaphone. I stop to listen, wondering if he is shouting to me, and, without any warning, there appears a long low flash and the sound of a report. I almost jump out of my boots with fright, then three other flashes and reports, the last one only about ten yards away. Well, that gave me a start—a battery of guns and I almost walked into them. One has to be careful here, I can see. There's no "Keep off the grass" signs in these quarters, so I make to skirt round the back of them and become entangled in some telephone wires, then I'm no sooner clear of them than I slip into a shell-hole with a foot of smelly water at the bottom. Up I scramble and run right into a pile of empty shell cases, several of which come clattering down at my feet and somebody wants to know:

"Who the hell's that mucking about?" but I don't wait to enlighten him. No, I'm getting a little fed up with this dozing around in the dark, and am overjoyed when the next fellow I ask tells me I'm at the beginning of the ramparts and my battalion headquarters are just along the road.

Ten minutes later I have reported and am waiting outside a dug-out for a runner to take me to the company. A sergeant emerges from behind the blanket which flaps at the dug-out entrance, followed by another figure, the runner, I suppose.

"Here you are!" he tells the second figure. "Take this fellow to A Company, Sergeant Wintrop's platoon."

Then to me: "Report at the company's office in the morning."

The runner approaches:

"Come on, soldier, we don't hang around here, it ain't healthy."

"Streaky," I find myself shouting.

"Well, strike me 'andsome if it ain't Jock. Put it there, old dog's body; come on, the boys are over here. We've had your bunk fixed up since yesterday; we knew you were coming."

We go about a hundred yards further up the road, Streaky talking thirteen to the dozen, then he stops and lifts a blanket similar to the one at the dug-out entrance we have just left, and I follow him into a dark narrow passage, where we turn left then pass some cubicles well lighted and packed with troops. At one of these Streaky halts and shouts :

"Gentlemen, the King," and pushes me forward. Somebody yells "Jock," and my back is thumped, my hand shaken, and enquiries hurled at me from half a dozen different sources. It is a full hour before I have satisfied their hunger for information, and another hour before I have appeased my own, then when it is all over I climb up on my bunk and take stock.

Well, here I am with the crowd at last, all those who left Blighty three months before I did, and those of my own draft who left me at Division when there was that hitch about my age. We are all together again : Mac, Webby, Streaky, Ginger and a host of others. This is the life, and to think I am actually at the front at last.

A louder explosion than usual, just above our heads, makes the whole place tremble, and Mac looks up from his game of cards :

"It's all right, Jock, we are as safe as the Bank of England down here, tons of earth above us, direct hits don't count."

"I'm not worrying," I make haste to reply. I mustn't let them think I'm afraid, and to be honest with myself, I'm not.

An Australian pops his head into the cubicle and enquires :

"How's the light, boys, that was a direct hit up above."

"Fine, Digger," Webster shouts back. "You're a great electrician, and when this bloody war is over, I'll get you to fix up the old ancestral home, all of it, both rooms."

I look up at the light and am mildly surprised to see it is an electric globe. I hadn't noticed it before. Fancy, electric light in a dug-out at the front. Gee, this is fun.

The game of cards comes to an end and the others depart, leaving six of us in the cubicle. The wire-netting bunks are arranged in tiers of three on either side, leaving a space of about eighteen inches up the centre. My bunk is at the top of one tier and Mac is my opposite number. We smoke and talk for a bit, then get down to sleep, while the faint crashing of explosives goes on above incessantly.

I must have fallen asleep almost immediately for I remember nothing more until I am awakened by the most unearthly racket, like somebody hammering away at a metal canister. The others are awake too, and I notice the light burns all day and night here.

"Get your gas-helmet on, Jock," Mac yells across at me, and someone else comes along the corridor shouting into each cubicle: "Gas, stand to."

I know exactly where my gas-helmet is; I placed everything handy last night, and in a couple of seconds it is on. The others, I see, are putting on their equipment, so I do likewise. Rather a difficult job to manage from a sitting position, but after a little twisting and turning I get the last buckle fixed. Just as well we sleep fully clothed if this happens every night.

Half an hour goes by and we are just attempting a game of cards, when the "all clear" is given, and the order comes along to "stand down." Thankfully I pull off my gas-mask. It was becoming a little uncomfortable. I certainly shouldn't care to fight in that contraption. We strip off our equipment again, hauling it up with us into the bunks, and try to finish our disturbed sleep.

I can just remember thinking how exciting this war is going to be and wondering if we'll be called out of bed to make a bayonet charge or something, when another call comes along the corridor:

"Breakfast up, A Company."

Well, that's my first night at the front, and I've slept like a log. I'm thoroughly enjoying it.

A whole week now since I arrived at the ramparts, and what a week it has been, shelling day and night, never silent, hustle and bustle all the time. I'm told I'm unfortunate because I've just arrived in time for the offensive, but I think I have the devil's luck. I wouldn't be out of it for anything.

I've had to learn an entirely new set of rules, too. All those things we were taught back home in Blighty go by the board out here. I'm afraid the training manual is sadly out of date.

We are supposed to be in reserve at present, resting for the show which commences some time within the next three days, but we work harder than the fellows in the actual front line. Fatigue parties, carrying parties and working parties, it's work the whole time, and, so far, I haven't fired a shot and only saw the actual front line to-day for the first time when I went up with Mac and Webby with some acid accumulators to a wireless station which will be in the front line when we go over.

Webby shows to good advantage here. He is a regular soldier, and although only twenty years old, was out at the very beginning, and has already been wounded twice. He knows all there is to know about war, and has many quaint sayings, two of his favourites being: "If you hear a shell there's nothing to worry about, it's the one you don't hear that causes the trouble." The other:

"A gun never drops a shell on the same spot twice, so the safest place is a shell-hole." All very true, as I am slowly finding out. He has taught me more of actual value in a week than a training manual could in a lifetime.

The front line in this sector is only a breastwork of sand-bags. You touch water, I believe, at two feet, so trenches are out of the question. When in the firing line I had the strongest desire to have a look over the parapet and see what was beyond. Just one peep would have satisfied me, but I've heard too many tales of fellows who took just one peep, so I kept my head well down, and I'm still alive.

We had a bit of a rush to get back before Jerry started his tea-time hate, but barely managed it and got caught by the first few salvos. Mustard-gas shells, Webster says; something new, evidently. When the shell bursts it spews a gas that burns, not an acid that eats away, but a gas that blisters the skin and causes swellings. I suppose the same would happen to your innards if you breathed it. Oh, it's a great war, but I'm not bothered.

Tea tasted good after the excitement of our rush, and now we are standing at the dug-out entrance. There's a daylight raid taking place to-night; a whole battalion is going over to hold Jerry's front line for an hour, then they are coming back. What the idea is I don't know, but it will certainly put the wind up the Boche. We wait for the bar-rage. Only a few more seconds to go and Mac counts them off. Crash, dead on time, it drops like a thunderbolt. I've never heard anything like it before. Just one continuous rumble. The sound and the very thought of what is taking place makes my skin tingle. This is a thrill.

Just think of it, a Saturday night; at home the streets will be crowded, people going to the theatre or pictures, others out for a stroll, everybody happy and carefree out to enjoy themselves, and we here, huddled at a dug-out entrance, listening to the screeching of innumerable shells flying overhead and bursting in a continual rumble on the Jerry trenches beyond. Shells keep dropping amongst the ruins facing us. They have a peculiar sound of their own. I think it must be the echoes among the ruins that make it so different to a burst in the open.

One of our crowd comes back from the signal office with the news that the boys are over all right with very few casualties. That sounds good to my ears, but some of the older ones, Webster among them, seem more anxious about the coming back.

I can hear Webby telling somebody:

"If he gets a machine-gun on them coming back, it's domino; that's the worst of these daylight raids."

The hour slips by quickly and the barrage fire fades away. We hang about the signal office for news, but it's a long time in coming. At last a signaller pops his head out of the dug-out and shouts:

"Raid a complete success, fifty casualties."

"Success my bloody backside," Webster replies.

The signaller's head pops out again:

"And here's another bit of good news for you, my hearties: we take over from the front-line battalion to-morrow night. You know what that means, so put it in your tea and stir it." With a big guffaw his head disappears into the darkness of the dug-out.

I repeat under my breath: "To-morrow night." That means the following morning we go over. Well, what about it, I'm ready.

Zero day has come and gone and I have lived a hundred years.

Four short days ago I was a youngster with all the ideals of youth, looking upon war as a glorious adventure and revelling in the part I was playing, but now I have changed, everything seems different. I doubt if life can ever be the same.

The one-time omnibus sways and jolts over the uneven ground as it carries away from the line what is left of our platoon. Where we are going, or what is to happen to us next, I know not and care less. It is sufficient that we are leaving that hell behind.

The lurching of the bus doesn't induce slumber, but my weary, sleep-starved body has become attuned to physical discomfort, and I doze fitfully until a more severe jolt knocks me off my balance, and I bang my head against a wood support. After that sleep evades me and I linger at the half-way stage, my thoughts returning to the scenes of the last four days, and try as I might to banish them, I cannot. They are all too fresh in my memory. Everything is so vivid I might be living those hours over once more.

I am back again in the shell-hole, fascinated by the glassy staring eyes of Rice who had been wounded in the stomach. His continual groaning got on my nerves, and I thought how childish and weak he was, making such a fuss over a little puncture in his belly. In my ignorance I didn't realise how painful and serious that little puncture was. The two dead Jerries we placed on the lip of the crater to provide better cover for ourselves and the interest I took in watching the bullets smack into their already lifeless bodies until a spot of cold blood from one of them splashed on my face. The terrific din and the terrifying vibrations of the earth caused by bursting shells; the vicious hiss of shrapnel and the phit-phit of bullets passing by my ears; the peculiar stumblings of wounded men and their curses; the clods of earth that thumped down on me and rattled against my steel helmet; the gaping wounds and the blood.

Later on, the artillery coming forward, and the use they put those dead bodies to, forming a road over that marshy piece of ground. They said it was the nerves that made those limbs twitch underneath the horses' hoofs and the gun wheels; they were quite dead—I wonder!

Then our next advance and that bloody mess of Ginger's arm with its inside folding out, looking for all the world like a piece of raw steak, his hot blood running over my hands as I tried to fix on a dressing, and the parting wave he gave me with his sound arm just before the shell got him; his leg which fell so near to me, stripped of all its covering and looking like a lump of pork, the flesh was so white.

That stretch of uncut wire and the fellows who were caught on it. Will I ever forget their struggles to free themselves as the Boche machine-guns pumped bullets into them, the curious jerks of their limbs as the bullets smacked home? I can see it all now like a ghastly panorama.
. The first Jerry I almost ran into and the way we tried to avoid each other, then the one I met so suddenly as I rounded the traverse in the trench, that second of panic when I almost turned tail and made a bolt for it, the vicious lunge he made at me with his bayonet, and the bullet from Mac's rifle which whistled past my side, just in time.

All these things are coming vividly to my mind and keeping me awake, when all I want is sleep and forgetfulness. Try as I may I cannot get rid of them or the feelings they awoke within me.

I can recall clearly the change that came over me as I watched the man Mac's bullet had stopped sink slowly down at my feet, while a queer croaking sound came from his throat. All fear seemed to leave me, and in its place came an overwhelming feeling of vindictiveness. This man had tried to kill me; so be it; I would kill too. I gripped my rifle more firmly and strode on.

The rest is a little hazy, but I can still see the clutching of those fingers as they grasped the bayonet I strove to withdraw from the sucking flesh. Whether he was young or old I'll never know, short or tall, fair or dark, I didn't notice, everything else was blotted out by those clutching fingers.

I am not surprised that I begin to wonder if I actually did take part in these things, or if it is just a trick of my memory; but no, they are all too vivid for that. No trick of memory could recall so clearly those clutching well-kept fingers, so lean and tapering; more the hands of a student than a soldier, nor the outlined details of that head battered in by a rifle butt, the look of agony and despair in those eyes, the viciousness of it all. No, there is no trick of memory, they are the ghosts of fellow creatures who will be with me in moments such as these for the rest of my days.

Chapter Two

OUT ON REST

August 5th, 1917, POMMERN REDOUBT, YPRES. *Relieved at last. I know now what war really means. Discovered I'm lousy.*

August 7th, AUDRICQUE. *Billeted in a barn at a farm-house a few miles from Audricque and near Calais. Golden days these but already dreading going back to the line.*

August 9th, THE BARN, AUDRICQUE. *Had an exciting eel hunt yesterday. Stewed apples and eels for tea—glorious. Put in a disturbing night afterwards.*

THE war seems very far away now. We could be supremely happy if only we didn't know that this is merely a respite, that some day, perhaps a week, perhaps a fortnight hence, we shall have to return to it. But let to-morrow look after itself, to-day we live, yes, every second of our lives.

The filth of the trenches has disappeared from our uniforms; we are once again the amateur soldiers of our training days.

We stroll along the quiet country lanes, or lie in the fields, bareheaded, tunics open at the neck, the blue sky above us, the scent of clean earth and the hundred other perfumes of a countryside playing havoc with our senses, the droning of bees, the song of birds, welcome lullabies to our weary nerves.

Golden days these. We had almost forgotten such peace existed.

We are billeted at the usual French farm with the usual full-sized midden occupying the whole of the farm-yard. During the day it is the pigs' paradise, and at night it becomes the happy hunting-ground for the numerous farm rats. On both sides are byres and pigsties, while at one end is the farm-house in which the sergeants are billeted, and at the other end—the direction the wind always seems to blow—our barn.

It is roomy, however, and boasts an abundance of clean

straw, and at night, with our cigarettes and pipes aglow, we enjoy our sing-songs and discussions.

Amongst those in our company Webster and Mac are my closest friends. Webster is an old "sweat," and has all an old soldier's virtues with few of his vices. His vocabulary is two-thirds cuss-words, but there is something so peculiarly humorous in the way he curses that nobody could take offence. He always greets one in the morning with a cheery: "Well, how the bloody hell are you?" No matter to Webster whether the sun is shining or whether it is raining like blazes, it is always—"A hell of a bloody fine day." He is the finest pal a man could have out here. I shouldn't fancy him as an enemy. A great lover of animals, he has an utter disregard for human life and boasts he has never taken a prisoner. Possesses a wonderful eye for the ladies, and an unfailing nose for grub and cushy jobs.

A peculiar cuss, but I like him, full of trench philosophy; he has taught me all I know of the things that count out here, the little things that mean all the difference between life and death.

Mac is a countryman of mine and nineteen years old. We are very clannish and almost inseparable.

The other fellows hardly understand us. We are Scots, yet we never get drunk and actually fortify Webster with our ration of rum. To them, a Scot who prefers water to spirits is a curio, but then, they have never visited Scotland. Mac, however, saves our nationality with a shock of red hair and a photo of himself in kilt and sporran complete, even to a dirk stuck in his hose. The dirk is most essential, and is to our English comrades the hall-mark of a wild uncivilised Highlander.

Mac has the broadest shoulders I have ever seen on a man and is the strongest in our company and, despite a temper as fiery as his hair, he is a great favourite. Before the war he was apprenticed to his father, a butcher, and is our master of ceremonies when we go for a scrounge round any of the neighbouring farms.

Naylor was a schoolteacher before he came out here and receives letters addressed to Private Naylor, M.A. He is a bit of an idealist and doesn't take kindly to the filth of the trenches. To make matters worse he is a battalion scout and spends many a miserable night crawling on his belly in no-man's-land.

Bacon is a Cockney and as chirpy as a sparrow. We call him "Streaky." At one time he sold vegetables from a barrow, and swears he only joined the army to get a decent suit to walk out in with his girl. Common clay is Streaky, but he has a ready tongue and a cheery smile.

The father of our company is Bellchamber. He is almost old enough to be my grandfather. He enlisted after his son was killed and knocked a dozen years off his age to accomplish it. He is a quiet man; one never knows what he is thinking.

Erskine is our pigeon-man. He takes the carrier pigeons up the line and sends them off with messages. In our last attack he disappeared and only turned up in time to be relieved. He is a bit of a mystery. Nobody knows what he was before the war. For a nickname we call him "Bumskin."

Taffy, a Welshman, is the brother of a bishop and is waiting for a commission. He is religiously inclined and sincere in his beliefs, and although at first we all stood in awe of him, we rather like him now, and at times I believe his sermons do us good. He never joins us in our smutty songs and never swears, but he is no spoil-sport.

The remainder are mostly recruits who came up with the last draft six weeks ago.

And myself, small but sturdy, I joined the army a few months after leaving school and am now sixteen years of age. Officially, I am nineteen and resent any reference to my youth. Like Mac I am a Scot and proud of it.

We provide a queer mixture of opposites, but we have one thing in common, we are all volunteers. Men who thought war a glorious adventure, but have learned otherwise only too late, men who would now give everything they possess to get out of it honestly and honourably. We all believe this war was thrust on us, it was inevitable and had to come. It came in our time, and we have taken on the job, so there is nothing else for it but to see the thing through. We all have a feeling that this is a war to end war; how can it be otherwise? For all times, war has been stripped of its false glory and revealed as something foul and obscene, bestial and uncivilised. Surely there must be some other means of settling disputes in the future. But the future means little to us; we are here, and no matter how eager we may be to get away from it, deep down in our hearts is a feeling of pride that when the call came we answered it.

When we are true to ourselves these are our thoughts, and yet at other times we call ourselves a lot of damned fools for allowing ourselves to be eyewashed into it. Let those fight who like it; for us, a cosy corner by a fireside.

Bumskin is due for leave, and, although his train doesn't start for another six hours, he is ready for the eight-mile tramp to the railhead. His excuse, that he is determined to be up to time for once in his life, we ignore. The chance of an enquiry into his mysterious disappearance last time up the line prompts him to "get" while the getting is good, only he hasn't got the guts to say so.

"You'll have hours to wait if you make a start now, Bumskin," I remark.

"Hell, and what about it," he snaps back. "I've waited fourteen months for this day, so a few hours at the station won't hurt me. What do you say, Webster?"

"Quite right, sonny, a man who is late for his leave train ought to be shot at sight. Damn it, but you're some soldier, shoes and buttons polished, not a spot of Flanders mud for a souvenir, just shining like a shilling on a darkey's behind. Ye Gods, won't the girls stare! What do you think of him, Mac?"

"Och, no so bad," Mac replies with just a touch of sarcasm in his voice, "I've seen worse growing out of a cow's platter." "And I've stuck my foot in better," Streaky joins in, "but just to show you there's no ill feeling, Bumskin, I'll give you a wrinkle. Let's see your toaster." Drawing Bumskin's bayonet, Streaky shoves it into a great lump of beef that our cook has got hold of. He twists it round and round until it is nice and bloody with little bits of flesh sticking to it, and hands it back.

"There you are, now. When you're spinning the yarn to-morrow night just show them that and tell them all about the Great War, and if it doesn't fetch free drinks every time, I'll eat my tin hat. And by the way, got any spare fags," he enquires meaningly.

The idea of our gallant, disappearing pigeon-man displaying his bloody bayonet, and describing to an interested audience how he bayoneted a dozen or two Jerries single-handed, brings forth howls of derisive laughter.

Realising we are pulling his leg, Bumskin snaps his bayonet into its scabbard and starts off down the road.

"Remember me to Blighty," come half a dozen different voices. "Thank your mother for the *Christian Herald*," Streaky shouts. But Bumskin is already almost out of hearing, padding it along the road to the railhead, before him fourteen glorious days of peace and comfort.

We lounge about the farm-yard, all a little homesick, I think. It is not felt so badly when a fellow goes on leave from the trenches. We envy him; he is a lucky blighter, and when he disappears down the communication trench, he is gone; other things take up our attention. Out here on rest it is different. We have nothing to do but think.

Mac is the first to break the silence:

"Well, Bumskin is damned lucky getting away so quietly. He'll be for it all right when he gets back."

"Oh, he isn't such a bad sort," Webster replies. "Got a bit windy about his leave and made sure he was alive to go. Others have done the same, only he was unlucky and got nabbed dodging the column; that's his funeral. Let's do something, I'm fed up moping about this midden heap."

"Yes, come on, what about that bathe we promised ourselves twelve months ago. Just the idea," Streaky suggests. Accordingly we all troop down to a little stream we have discovered in a field at the back of our barn. It emerges from an orchard, through an archway, covered with netting, in the wall. The netting catches all the dirt and dead leaves coming from the orchard. It is a lovely bathing spot. The water is only five feet at the deepest part in the centre and as clear as crystal, while at the sides near the bank it is barely a foot in depth. We wouldn't swop it for all the tiled and gilded baths in the world.

Soon we are stripped, and with our shoulders propped up against the bank and a hollow scooped out for our rear position, we sit for hours in its cool, clear embrace. Occasionally we have a swim or come out for a sunning on the bank. This occasions shrill cries and laughter from the farm girls on the other side of the field, who keep one eye on us and the other on their hay-making.

Mac and I are by ourselves lying stripped on the bank, engaged in the all-important though hopeless job of trying to delouse ourselves. An engrossing task this, but I have a method all my own for dealing with these friendly little fellows. With my two thumb-nails as a mopping-up party I kill everything I can find on my shirt that crawls, then with the lighted stub of a candle I make a perfect creeping barrage up the seams, putting a special box barrage on the nest of eggs out in the open. At first I spoilt two good shirts this way, through holding them too near the flame, but I am an expert at it now and seldom leave a scorch mark.

"I wonder where all these blighters come from Mac?" I enquire.

"Ask me another. Who put the lavatory seat up, in the nunnery? Answer that one, Jock, and you've solved the whole mystery."

"The blasted things do keep on turning up though, here's a bounder I could swear I sent west a week ago. I could tell him anywhere by these grey stripes on his back."

"Here's a fellow," I reply—crack, as my thumb-nails close on him; "by the colour of him he must be a week old at least, and I thought I had cleaned the whole damn' family out two days ago. Ah well, I think I'll about do now, Mac, we'd better get back into the water, those females are gradually getting nearer."

"What's Webster making all the noise about up there?" I enquire; then noticing my braces in the water I jump in and endeavour to catch them as they glide downstream. I just manage to grasp the end of them, but they are slimy and slip through my fingers. The braces seem to come to life and dart, wriggling, down the stream. I can only gasp and stare.

"Your braces are on your pants," Mac shouts.

"Well, hell knows what that was, I don't," I reply. "It was the biggest worm I have ever seen. Did you notice it, Mac?"

"Not me," Mac answers. "Sure it wasn't a louse?"

The commotion further up has increased. Webster and Streaky come splashing down the stream. Naylor with only his socks on is running down the bank alongside Taffy clad in his shirt. "Eels," shouts Webster, "did you see them? They came down this way, two whoppers, they'll make a bloody fine feed."

"A feed," Mac roars. "Jock thought they were his braces."

"Braces, be damned," chimes in Streaky, "let's get after them."

Off we all go, Mac and I following Webster and Streaky down the stream, while Taffy and Naylor run on in front along the bank.

The girls in the field are roaring with laughter, but we hardly notice them. I get as excited as the others. The spirit of the chase has taken hold of me, or, is it just the lust to kill? Strange how that often crops up in me now. Under a bridge we go, yelling and splashing, over a road and past some houses.

"Here they are," yells Naylor, jumping into the stream. "Head them back," commands Streaky.

"Hit them over the bloody head," directs Webster.

I break a branch off a tree and join in the mêlée. The eels are darting in and out amongst our feet and it is difficult to get in a telling blow despite Webster's repeated instructions to hit them over the bloody head.

"That's my behind," I hear Mac shouting, as somebody else clouts me on the leg.

At last we've got them. They are still wriggling, but Streaky, who seems to know all about them, says that it is only their nerves; they are quite dead.

"Beauties, aren't they?" he remarks. "Three feet if they're an inch. We'll have the tea of our lives to-night, boys."

I don't exactly fancy the look of them, and tell him so, but perhaps, as Streaky tells me, that's because I don't know a good feed when I see it.

"Anybody got a knife?" someone enquires. Instinctively our hands go to where our pockets should be. We have all forgotten we are in our birthday suits with only a shirt and a pair of socks amongst us.

Our hullabaloo seems to have brought all the youngsters in the neighbourhood around us; they are enjoying the fun. We try to chase them away by splashing water on them, but to no purpose. Taffy makes a gallant attempt, but the sight of him chasing a crowd of French kids with his shirt-tails flying in the air, only makes matters worse, and we are convulsed with laughter.

The noise and the yells of the children have brought the women out of the houses. They stand at their doors jabbering and gesticulating. There is nothing else for it but to try and slip past them, so, bent almost double, we wade up the shallow stream towards the houses.

The youngsters have by this time returned, and as retaliation for Taffy's assault on them, commence pelting us with stones and anything else they can lay their hands on. The women, now thoroughly excited, come over to the side of the stream and stand roaring with laughter at our sorry plight.

I hear Webster saying: "To hell with this. I'll spoil their sport." Making one dash he is up on the bank and into the middle of the road. The women turn and with shrill screams make towards the houses, but seeing he means no harm, the more immodest stand by their doors pointing and laughing at him.

The trick has worked, however, and allowed the rest of us to go splashing past the houses, but we still have the road to cross further up where the stream passes through a culvert. As we emerge from the cover of the banks, the girls in the field take to their heels, stop, then return and chase us across the road and field with the handles of their hay-forks. One Amazon endeavours frantically to tear the shirt off Taffy, who is doing his best to hold both tails together in front of him with one hand and beat off his tormentor with the other.

At last we have reached the safety of the barn, breathless, but still in possession of the eels, and determined in future to do all our eel-hunting fully clothed.

Tea over, and I've quite decided that eels, as Streaky foretold, make a splendid feed. I am not sure whether they are the nicest fish I have ever tasted, or whether it is the lack of fish in our diet which made us relish them so much. Our cook excelled himself and fried them to perfection.

Real bread arrived with the rations by way of a change from army biscuits, and Mac and I paid an informal visit to the orchard.

What a tea : fried eel and bread with stewed apples to follow ! "Napoleon once said an army marches on its stomach," mumbles Streaky, "but I'm damned if I could crawl on mine. Oh, why did I take that fourth lot of apples?"

One by one we are awakened from our over-fed slothfulness and rush, unbuttoning our pants, to the rear. What a feed, but oh, what a night !

We have all decided that fried eels and stewed apples, however nice, are not good for a fellow's peace of mind.

Chapter Three

SHELL FIRE

August 10th, 1917, HAZEBROUCK. Entrained this morning for the front again. Making towards Poperinghe. In an awful funk at going back to that part of the line.

WE are *en route* for the front. What has happened nobody seems to know, but we all have a feeling there must be something wrong, otherwise they wouldn't send us back without our replacements and only a third of our strength.

All those rumours too which we had so willingly believed about being out for a month's rest, and here we are, after four days, once again nearing the front.

The long train rumbles slowly on. With the doors of the cattle trucks wide open we try to get a little air into our cramped stuffy quarters. Some pass the time playing cards, others sit at the doors dangling their legs and carrying on conversations with the civilians in the fields and villages through which we pass. Every level crossing is lined with country women and children who clamour excitedly for "bisceet" and "bullee beef." I am mildly surprised at the eager greedy way they snatch and scramble for the army biscuits we so carelessly throw them.

The train never seems to get past the starting speed. Dozens of our fellows jump down and relieve themselves behind hedges, then race after the slowly disappearing train and regain their truck. We take it in turns to catch up with the engine and obtain hot water from the driver with which to make tea. As we pass an orchard we scramble down and fill our pockets with whatever we can lay our hands on. The sergeants and officers turn a blind eye to these little misdemeanours.

At last we glide into the goods yard of a large town. My heart sinks a little further as I recognise the station, Hazebrouck. We are going back to the same part of the line we left a few days ago. With a clanging and grinding of brakes we come to a stop, and instantly we are out and rummaging under the covers of the open wagons on either side. We are inveterate scroungers.

This our officers do not overlook, and with much taking of names and many threats, we are herded back to our trucks.

The rat-tat-tat of a machine-gun is suddenly heard, then another and another, until it sounds like a miniature war. An anti-aircraft gun joins in the chorus, and following the white puffs of its bursting shells, we notice several little dark specks high up in the heavens. There are heavy detonations as the bombs are dropped on the town, then the small specks turn and make for their own lines, and our train starts once again.

We pass the now familiar hop-fields, the same old ruined villages and come to a halt at the same well-shelled railhead. Out we tumble, form up in companies and march off down the well-known dusty grey Poperinghe-Ypres road, flanked on either side with poplars.

We try a song or two but fail rather dismally. This place holds too many recent memories for light-heartedness.

I already have that empty feeling in the pit of my stomach, my appetite has gone, and I know my bowels will refuse to function. It is always the same when I go up the line. The front has an atmosphere peculiarly its own. We sense it more acutely the nearer we approach. We cannot define it, but know it is there, all around, ready to engulf us. Strange how it affects fellows differently.

Webster as usual takes everything for granted. Only a few more adjectives slip unconsciously into his already wonderful vocabulary.

Mac becomes a little more fiery, while Streaky chatters away like an old sweetie wife.

Everywhere is bustle and noise. On either side of the road are camps and huge dumps, artillery parks and training grounds. The road itself is fairly clear of heavy traffic, but at dusk it will be one seething mass of activity.

Our leading company turns into a field already dotted with bivouac tents. Joy of joys; we are not going into the line to-night. I start to live again, another respite if only for a few hours.

As our platoon wheels into the camp we break into a popular ditty. For us the sun begins to shine once more.

Mac, Webster and I are at present attached to battalion headquarters as emergency signallers, and accordingly we get a billet in a Nissen hut. Not for us the hard ground and canvas bivouac of the common soldier. We have a palliasse, albeit of doubtful cleanliness, left by the former tenants, and an iron roof above our heads—we are on the staff. In our battalion it is an asset to know the value of when to be able to do a little signalling; it relieves the monotony, allows us to escape a few fatigues and working parties, not to mention the little luxuries one can pick up away from the herd. Just the natural perquisites of old soldiers who can draw a dividing line between what to know and what not to know.

Sergeants are wily customers to deal with when they are looking for men to do unpleasant jobs, and it takes all our cunning to nose out the false from the genuine. An admitted knowledge of signalling we have never regretted. Twice, however, have our instincts played us false, once when our sergeant asked for volunteers who knew something about gardening and put us on burying some dead whose planting was long overdue, and again when the same sergeant offered us a painting course and gave us the job of whitewashing latrine buckets when we should have been out on rest. I don't think he will catch us a third time.

As soon as we have dumped our kit, the sound of our regimental band playing popular musical-comedy airs draws us outside. The troops sit or sprawl in a circle round the band. It is a treat we older soldiers have come to associate with our last night before going into the line. We hum the familiar tunes which recall such happy memories and almost forget there is a to-morrow.

From far behind the enemy lines, and dominating the noises of even this part of the front, we hear a dull boom-m-m, then the faint shriek of a heavy shell, gradually getting louder and nearer, a hissing whistling menace; we can almost follow its course by the sound as it grows in volume. Nearer and nearer it comes, ending its flight like a thousand rushing shrieking devils. The earth spouts up in a field next to the camp followed by the crump of the explosion.

The band plays on.

One or two of the men rise and stroll over to some slender artillery dug-outs on our left, but the majority of us disdain such a precaution and lie more leisurely on the ground, our eyes on the band but our ears on the alert for that warning boom from over the Boche lines. A minute or two elapses and again we hear it. This time we sit up and strain our eyes as if we expected to see the missile. The hissing grows louder; we don't wait any longer but with one rush make for the nearest shelter. Cr-r-ump—clods of earth fall around us, but nobody is hurt. I look for the band and can only see their scattered instruments, tokens of the smartness of their discretion.

We lie low for a quarter of an hour but there is no more shelling, the enemy gunners seem to have knocked off for tea, and our bandsmen take the opportunity to recover their instruments. We greet them with howls and encores until our own tea, arriving on the scene, puts an end to our fun.

Tea we find is conspicuous by its absence. The field-kitchens have been lost *en route*; there is only bully beef and marmalade. However, there is plenty of that, and we all get a tin of each. Much to my surprise I find that beef and marmalade taken in alternate mouthfuls makes quite a pleasant and appetising meal, providing you haven't eaten for a matter of eighteen hours and there is nothing else to be had.

After tea the band major once again collects his followers and starts another programme.

Dusk is falling. I close my eyes and again I am sitting in the park at home listening to the band. The noises of the front are just the rumble of traffic outside the park gates. I am loath to come back into this world which has absorbed me. Slowly I open my eyes again, and am just settling myself more comfortably when the ominous boom-m-m I distinctly hear, or am I mistaken? No, Webster and Mac I can see are listening, others I notice are more alert-looking.

"It's coming," someone shouts. Instantly we are on our feet. The terrifying hurtling thing appears to be coming right into our midst.

"This way," shouts Webster, and we follow him in a rush for the nearest hut. We seem to be running right into it. The earth trembles as the shell buries itself behind us. We fall flat, there is a deafening explosion and we hug the earth more closely. There is the sound of falling debris, then another shriek as of an oncoming express followed by an explosion near the dug-outs. There is a queer silence, then :

"Stretcher bearers."

Somebody has got it.

We have had enough of band concerts for one night, so return to our hut and lie down.

"I don't mind a war," Streaky remarks, "but this bloody murder is getting my goat. After all, we were only listening to the band."

"Quite peaceable like," Mac chimes in. "It ain't playing the game. By the time the next band concert is due we'll be kicking up the daisies in some rest camp and making damned good manure for the Roses of Picardy that Taffy's always singing about."

"Talking about dung," Streaky interposes, "I'd give ten years of my life to get some of those gents, who started the war, up to their necks in a latrine and watch them duck each time I threw a brick at them."

"I wonder if they would duck?" enquires Mac.

"They'd duck all right. Hell, when I think of them sitting at home, with a comfortable bed to slip into at night, and a decent breakfast in the morning, ready to jump out of their shirts for a lousy air-raid, and us—living like sewer rats. Oh, they'd duck all right," continues Streaky. "They've nerve enough for anything. Why, the folks at home tell me the munition workers are coming out on strike; on strike, mark you, and a war on. It makes me wonder what would happen if we came out on strike."

At that moment our sergeant's head appears in the doorway.

"Parade in a quarter of an hour outside," he bawls; "battle order, we go up to-night. Get a move on now."

"Hell; yes," muses Streaky, "I wonder what would happen if we went on strike now. I reckon sergeant would have his pants full, boys, don't you?"

We are in reserve and have taken over our old front line near the Potidjhe Road. It is quite cushy.

I have such a dread of the actual front line that I feel I could almost stick the war if it was always like this.

An occasional shell bursts, but not near enough to become uncomfortable. Out in the open the Boche gunners are searching with shrapnel, but I have no uneasiness. Around us the guns from both sides are as noisy as ever, but then they are never silent in these parts, and I have known no other sector of the front.

Our trenches here are little more than sandbag breast-works, the country being too waterlogged to allow of deep digging. As it is, the rain has turned our shallow trenches into little streams and made of the surrounding country a sea of mud, pock-marked with shell-holes.

We are by now inured to these discomforts, and once the rain has ceased and we begin to feel the welcome warmth of the summer sun, we soon forget them.

An enemy aeroplane flies over our lines, and we flatten ourselves up against the spongy sides of the trench or disappear into the small funk-holes built in the breastwork. The plane passes over, turns in a wide circle and flies along our length of trench. We follow its flight and can distinctly make out the figures of the pilot and observer.

"What the hell are you fellows gazing at?" bellows a sergeant. "Do you want that perisher up aloft to spot your white-livered mugs? Get under cover, or we'll have every gun on the front potting at us."

We disappear like rats into our holes and listen to the drone of the engine as it returns again. They are evidently hunting for some target. There is a battery of field guns at our back; no doubt it is that. The sound of the engine gradually gets fainter, and we crawl out of our funk-holes as the whistle blows the "all clear" signal.

A shell bursting a few minutes later in front of our trench arouses our curiosity. We give a look to see where it has fallen, then promptly forget about it. Another comes over, this time a little nearer, then another whistles over and drops to the rear.

"Ranging," remarks Webser; "we'll be getting it in the neck shortly. I thought there was something fishy in the way that 'skylark' flew up and down this ditch."

We notice our officers and the sergeant-major comparing notes and anxiously scanning the newly-made shell-holes.

Webster gives me a wink. "Come on, Jock, get Mac, it's about time we were patrolling those signal lines." Then in an undertone :

"It's going to be hot here shortly."

As linesmen temporarily attached to the signallers it is our duty to patrol the lines occasionally, and to Webster this seems an opportune moment to make a start. I trust Webster implicitly in these matters as he knows all the ropes.

We look in at the signal office, an old shell-hole with a corrugated iron and sandbag roof, and report that we are going to patrol the line to battalion headquarters.

"Right-o; see if you can scrounge a candle when you are there, we've only two left."

"As good as done," replies Webster. "I'll——"

The rest is drowned by an explosion just at our backs. We crouch down and wait. There is another, more to our left, and then the storm breaks.

Every nerve in my body seems to be alert, and yet I lie

at the bottom of the trench unable to decide whether to move or stay.

The air is filled with the angry vicious hiss of approaching shells, and I am continually struck by falling bits of wood and iron. Something drops on my shoulder, a warm hand is against my cheek. I half turn my head and the arm slithers down at my feet, the fingers still twitching. The smell of high explosives is almost suffocating.

Suddenly I remember the iron roof of the signal office and make a rush for it, but the trench has collapsed, and I have to get out into the open. The earth spouts up at my very feet and I am flung into the air, then find myself lying on my side. A dozen missiles strike me. My neck feels as if someone had tried to break it—this is the end.

I am surprised that I can still move. There's no blood, yet I'm sure I am desperately wounded. My neck is painful and stiff and my helmet has disappeared. Strange that I can move all my limbs. It seems an age before I realise I have only been blown up and struck by bits of the upheaval.

An officer comes crouching along, looks at me with unseeing eyes, shouts to somebody in the trench to come out and lie in the open, then gives another look in my direction and moves on still shouting orders.

Figures pass me bent double, so I get up and follow, then flop down beside them in a shell-hole. We lie huddled together, clinging closer to the earth at every explosion. My eyes are staring straight in front of me. We have stumbled into a shambles.

The stench is nauseating. A disembowelled belly is within three inches of my nose, black and obscene-looking. It is covered with a mass of flies and blue-bottles that don't seem in the least disturbed by the bombardment. They buzz and buzz while they explore its filthy depths. The sight almost sickens me, yet I can't tear my eyes away. One great purple-green monster seems to fascinate me as he moves further and further into the black mass. With a shudder I force myself to look away, but all around are the same grim reminders. A foot sticking out here, an arm there; beyond that, and almost on the lip of the shell-hole, part of a back, grey and jelly-like with half a shirt still covering it. Then a head and shoulders, while lower down part of a limb is visible, and a strip of a familiar tartan kilt catches my eye. Unconsciously I glance at the numerals on the shoulder strap, then to the head. The face is black and fast decaying, giving an unreal and artificial look to the fair hair above it.

I find myself thinking: this is what I'll look like when my time comes, and shudder at the thought. I don't want to die, but oh, God, if I must, let me die whole and clean. Once I am buried, let me lie in peace.

My thoughts are interrupted by an explosion almost on top of us. Something comes stumbling and gibbering into the shell-hole and falls on top of me. I am too dazed even to curse. The gibbering comes to a stop. There is a strange gurgling sound, then silence. I ease the thing up; somebody gives me a hand to free myself from it. There is a great ragged bit of steel embedded in its chest; the blood is still spurting out.

"Got him all right," somebody remarks, and I recognise Webster's voice.

The bombardment shows no sign of abating. The place reeks with the smell of explosives, the noise is deafening.

Webster suggests we should shift into a newly-made shell-hole, but nobody makes a move. We are loath to leave what cover we have. It is too terrible out there; every minute we expect to be our last.

"Well, I'm going"—and Webster scrambles up and dashes for another hole. Like sheep we all follow, dreading to be left alone. Somebody stumbles, and we turn and drag him down into the bottom of our new hole. It is old Bellchamber. His side is shattered—an awful mess. The wound is too huge for our small field dressings. Luckily he has fainted and this makes our job easier. Tubes from his inside keep slipping out, and I shove them back with my fingers, but cannot get the bandages on before they are out again. In the end we have to turn him further over on his opposite side. We manage better, but just as we get the elusive tubes into their proper place, a shrapnel burst immediately above our shell-hole makes us cower down, and out the tubes slip. At last, with the use of a cardigan as a padding, we succeed and tie it round with our dressings. A poor job, but our best.

The shelling, though still as heavy, becomes more muffled, and we recognise the explosions of gas shells. In the distance we hear the gas alarms giving out their warnings. Haste means everything as already we get whiffs of the beastly stuff. It's like pine-apples, I always think. Strange that such a pleasant smell should be the accompaniment to such a hellish death.

I'm thankful I've no helmet, but expert as I am in the use of gas-masks I fumble with the straps and waste a precious second or two. I'm holding my breath now, but still I have difficulty in fixing the straps. At last I get them adjusted just as my lungs give out and I almost draw the mask down my throat. I haven't got the nose-clip or mouth-piece in position, but that's the work of a second. Now I'm right. I feel cut off from the world, merely a looker-on through a pair of round loopholes. The glasses are already steamed, the result of my first impulsive breath, but I can see through them all right and watch the others readjust-ing their helmets. I feel rather bare and unprotected with-out mine.

The sight of a white face in the midst of the weird row of masks draws my attention.

Bellchamber—God! we've forgotten him. I start rum-maging about amongst his equipment for the mask. Where the hell did we put it? Others realise what I'm after and give a hand. We find it and try to fix it on. There is no time for gentleness. The movement makes his wound bleed again, but the mask must go on. I am covered with his blood. I feel it soaking through my tunic. At first it is warm, then it becomes cold and sticky. We prop him up and try to stop the bleeding, more in the desire to do our best for a pal than in the hope of saving his life.

The enemy fire slackens a little, and cautiously we look over the lip of the hole. The fumes of explosives lie like a fog around us. Figures flit from shell-hole to shell-hole. We lift the sides of our masks and sniff suspiciously. Opposite me someone strips the mask off, then others follow his example—it is "all clear."

Bellchamber, without his mask, looks ghastly; every drop of blood seems drained from his body. The stretcher bearers come forward, so we give them a shout and leave them to their job.

The sun disappears behind a cloud, and the rain falls, gently at first as if to soothe the tortured earth, then in a fury it lashes down in sheets.

Our trench is no more. We lie about numb and bewildered waiting for the roll-call, while our sergeants try to herd us together in companies and platoons.

My eyes hover on a disembowelled body, the rain-drops patter on the uncovered bowels. I marvel at their colour and the compact way they are folded into the small space—there must be yards of them. His helmet has fallen over his face, but there is something youthful looking about the cut of his limbs. Yes, I think he must be young—we mostly all are out here.

Death itself hasn't much sting. It would sometimes be very welcome, but to lie like that fellow with the rain-drops pattering on your bowels! Hell, if only we knew how we were going to die it might make things easier to bear.

Strange how sometimes I think I'll never come out of this war alive. How can I? If I live to-day there is always a to-morrow, and yet at other times I am confident I'll see it through.

Death lies about in all its forms, a limbless body there, the tunic fitting the swollen trunk like a glove. He may have wanted a tunic to fit like that all his life—he gets it in death. A body without a head, like a jar without a label. A form, fast turning green, lying in a pool of greeny-grey vomit—*gas*. Death in a thousand different masks, the harvest of the devil.

A youngster not much older than myself is bringing his inside up. Poor blighter, it's a pity. Heaven knows when our next rations will arrive.

Away to our left a rainbow stretches, curving well behind the enemy lines, while in front of me the rain still patters on the bowels of what had once been a man.

Chapter Four

COMRADESHIP

August 12th, 1917, WIELTJE (THE SALIENT). Took over from an Irish crowd, the 16th Divn., I think. Rain, rain and more rain. Naylor killed. Telephone wire ran into a shell-hole occupied by a dying sergeant. Both his legs off. Can't get him out of my mind.

THE war has given me four things—a healthy body with a love for the open air, a knowledge of my fellow men with the art of understanding them, cuss words and smiles when things go wrong, and comradeship.

I could almost count this war worth while if comradeship as we know it is strong enough to survive when the stimulant has ceased. Those at home could never realise what a prize it is. I doubt if we do ourselves. To live amongst men who would give their last fag, their last bite, aye, even their last breath if need be for a pal—that is comradeship, the comradeship of the trenches. The only clean thing born of this life of cruelty and filth. It grows in purity from the very obscenity of its surroundings. It is a flower in a bed of fungi. It brings out the good in every one of us; but seldom seeks to receive.

Call it what you will—teamwork, unselfishness of a common cause, or anything else you fancy. We know it as a sublime trust which is never misplaced—just comradeship.

Preparations are going on for another attack, towards Passchendaele, and as a preliminary we have captured a section of the enemy front trench.

Naylor and I have laid a signal line from our front posts across the old no-man's-land to headquarters.

How Naylor wangled this job I don't know. He evidently prefers it to being a battalion scout, and is bent on impressing the signals officer.

Like the schoolteacher he is, everything is worked out on paper. His schemes for maintaining the line would be marvellous if only we could put them into operation. It was his idea to run the line from shell-hole to shell-hole and thus obtain the maximum of cover when we patrol them. If Webster was on the job he wouldn't bother about such a trifle, it is the quickest and shortest route for him—"Get the bloody job done," is Webster's motto. Naylor, however, thinks and calculates all the time, and, somehow, it pleases me to let him have his own way. After all; it certainly is much safer to dodge a long way from hole to hole than to sprint a short distance across the open. It has its drawbacks, however, although Naylor can't see them. We have twice as much wire out, and shell-holes, after an attack, are usually inhabited by wounded.

In one we come across a sergeant. Poor fellow, he has lost both legs above the knee and has a nasty wound in the stomach. At first we think he is dead, but a movement of the eyes assures us he still lives. With strands of wire we encircle both thighs and twist each one as tight as possible; this stops the bleeding. The puncture in his stomach doesn't look bad but makes it impossible for us to move him without a stretcher. His glassy staring eyes follow our every movement, not a groan escapes his lips. We talk encouragingly to him, but cannot tell if he understands or not. There is something uncanny in the way he follows us with his eyes. His look seems to be one of antagonism : I almost believe he resents our presence.

I suggest to Naylor that we should get stretcher bearers. We can't possibly move him without, or the hole in his belly would kill him. It is then I think I understand the look in his eyes. I wouldn't want to live myself without my legs, to have to crawl on my stomach like a worm; that isn't life but a living hell. Ahead of him he has months of agony lying on his back, providing the hole in his stomach allows him that chance, months of gnawing pain, months of stabbing pain, then years of mental pain—pain and misery all the time.

Just now he is all numb—drowsy, as if he was slipping away into a void. If we take off those strands he'll just fade away. But following on these thoughts come my own when life has been a matter of seconds or inches. Yes, life can be very very sweet when we feel it slipping from our grasp.

"Come on," I urge, "let's get the stretcher bearers, Naylor, this fellow is about all in."

We haven't far to hunt for them. In a shell-hole we find two R.A.M.C. men, a broken stretcher lying between them. The supports are splintered in several places, it could never bear the weight of a man. We learn they have been sniped at for the last half-hour, and are not keen to leave their present shelter. However, after a little persuasion they follow us towards the shell-hole in which the wounded sergeant lies. The last few yards we crawl on our bellies as a machine-gun sweeps the ground.

The orderlies are soon at work. They put the professional touch to our amateurish job, but even they can do little more than we have attempted.

"Besides," one remarks, "he can't live longer than a quarter of an hour, he's lost too much blood already. Even if he had a chance we could never get him across the open in the daylight. When it's dark, we'll have a shot at it." Then as an afterthought: "If he still lives, poor blighter."

There's nothing else to be done. We have seen too much of this forced callousness to worry about it. Our turn may not be far distant.

Naylor and I carry on with our job.

It is late afternoon, now, and I have visited the shell-hole in which the sergeant lies many times; I dread whenever I have to approach it. His staring eyes haunt me. Why the hell did Naylor lay our line to that particular hole? Next time, I'm going to haul it out; I won't look at that poor blighter again. It isn't so bad when he is unconscious, but when his eyes follow me, when they stare at me when I crawl into the hole, stare at me when I tell him they'll soon have him out of this, stare at me as I test the line and are still staring as I crawl out again, I feel as if I had been intruding, almost as if I had been violating the sanctuary of the dead and been caught in the act. Yes, I must shift that wire; to hell with Naylor and his systems.

As the day wears on, our little part of the front gradually becomes more unpleasant. Casualties keep on mounting and we are forced to patrol the lines single-handed instead of in pairs.

The shelling is so intensive that our signal lines are never unbroken for more than a minute or two. The Boche counter-attack is expected at any time, and we are still out of communication with battalion headquarters.

Naylor, who is outside on the line, hasn't reported for almost forty-five minutes. He should tap in and do so every half-hour if possible. If there is no word from him in five minutes I'll have to go out into that hell and try the impossible. I watch the minute hand of my wrist-watch tick round, while the signaller taps away unsuccessfully on his buzzer. The corporal signaller gives me a nod, and grousingly I get up, loop my field telephone over my shoulder and make towards the entrance of our captured pill-box. Before I reach it the S O S comes in from our advanced posts, and as I hesitate at the entrance before bracing my nerves to go out amongst the general upheaval, I hear our operator's excited voice :

"I'm through, I'm through to battalion, corp."

I return into the signal office shouting: "Good old Naylor," while to myself I think: I won't have to go out now, after all, I'll be able to stay here where it's safer.

I watch the operator send through our messages for more artillery support and a request for bombs to be sent up, and congratulate myself on having escaped a nasty job.

"How do you find the signals?" enquires the corporal.

"Pretty weak," answers the operator, "can hardly read them at times, seems as if there's a 'short' somewhere."

The corporal listens at the earphones for a minute or so, then turning round :

"Jock."

"Hello," I reply.

"Better go out and give Naylor a hand. Look for a short circuit and use plenty insulating tape. By the way"—as I make for the entrance—"tap in when you find Naylor, and let me know how things are."

"Right-o." As I leave the pill-box the Boche barrage falls with surprising suddenness on our support lines. Picking up the wire outside I trail it through my hand as I stumble along in the gloom, mending numerous new breaks as I go. The barrage has lifted and is now falling on our reserve lines, and I hear our Lewis and machine-guns joining in the argument and know the Boche is attacking.

I am nearing that accursed shell-hole. I don't recognise it from the hundreds of others, I can't even see it through the gathering dusk, but I know I am almost on top of it. Yes, as surely as if it was the only one here. Those eyes will stare at me again as I slide down and stop for a breather, stare as I crawl out.

This is it, no, it's not. That's not the sergeant; another occupant. My God, it's Naylor.

I am beside him in a second.

"Naylor, Naylor, old man, where've you got it?"

I shake him, but it's no good. A gash in his neck tells its own tale; blood is still trickling out of his mouth. Poor old Naylor, suffocated in his own blood. I shake him again and feel for his heart, but already I know that dear old Naylor, with all his schoolteacher airs, has gone. I'm glad now that I let him have his own way so often. His fads annoyed me at times, he was always so particular about the little things, but after all he wasn't a bad spud, far too good for a death such as this.

Old Naylor's turn, I reflect. I wonder who will be next, there aren't so many of the old crowd left. Hell, mooning like this won't get me anywhere.

I unstrap the telephone, fix my leads, and calling up the company headquarters, find that part of the line is in working order and my signals getting through.

"Hello, that A Company? Jock speaking. I've found Naylor. Yes, hit in the neck. Oh, he's got it all right, certain. You'll send somebody out for him? Right, can't miss it, the line runs right up to it. I'll bring in his pay book."

Then:

"Hello, d'you hear me all right? The fault must be forward, so I'll tap in as soon as I find it. Cheerio."

I unfix the telephone, insulate the scraped wire where I have tapped in, and turn slowly towards Naylor. I've never quite mastered my natural shyness of touching a dead man, but, after all, this was Naylor, he wouldn't mind me going through his pockets. I undo the buttons of his tunic pockets, take out everything I find, gingerly slip my hand into his trouser pockets and do likewise. The lot I cram into my own already bulging pockets. A last glance just to make sure I am not mistaken about my old comrade, then grasping the line I start off.

Twenty yards further on I stumble over something. Curse it, the line is right underneath. Why the hell must they come to my line to die? But perhaps he is only wounded, so I look closer and turn him over—the sergeant. Yes, it must be him, there can't be two sergeants with their legs shot off and a wound in the belly within twenty yards of each other. Damn it, but that's strange. How did he get here? What does it matter anyway, he's dead.

I step over him and grope round for the wire. It's not there. I return and pick it up a yard or two on the other side of the corpse. I trace it back to the dead sergeant, but lose it again on the other side of him. I roll him over and the wire goes with him. Grasped in his hand I find it and begin to understand. I go round in a circle and soon discover the other end of the wire, then I repair the break and once again we are in communication with head-quarters.

I can only surmise what must have taken place in that shell-hole between the wounded Naylor and the dying sergeant. It was obvious that the sergeant had crawled those twenty yards with the broken wire in an endeavour to find the other end. How he had managed it, crippled and maimed, I cannot tell. The fact remains he had got far enough with one end of the broken wire in his hand to allow the signals to pass through the earth to the strands of the other part. The break was joined and our S O S message had got through.

An unselfish act for a dying man—just a gesture of true comradeship.

Chapter Five

OUR SERGEANT-MAJOR

August 14th, Pommern Redoubt, Ypres. Our C.S.M.
"gone west." Don't think he'll be missed.
It never seems to stop raining here.

We have just put the finishing touches to the grave of our
sergeant-major. He lies behind our dug-out beside the
latrine. Not buried there to emphasise our feelings towards
him, nor yet in a sense of humour. Feelings are submerged
when you have to shovel the earth on top of a fellow, and
there's not much humour in burying a comrade, no matter
how strict a martinet he may have been in life.

It was the best spot we could find in the short time we
have at our disposal, not under enemy observation. We
leave here to-night, otherwise he might have been buried
in the cemetery near the ramparts of Ypres.

Poor major, I can forgive you now all your unwarranted
fatigues and vile epithets. No doubt we were a bit of a
handful for your disciplined ideas.

I first came into contact with our late sergeant-major
in the training camp at home. He was a regimental quartermaster in those days, and as such, was entitled to a servant.
Why he picked on me to fill that capacity, I never found
out. However, the job was all right and relieved me from
all parades and fatigues, but like all cushy jobs it had a
snag.

Our quartermaster believed in a chamber. The porcelain
contraption I found under his bed the first morning I
arrived to take up my duties rather took my breath away. I
promptly shoved it out of sight and left it.

The next morning it was in its usual place filled to over-
flowing. As we were camped in tents without floor boards,
I emptied half its contents under his bed, and imagined I
had found a way out. Our worthy quartermaster was not
deceived, however, and I was severely lectured and ordered
to empty the pot each morning in the camp latrine. I
argued that I had joined the army to fight and not to

empty night-pots, but this only roused the quartermaster to greater fury, and I realised that short of actually disobeying an order, I would be obliged to empty his pot.

All night I thought over the matter, and just before falling asleep, I decided, with Màc's help, on the course I was going to adopt next morning.

Accordingly, while the full battalion was on parade and waiting for the colonel's order to "carry on," I emerged gingerly from the tent carrying the pot carefully in front of me, and walked the whole length of the parade to the latrines. After emptying it, I carried it back in my right hand, saluted the colonel with my left, and disappeared into the quartermaster's tent. I had heard the muffled sniggers as I passed along the lines, and felt quite pleased with myself. I resolved to give this little performance each morning until the quartermaster found other means of emptying his pot.

For three mornings the quartermaster ignored my show, and I began to wonder if I'd ever outlive the name of "Piss Wallah," which the battalion soon fastened on me. On the fourth morning an unrehearsed event settled the whole question.

As usual I walked towards the latrines, in full view of the parade, looking as innocent as possible, but an unseen tent peg proved my undoing, and down I went, pot and all. The discipline of the parade was greatly shaken, and amidst shouts of "Eyes front, there," "Take that man's name, sergeant," and a host of other orders, I ignominiously picked up the fragments of the broken pot and disappeared as quickly as possible in the direction of the camp rubbish heap.

That night, after a good dressing down, I lost my job— as a batman I had been a failure.

I had also become, in the quartermaster's eyes, a marked man. There was no way of escaping his wrath. In a hundred different ways he found means of making things unpleasant for myself and friends.

When we came out here we thought we had escaped him, but found to our horror he had reverted to his permanent rank, and was our company-sergeant-major.

Actual warfare proved him a bully and revealed him as

falling short of our standard of a brave man.

Far from actually being a coward, he possessed, however, the knack of getting out of a dangerous position without seeming to be running away, quite in order in a private soldier if not endangering his comrades' lives, but unbearable at all times in a sergeant-major.

On one occasion, after an attack, our company held an isolated strong point with orders to hold it at all costs. Yet just before the enemy put down his barrage prior to a counter-attack, our gallant sergeant-major went back to a dressing station to have a septic knee dressed. We all, more or less, had received nasty cuts from the barbed wire Webster had a knee swollen twice its size, yet, cunning ol' fox that he is, he never thought of going back to have it dressed at a time when every man was required.

When things were quieter and the attack had been beaten off, the sergeant-major returned with a knee well bandaged, bawling loud enough for everyone to hear that he was glad to be back with the boys, damn' sorry he had missed the little scrap, curse his luck. If only he hadn't been forced to go back for a dressing, instead of waiting for Jerry to come over, he would have gone and knocked hell out of him first. Now he was back, however, there was nothing to fear and he was pleased we had managed to do so well without him. We grinned to each other and let him mouth on—the damned hypocrite.

Previously I had not seen through his mask of bustling, bawling bravado. His advertised conceit and confidence had me gulled, but from then on I saw the man as he really was.

A few nights later I again experienced the sergeant-major's cunning. An identification raid on the enemy trenches near Wieltje gave him his opportunity.

Our orders were "a prisoner at all costs," and by good fortune I stumbled on the only Jerry who hadn't managed to make a bolt for it. While the others covered my retreat I hustled him across no-man's-land. On the way over, my prisoner, a big burly fellow, unsuccessfully tried to turn the tables on me with a small automatic he had hidden about his person, but I was too old a hand to be caught that way.

In front of our wire I met the sergeant-major and excitedly blurted out the story of the little automatic. The sergeant-major fairly bristled with importance.

"Hand him over to me," he ordered, "I'll see him safely to headquarters. Trying to start something, was he. Well, there will be no monkey tricks with me."

The bewildered prisoner was roughly shoved along the trench while I followed meekly behind. Arriving at the headquarters dug-out, the prisoner, with his gallant escort, disappeared behind the anti-gas blanket which served as a door. I saw no more but heard the sergeant-major:

"Your prisoner, sir."

"Splendid, major, splendid. Who brought him in?"

"I brought him down, sir."

"You brought him down?"

"Certainly, sir."

"But you weren't detailed, major; you know the regulations?"

"Can't help that, sir; where the boys go, I go too; just had to see things were going right. Can't expect the boys to go on these jobs always without their sergeant-major, sir."

And so he careered on in his brusque easy manner.

"We can't afford to let good men like you go out on every minor raid, major," I heard our captain say.

"However, seeing you've brought back a prisoner, we'll have to overlook it this time."

I turned away and met the remainder of the raiding party coming down the trench. To them I related our sergeant-major's latest exploit, and learned that as soon as we had penetrated the Boche trench, our own front line became rather uncomfortable, and our sergeant-major, finding things too hot for him, had quietly slipped out in front of our wire where it was safer. I had inadvertently blundered into him, and the rest he had seen to.

A few weeks later there appeared on the left breast of the sergeant-major's tunic a nice new ribbon, while his name, rank and number along with the decoration received, appeared on Regimental Orders.

Poor bombastic fool: he had gained the decoration he had so often promised himself, but in doing so had played

into our hands. He was right where we wanted him and
hanging plumb. Undeserved fatigues became fewer, and
though his tongue was just as sharp as ever, he was careful
not to overstep the mark. He realised he had made a slip
and tried hard to trap us into disobedience, but we never
openly disobeyed orders, neither did we mention the
prisoner he brought in, but as Webster said, it was a fine
piece of silent blackmail.

And now we have smoothed over the mound, and stuck
a wooden cross over all that remains of our sergeant-major.

His overbearing assurance couldn't ward off the inevitable, his petty excuses didn't help to eke out his existence
a second longer than fate decreed. He fell with a neat little
hole between the eyes in a foolish attempt at bravado
before a recruit when he thought danger miles away; a
victim to his own vanity.

Poor fellow, he is dead.

To-morrow we'll talk of that bloody swine, the sergeant-
major.

Chapter Six

RUMOURS

August 16th, 1917, IN SHELL-HOLES BETWEEN ST.
JULIEN AND ZONNEBEKE. *Another attack, and as usual
raining. Mud everywhere; we live in it, sleep in it, and
eat it. I now know what a mud-lark feels like.*

*Hot tea arrived from the transport lines to-night, real
sergeant-major's, sugared and milked. Never tasted tea
like it.*

RUMOUR, always a lying jade, has become active again.
A corps intelligence man has brought us the latest latrine
tales from the rear, and they are as varied as only a corps
man could make them.

A well-known "Brass Hat," anxiously waiting to get

news from the front line, was overjoyed to see a carrier pigeon alight at its loft, and stood watching the pigeon-corporal as he deftly caught the bird and extracted the slip of paper from the metal holder attached to its leg. The corporal glanced at it, then, obviously ill at ease, began to inspect the bird as if trying to locate something that wasn't there.

"A bird in, corporal?" enquired the "Brass Hat."

"Yes, sir."

"Any message?"

"Well, a—a—not exactly, sir," stammered the corporal.

"What the devil do you mean, man—bring that paper here."

"Sorry, sir, there's no message that I can see, only this," And rather shakily the corporal handed over a sheet from the usual official message pad.

In rather scrawly writing, but quite legible, the "Brass Hat" read:

"I'm darned well fed up. I'll carry these blasted poultry no longer."

What the General said our informant doesn't divulge—he is too eager to get the other rumours off his chest—but we surmise from the hints he drops that even a "Brass Hat" can curse.

His next yarn is of wounded Jocks on our left who have been found with their kilts torn off and cruelly mutilated. Then a brigade, this time on our right, who seem to have got tired of the whole business, packed up and retreated.

Further south the Boche is on the run, so troops in that sector are being issued with shorts and running-shoes to keep up with him.

He has vague tales of some coloured regiment, negroes from darkest Africa, who go out into no-man's-land at night and collect ears and noses.

Eagerly we take in all his yarns and seek more. How we enjoy trying to believe these rumours! The only disturbing factor is we can never find an eye-witness to any of them. It is always a battalion on our left, a brigade on our right, a machine-gunner who has a brother who knows some-body in the Intelligence Department, or, by way of a change, and more in keeping with the natural birth of all rumours, a batman who passed the officers' latrines and overheard a secret of the war. Rumours—but what matters that? Fondly we snatch at them, enlarge on them to our own fancy, then pass them on.

The tale goes that our battalion pigeon-man is minus a bird, and it might be his which carried the news of battle to our General, but this he stoutly denies, reminding us that he isn't like Bumskin, our late pigeon-man who lost his memory and his birds last time in the line.

"No, maybe I ain't no hero," remarks our worthy keeper of birds, "but at the same time I ain't no Bumskin and gets blown up and loses my memory for five days, only finding it again when the relief turned up."

"The poor blighter was due for leave," somebody remarks. "You could hardly blame him; he only made sure he was alive to take it, and forgot the rest of us might require his pigeons. His trouble starts when he returns from leave and tries to explain away those five days."

Our conversation veers round to court-martials and shootings, and from that to Webster's emphatic statement that there are always battle police detailed during an attack. Some of the boys don't believe him, but I think he is right and tell them so.

"Listen, fellows, when I took that first message back to our old front line, I came across two chaps in a shell-hole. Thinking they might be wounded I went over, but as soon as they saw me approaching they started shouting and waving me back. I couldn't hear what they said, but their actions plainly told me I wasn't wanted. They were watching something or somebody in front, and reckoning it might be a Jerry sniper, I carried on, although, now that I think of it, I can't say I noticed what battalion they belonged to. They certainly had no equipment and only carried revolvers."

"Bloody red caps," yells Webster in glee. "Battle police. I told you so, boys. That proves what I'm telling you. Then there was that sergeant-major who came round the pill-boxes. What do you think he was asking all those personal questions for? Not because he was anxious about your health. Oh no, he was on the hunt for scroungers, prisoners' escorts and chaps who had taken a wounded pal to the dressing station and sort of lost their way back to the front line. Battle police, boys, I know it. They think of everything in this war but the quickest way to end it."

"You're right, Webby," shouts Mac, as our ration party appears in sight, struggling along the shallow communication trench, "they do think of everything. Look what's coming! Heavens, it's tea, boys, and real sergeant-major's at that."

"Good old Santa Claus," chimes in Streaky. "The A.S.C. are beginning to realise there's a war on."

We can hardly believe our good fortune—hot tea, brought up in petrol tins wrapped round with blankets, and such tea, truly a sergeant major's drink! Here are we, right up in the front line, first evening of a push, being supplied with hot tea, milked and sugared. How many lives it has cost to bring it up we don't know, how many lives it has probably saved we can guess. We have a feeling we are not forgotten after all.

Webster calmly remarks:

"If they'd dish out the rum the same way, it wouldn't be such a hell of a bad war after all. They've worked one miracle and, who knows, they might manage another."

"Aw, chuck your jawing, Webby," advises Mac, "and let's have a taste of that sludge before it gets cold."

Webster ladles it out as we all crawl round him in our little funk-hole. The water and mud is half-way up to our knees but we've forgotten that. Never have I tasted such tea before, and I drink in big gulps, letting the hot fluid flow down into my stomach. Its warmth pervades my whole being, and a feeling almost of contentment creeps over me. I hasten to finish what I have, and qualify for any more that may be left in the tin.

"Stand to" is passed down the trench. There are more serious things in hand than tea drinking.

Chapter Seven

DUTIES OF A LINEMAN

*August 18th, 1917, IN THE MUD IN FRONT OF YPRES.
Put in a hellish night on the lines with Webby. Fed up
with the whole business.*

*Saw a battery of our field guns get it in the neck from
Jerry.*

The poor horses get the worst of it.

OUT on the lines isn't quite as cushy a job as I had always
imagined. There are many little annoyances in the shape
of shells and shrapnel, which, in all this huge area, pick
on our eighth of an inch wire to practise their destructive
abilities. Still, the job takes us away from the firing step,
and that is sufficient compensation.

Soaked through and sweating like horses we plough our
way in the darkness backwards and forwards through this
wilderness of mud. Running the wire through our hands
we flounder in and out water-logged shell-holes, stumble
over foul-smelling heaps of putrefying flesh, or, as
machine-guns sweep the ground, crawl over the more recent
dead of the morning's advance, which emit strange noises—
half groan, half sigh—as the weight of our bodies presses
the air from their lungs.

When we find a break we scout round on hands and
knees in a circle to try and pick up the other end, which
may be anywhere within fifty yards, but at last it is found,
the join made and insulated, then on we go.

Shells, machine-guns, the nearness of these still forms,
and the darkness, all add to our misery and fear, but the
line must be kept clear. As soon as one break is mended
another is made; the task seems hopeless. Physically we
are beat, but the boys in front rely on us to keep going and
we cannot let them down.

And so on throughout the night, we trudge to and fro,
seldom meeting a soul, although there must be thousands
all around us.

The road to our right is alive with transport, but here

between the captured Jerry first and second lines, we seem to be the only two living beings amongst the dead. Away from the roads and tracks a battlefield can be a very lonely spot.

Towards dawn the usual Jerry hate increases until we find ourselves just within the limits of a truly terrific barrage. A wall of smoke and up-flung earth blots out all landmarks, but just ahead of us should be an old trench, and we make a dash for it. Loaded with equipment and field telephone I stumble on after Webster, my legs sinking up to the knees in mud at every step, until the stumbling gradually becomes a slithering and floundering amongst the vindictive morass. Occasionally I come across a yard or two of firmer ground and try to sprint over it, bent double as the shell splinters and clods of earth whizz around me, then, without warning, down I flop into another stretch of squelching mud. I try wading through it until at last I can go no further and drop exhausted into a newly-made shell-hole, where the explosion has unearthed fairly solid clay, which I don't immediately notice, being only faintly surprised that I am not sinking gradually down and down into its churned-up slimy depths.

The ground beneath me is in a continual state of trembles. Fifty yards further on I can see the comparative safety of the edge of the barrage, but I have ceased to worry over these things. Utter exhaustion has made me indifferent, and I care not whether I live or die as, unconcerned, I watch the inverted cones of earth soar skywards, and wait for the clods to clatter down on top of me. The blasts of hot air and lyddite fumes, the hiss and smack of flying splinters have lost their power to send me scampering for safer quarters : I am brave beyond my wildest hopes. It is a feeling I have never experienced before, this calm indifference of exhaustion.

I see Webster dodging between the bursts and smoke on his way towards me and try to wave him back, but he carries on until, with a rush and a jump, he is in the shell-hole beside me.

"Hurt, Scotty?" he yells.

"Not me, I'm just all in. I'll come along after I've had a breather."

"Breather be damned, let's get to hell out of this."

Snatching up my heavy drum of wire and telephone, he hauls me to my feet, and with a final "Come on," leads the way.

The short rest has given me back my wind and, relieved of my heavy baggage, I somehow manage, with Webster's help, to pull my weary legs along, and drop down beside him into an old trench just clear of the barrage.

"Phew, that was hot."

"Bloody hot," is all Webster replies.

From the safety of the trench we watch the landscape changing, then as suddenly as the barrage dropped, so it lifts, and once more we climb out into the open and the eternal breaks in the wire.

The shelling has cut our signal line in so many places that it could never be repaired, so we decide to run out a new wire from the extra drum I have lugged about all night. Before we can get started, however, our relief, Mac and Streaky, arrive, and are rather surprised, I fancy, to find us still on our feet.

We slip into a hole and swop the latest rumours, then, with a cheerio, Webby and I make for the captured pill-box which is now our battalion headquarters.

The entrance, facing the Jerry lines, has had a direct hit but has withstood it well, only a slight crack being visible and proving beyond doubt that whatever the Germans have been forced to find substitutes for, concrete certainly isn't one of them.

As we enter we notice the walls are splattered with blood and fragments of flesh, while on the narrow floor lies an artillery man with a badly mangled leg, and beside him a comrade holding a rosary in his hand. As gently as possible we step over the wounded man, but the passage is only two feet wide and is lined on either side with men. Our effort is rather clumsy and evokes groans from the figure on the floor and curses flung at us from his pals, which we treat with true soldierly indifference.

In the signal office lie what is left of three more artillery-men and one of our runners. We are told they were standing in the passage-way when the shell burst and were blown there. We merely glance at the gruesome sight as we pass by, knowing that shortly somebody will cover up the pieces with sandbags.

On reporting to the sergeant we are told to go and lie down in the rear compartment, and with visions of a sleep, we grope blindly along an alley, eventually stumbling down four steps into a square emplacement with machine-gun slots in each wall. The last step down lands us into a foot of water, and our curses are answered from the semi-darkness with:

"Don't disturb the goldfish," "Mind your feet on the lobby gas," and "Watch your head on the door mat"—all of which we ignore, as we scramble back on to the last step above high-water mark, and view our bedroom with mixed feelings.

A solitary candle, stuck at a perilous angle on the wall, throws a half-hearted flickering glimmer of light round the place, revealing, perched along each wall on a narrow ledge—for all the world like hens gone to roost—the usual miscellaneous mixture which comprises the normal head-quarters staff. Occasionally someone's foot slips off the six-inch ledge, and down he comes with a splash which is greeted with loud guffaws by those who have already undergone the experience.

The game seems to be to cling to the ledge as long as possible and thereby keep your legs dry, but once you have slipped you adopt an air of utter contempt for dryness, and with the exception of lying full length in a foot of water, disport yourself in the most uncomfortable and wettest way possible, and feign sleep.

The stumble at the last step has decided the matter for Webby and I, so we wade over to the only vacant space on the ledge, light a fag, fling a few queries at a couple of optimists who are attempting to bale the water out with empty cigarette-tins, then with our equipment and rifles over our knees, we settle down for that well-earned rest.

In those far-off civilian days such an experience would have laid us on our backs for weeks, but the exposure and discomfort now only seems to harden us for worse things ahead.

Somehow I manage to doze. The exploding shells and the rattle of machine-guns outside are vague muffled sounds in the background as my head drops farther forward. Sleep is coming at last, the only sanctuary I ever find up at the front. Far away somebody seems to be calling my name. Surely it can't be time to get up. It's mother, I imagine, calling from the foot of the stairs, so that's all right—I've fifteen minutes yet; I never get up until she knocks on the door and tells me I'll be late again for school. The calling continues until someone knocks my elbows off my knees and my head comes down with a jar as my dream disappears. It is time to relieve Mac and Streaky on the line.

We hitch on our equipment and wade out of our sleeping-quarters. The place is just as crowded as ever, but I notice the mess in the corner has disappeared, and in its place, standing in a pool of blood, is a large tin of biscuits. There is nothing else to be had in the eating line, so we cram our pockets with them and go in search of something to drink, as the issue of cold tea in our bottles has long since given out. There isn't a drop of clean liquid in the place and it is hardly likely we'll find a water-cart so far up, but we needn't go thirsty—it is still raining.

Outside the ground is like a sea of mud covered with depressions and miniature lakes. The landscape has changed entirely and we cannot walk two yards in a straight line without skirting the lip of one of these craters fast filling with water. It is a relief to get to the more open and less tortuous ground of the old no-man's-land.

In the trench we have marked as our half-way point we find Mac and Streaky. They have had a fairly uneventful day, and the line has held for the last two hours. That sounds good to us. In return we can only tell them that the pill-box is still anchored and holds about eighteen inches of dirty rain-water, without showing any signs of a leak. The safety ledge is still half an inch above high-water mark, and the rats have stopped dropping from the roof. This we found rather annoying last night as the cold water splashing on our faces continually woke us up, otherwise it is pretty much the same old war.

"Have the rations come up yet?" Mac enquires hopefully.

"Only a tin of biscuits as far as I could see, but we got

three tins of bully out of the packs of those fellows over there, and a loaf of black Jerry bread. It's damnable-looking stuff, but not so hard as biscuit and will fill up a hole quicker. There's a loaf left in his haversack, Mac; you can't miss him: there's about a dozen lying around a machine-gun, but it's the big fellow sprawling over the gun who's got the doings."

"Right you are, Jock, we'll have a scout round while it's quiet. Cheero."

They climb out of the trench, and Webster and I make ourselves as comfortable as possible. So long as the line holds and we are in communication with battalion headquarters, we don't require to move from here—we pray for a quiet night.

These trenches, so full of activity a few hours ago, are now only occupied by rats and those other things. Occasionally a runner comes our way, lost as usual, and enquires where the White Ruin is, or Uhlan Farm, or some other spot we have never heard of. Just the same old ignorance after every advance; outside our own immediate front we are all lost.

The little funk-hole where our field telephone has been installed seems very comfortable to us after our cramped quarters in the flooded pill-box. The corrugated-iron roof keeps the rain out, and Mac and Streaky seem to have searched the whole front for blankets as a flooring. I count sixteen and then give it up. There is just room for the two of us and our telephone. If we lie down our feet protrude into the trench and rain. If we sit up we have to keep our heads bent, but with its flooring of blankets it is dry and that to us is luxury indeed.

An hour passes and the line is still intact, the shelling being very moderate, so everything points to a quiet night. Webster is busy drying his socks over a candle, while I engage in a rat hunt. They are the only things that seem to thrive in this place of death. Like rabbits in size they have the audacity of the devil, loathsome creatures who live on the harvest of the battlefields. I have the whole trench as my hunting ground, and as it has been unoccupied for twenty-four hours, their foraging parties swarm everywhere, nosing around empty tins, tearing away at abandoned haversacks, slinking around every corpse; each funk-hole has its contingent. When they have cleared the trench of everything eatable, and in some cases uneatable, they'll evacuate the place for better feeding grounds.

It is just getting dark when my sport is interrupted by a battery of artillery taking up position in the open ground immediately in front of our trench. What a picture they make as they gallop over the uneven ground, wheel into line, unlimber, and go into action straight away. The horses are trotted off and tethered about a hundred yards from the guns. Semaphore signallers are already busy, while two more unwind a reel of telephone wire. I watch it all in amazement. Each man knows his job and goes to it, but planting guns in a spot like that beats me. There are no gun-pits, no cover of any kind, and worst of all, the Jerries must have every yard of that stretch of ground taped. However, that's their funeral. They've kept the gun teams handy, so they don't expect to stay long, and if I know the Jerry gunners, they won't.

Mac, on hearing the shouting and firing, has joined me. "Blasted fools, what the hell do they want to bring guns alongside our line for? There will be no peace for us to-night, Jock, unless we shift that wire."

Experience has taught us never to lay a telephone wire near a battery, as guns invite shell fire, and that is the worst thing possible for a signalling line.

"Well, Webby, I'd sooner be an infantry flag-wagger to-night than a gunner with that mob. Just wait till Jerry finds out they are there."

"Wait be damned," Webster replies, making towards our funk-hole. "Come on, let's get that wire fixed."

We have just sufficient spare wire to make a detour about two hundred yards to the right of the battery, then we curve in and connect again to the original line well in front of the guns. The direct line we then cut off at the join and roll up for future use. This done, we feel more comfortable and stop for a minute to admire the battery.

The gunners are now firing away merrily, while the horse teams are engrossed in their nosebags. One or two of the drivers, we notice, are exploring our old front line on the scrounge, and as things have a peculiar way of disappearing when there's no one around, we pick up our wire and leave the gunners to their job; our own little home requires our watchful eyes.

Webster takes first turn with the earphones, which gives me two hours to laze about, providing the line holds, so I settle the blankets to my liking, and, in doing so, unearth a bag full of letters; evidently the last mail before our boys went over. It has never left the trench, but that is just one of the many subterfuges practised on fighting men by those in authority. Before every attack we are given the opportunity to write our last mail, then it is religiously collected, handed over to an officer and promptly dumped in a corner. It has accomplished its allotted duty, and for a brief hour has taken our minds off the work before us.

Idly I scan over one or two of the notes. They are all much of a sameness. It is difficult to realise they are perhaps the last epistles of youths who a few short hours after were going on the great adventure. There is nothing very melodramatic in their wording. A few drop vague hints of something doing. Some make out the war to be a bit of a picnic, while others contain the usual army grousing and exaggerations. One poor fellow has had his Sunday dinner completely spoilt by the absence of mustard and has tramped the whole front line, but could neither beg, borrow nor steal a grain. Another bright spark is greatly upset by the mess the regimental barber has made of his hair-cut. All the French girls near the trenches are pulling his leg to an awful extent about it. Not one do I come across which affects the style of the last will and testament.

The letters might be prized and cherished by someone in far-away Blighty, who now will never know they were written. I wonder how many letters of mine lie hidden and unearthed in holes such as this one, the letters which I thought would give a little comfort to those at home if anything happened.

The paper slips from my fingers. In the trench a rat is half hidden in an empty bully-beef tin. Occasionally it emerges, looks at me half defiantly, then struggles to get further into the tin after some morsel.

My thoughts drift far away and merge into obscure

shadows as I slip into that state of semi-consciousness which serves me as sleep near the front line. The noises of the front can still penetrate my brain but have ceased to mean anything. The occasional crump of a shell, the spasmodic rat-tat-tat of a machine-gun, the buzz of Webster's telephone and his voice as he speaks to someone at the other end of the wire, the squeal of a rat and the rattle of a dislodged tin in the trench—I can hear them and recognise them, but my nerves fail to react to their message of activity. They are just part of the general atmosphere which surrounds me, even in my moments of sleep.

These are the only times of peace and contentment I ever have at the front. Even the growing tumult outside and the tremulous vibrations of the floor of our funk-hole fail to disturb my tranquillity. It is Webster's voice which eventually hauls me back to this world of action and fear.

"Wake up, Jock, the line's gone, and that battery in front is getting hell."

A second ago I was devoid of action or thought, not oblivious to what was going on around me, but just mentally indifferent to it all, but Webster's voice has the power to bring me back to my senses. I am instantly on the alert, muscles poised, ears straining and nerves tingling. No leisurely eye-rubbing and yawning such as accompanied my awakening in pre-war days, no gathering of scattered thoughts, but an instantaneous change which leaves me clear-headed and ready for action—the natural training of the front.

I crouch beside Webby while he calls up headquarters on the buzzer. Little bits of earth and stones fall from the roof and sides of our funk-hole as the whole trench shivers and quakes in unison with the explosions taking place on the strip of ground in front. Webster's buzzing is useless, there is no reply. No line could stand under such a shelling, and there is nothing we can do till things quieten down.

"Well, the line's gone sky-high by now, Jock," Webster at last admits rather reluctantly.

"Let's see what is going on outside."

We crawl out into the trench and look over the parapet, but nothing can be seen of the battery. Instead, where it should be, there is a wall of flying earth, smoke and flashes.

Watching other people being shelled has a fascination, and we strain our eyes and gaze into the darkness ahead, seeing little of the havoc that is taking place, but fully conscious, by the tumult, of what is going on. The battery is being shelled out, just as expected.

As we watch we become conscious of a sound totally different to that of shrieking bursting shells. We listen more intently and can pick it out quite easily from the general babel of noise. It has a rhythm about it which at first I cannot place, then suddenly it dawns on me: it is the thudding of hoofs.

"What the hell's that, Jock?" shouts Webster. "Do you hear it?"

"It's the horses, Webby. Look, there's two of them."

Rearing and plunging the terror-stricken beasts come out of the hell of shells and smoke. With necks outstretched they gallop on, making straight for the trench and the barbed wire in front of it.

"The wire, Webby, they'll be on it in a minute."

I am already climbing the parapet with Webster at my heels, but in our haste we miss the narrow pathway through and are soon caught in the maze ourselves, but struggle on while the strands catch in our uniforms and tear it to ribbons. We wave our arms and shout, but our voices can't be heard above the noise of shelling, and there is a tanging of wire as the half-crazed animals gallop into the tangle of cruel barbs. They rear and kick and plunge deeper into its depths, making every movement a torture to them, and very soon they are a mass of lacerations right up past the flanks. One viciously snaps at its tormentors only to toss up its head with a cry almost human, its mouth dripping blood.

Hopelessly we try to get at them, but have become so entangled ourselves that at each movement the wire tears our flesh, yet the piteous cries urge us forward, until we get to within four yards of them, but can get no further. We are close enough to see the mess they are in. Both are bleeding freely from dozens of ragged tears, while one has a huge slice out of its hindquarters.

"What the hell do we do now, Jock?" Webster enquires. "We'll never get them clear of this lot, they're too well anchored."

"We'll have to try, we can't shoot them without an officer."

"Officer be damned, Jock. I'm going back for my 'Bondook'."

As Webster struggles back to the trench for his rifle I speak gently to the two animals and try to stop their frantic struggles, but they are beyond control of human voice. Foam appears at their mouths, while steam rises from the blood that trickles from dozens of places on their torn bodies.

At last Webster is laboriously working his way back.

"Try and quieten them, Jock," he urges. "Get hold of that one's head and give me a chance."

"I can't, damn you," I reply irritably, as my foot becomes entangled and I trip over sideways on to the ragged wire.

"Well, look out," yells Webster.

Only four yards separate him from the beasts, but as if they know what is about to happen, they rear and plunge more violently, as Webster tries to take aim.

It takes three shots before the first sinks limply down on to its couch of barbed wire, and by now the second animal is struggling desperately in its terror, but by good luck Webster's second shot gets it between the eyes. It flops instantly and it is all over—poor hard-working uncomplaining friends of man.

We return to the trench, where Webster leaves his rifle. He slings the field telephone over his shoulder and I pick up the drum of spare wire, then over the parapet we clamber again and through the narrow lane in the wire. At the edge of the entanglements we slip into a shell-hole and wait for the shelling to slacken off.

The vibrant sound of thudding hoofs is something new to a battlefield; it has a nervous tension about it which conveys itself to us, and we become fidgety and windy. Galloping figures appear, then disappear again into the smoke. A band of a dozen are almost on top of us and past before we realise it. Shells burst in front of them and they wheel round in fright and come thundering back again. We jump out of our shell-hole and vainly try to stop them, a rushing mass of uncontrollable horse-flesh. We begin to fear their mad rushes more than we do the stray shells which are falling around us.

The bombardment subsides gradually, and we make a start on our broken line. It is difficult to tell in which direction the horses are galloping, and when we think a band of them are coming our way, we drop the line we are trailing through our hands and make a bolt for it, only to find it is a solitary animal going in another direction altogether. For an eternity we grope around for the dropped wire. It is no sooner found than off we bolt again at the approach of those thudding hoofs. This time they don't even come our length.

At last the uproar dies away and we get on more quickly with our job. It is too dark yet to see the effect of the shelling on the battery, but the upturned and twisted guns nearest our wire are just visible, and we hail them with the usual :

"Anybody hurt?"

There is no answer.

"Looks like they've all ditched it," remarks Webster, as we repair one of the numerous breaks in our wire. The detour we made to the right of the guns the evening before has certainly helped it, but, even so, it is pretty well cut up. Level with the guns and in front of them, we come across many wounded and dying horses. They are scattered all over in shell-holes, and at our approach attempt to get up and off, as if they mistrusted the very presence of a human being. One poor beast with back broken tries to haul its useless hindquarters along, while others just lie where they have fallen, colouring the sodden earth with their life-blood. A few are still galloping aimlessly about, foam-flecked and wild-eyed—victims of man's ruthlessness.

And so on throughout the night—endless breaks in our wire, flying figures, thudding hoofs and a moaning almost human in its intensity.

Dawn at last, and we plod wearily back for our spell of uncertain off-duty.

Standing near the debris of guns and limbers is a solitary horse gently cropping leaves from a low-lying hedge. At our friendly words it trots towards us as if pleased to have our company, but not sure of its welcome—poor faithful beast, how ill you are repaid for your staunchness.

I have long since become accustomed to wounded humanity. Their plight evokes pity and the desire to help, but a wounded animal leaves me with a feeling of loathing, loathing towards myself and the civilised humanity which I represent. Too often have I seen reproach in the eyes of a dying horse, and outraged frailty in the flutterings of a wounded carrier-pigeon.

We may understand; they never can.

Chapter Eight

RELIEVED

August 19th or 20th, WATTEAU, NEAR POPERINGHE.
Arrived dead beat in the middle of the night.
Had a bath this morning, the first for weeks.
Lice beginning to bite again.

WE have been relieved at last—by an Irish division. Everything has been handed over to the incoming troops, even to the quarter-of-an-inch stub of my last cigarette. Poor devil, he looked at it so covetously that I had no option but hand it over. His "Thanks, mate," rewarded me. After all, they are just coming in to this nameless thing of mud and death, while we are gladly leaving it for a spell. I can afford to be generous to the extent of a well-fingered stub of a gasper. We tarry a little over the handing over, as there is a good deal of shelling going on down the road we must take. Assuring ourselves that the new signallers are comfortably settled, we have another look at where the shells are falling, and with a final cheero, hitch up our packs and start down the trench.

At every bursting shell we duck down, and wait until the upheaval has settled itself. As Webster remarks : "There is no damned use in hurrying and running into a packet; we'll take our time and make use of every bit of cover."

We seem to be more often on our bellies than on our feet, but finally we file out of the trench and on to the road. For a minute or so we watch the shelling. They are coming over in threes at about half-minute intervals. One learns to take note of these things; they mean all the difference between life and death. Accordingly we wait for the first shell to burst, then make a dash past the crater. They drop at almost fifty yards' distance; so we regulate our runs to be well clear of the second and third shells, then of the third and the first of the next series of three; and so we repeat this manoeuvre until we are practically out of range. This will be our last run. Another sixty yards and we shall be clear of the stretch of road under fire, but we are so anxious to be on the safe side that we delay our rush just a fraction too long, and have hardly covered ten yards when we hear the shell approaching, at first like a faint hissing which gradually gathers in volume and takes on a more menacing tone, then like a rushing steam-engine coming straight for our backs. I am undecided whether to follow Webster or drop where I am. My skin tingles and my breathing almost stops as, with a hurtling roar, the demon arrives, and I fling myself clear of the road on to a mess that gives way beneath me, something which feels cold and slimy as I sink into it, and gives forth a suffocating stink. A disturbed rat scuttles away, and I press even closer to this nauseating couch as the ground beside me shudders and heaves. The clods of earth and paving-stone are still falling as I jump up, and, with Webster and Mac, finish that last dash down the road, the stench of dead mule still lingering in my nostrils.

Each step now takes us farther away from the shelling and our spirits rise accordingly, until, as we turn off the road and make for the outskirts of what had once been the thriving town of Ypres, we are as happy as schoolboys. We cross the moat and through the Menin gateway in the ramparts. Every inch of this road we know, and yet, as we enter the ruined city, everything seems different; it is so quiet, so ghostly. The rattle of a limber on the cobblestones is all we can hear. It gives us an uncanny feeling and accentuates in glaring relief the desolation that surrounds us. The ruins themselves, the constant whine of shells overhead, the sound of heavy detonations re-echoing amongst the stark gable-ends, the ever-present pall of smoke and dust, these things we know, but this silent, ghostly, ruined city of the dead is beyond us.

"It isn't the same place," remarks Webster, voicing all our thoughts aloud. "It's so cleaned up and quiet-like. Why, they have even got a Y.M.C.A. tent rigged up. Let's see what's doing."

Inside the tent a kindly old gentleman in a semi-civilian military uniform enquires if we will have a cup of cocoa.

"How much, dad?" I ask with native canniness, and am agreeably surprised when I am informed that we are welcome to all he has.

"Did you hear that, Webby?" enquires Mac. "The drinks are on the house; this war is becoming easy."

A cup of steaming cocoa is handed to us, along with a chunk of cake, and, joy of joys, a packet of real British Woodbines.

Many harsh things have I said of this institution, but for that one kindly act I retract them all. We thank the fatherly gent profusely, and with cup in one hand and cake in the other, hie ourselves away to a handy spar which we notice has already been rigged up, and give Nature the treat which has been denied her for the last five days.

That finished, we go in search of our battalion and are formed up in pitifully small companies and marched to a field on the other side of the town, where we are halted for an hour until dusk.

No sooner do our heads touch the ground than we are dozing off, but only seem to have settled ourselves comfortably when it is time to move again. On we trundle along the country roads, practically sleeping on our feet, past farmhouses, through villages, silent and shuttered, alongside beet and hop-fields and still we carry on, continually pushed into the muddy ditch at the side of the road to allow transport and army wagons to pass. Big country houses loom up inhabited by soldiers which, we guess, are divisional or corps headquarters. Where we are, or where we are going, nobody seems to know.

"Why the hell can't we doss by the roadside?" wearily

shouts Webster, but everybody is too exhausted to answer even that enquiry.

Night is giving way to dawn when at last we are marched off the road and into a field. A halt, some instructions are given in front, then a figure carrying a hurricane lamp counts us off in sections and leads us to a darker patch on the dark landscape, which blossoms into an erection of some kind. There is the creak of rusty hinges and we find ourselves in a barn of sorts. Our entry is greeted with the cackling of awakened poultry and the grunting of shocked pigs at this barbarian intrusion of their nocturnal privacy.

We sort ourselves out into our own particular groups, fling off our packs, and with a "to hell with the war, I'm going to sleep" feeling, stretch ourselves out on the straw which covers the floor of the barn, and are soon vying with the dislodged occupants for musical honours.

The next thing I remember is the opening of the barn door and a stream of sunshine on my face, while a leather-lunged sergeant invites us to show a leg. With much grousing and cursing we sit up and stretch ourselves, then realising how chilled we are, jump up and stamp some warmth into our bodies.

Breakfast puts us into a better humour, and we jostle and joke around the solitary biscuit-tin of water which constitutes the communal bath-tub. Razors are brought out and there is the usual scrimmage for odd pieces of scented soap and broken mirrors, but, thank Heaven, I am still spared that little bit of torture. A razor over my face once a month is all I find necessary to comply with King's rules and Regulations.

Spit and polish becomes the order of the day, and we scrape and brush until there isn't a vestige of the mud of the trenches left. Then bathing parade. With our towels over our shoulders we march singing down to the bathing-shed. The guns are only a rumble in the distance, and our spirits revive according to the number of miles we put between ourselves and their death-dealing nearness. It has become such a custom to live without a future that the knowledge we can now talk of to-morrow with some measure of certainty makes us light-headed. Pleasure is now derived from the common things in life that at home would have been passed unnoticed. The sun, the trees, the birds, green fields and the country people going about their daily labour; how peaceful it is, surely life as we were meant to live it, but we can only snatch these golden hours while we may and live them to the full.

Streaky's voice, as squeaky as ever, breaks up my thoughts :

"Now for the old wash-tub, boys; it makes me think of Friday night in Blighty."

We laugh gaily at the poor joke, and with one accord break into our company bathing song :

"Whiter than the whitewash on the wall,
Whiter than the whitewash on the wall,
Wash me in the water
That you wash your dirty daughter,
And I shall be whiter than the whitewash on the wall."

In we file, and, stripped naked, we are soon shoving and jostling underneath the dozen hot sprays. The flow of water isn't very generous, but by judiciously spreading each drop as it falls over as wide an area as possible, we fare not so badly. There is much spluttering and joking, and the hut is soon full of steam, lather and the smell of hot bodies, but how refreshing it is. Then, when the air is too hot to breathe, we make tracks for the delousing-shed, where we hand over our verminous shirts and pants and receive clean ones—part worn—in exchange, the past property, no doubt, of some now defunct Tommy.

Without the necessity of a good scratch I hardly know myself, but that blissful state lasts barely half an hour, then I feel a slight itch on my leg. Surely I'm mistaken, just a little irritation with those new pants, it will disappear in a second. I cannot console myself, however; I know that itch too well. Some skulking louse in the seam of my trousers has found his way under the pants, so the unequal fight must commence again. By to-morrow I'll be as lousy as ever.

Chapter Nine

BILLETS NEAR CALAIS

August 21st, NEAR CALAIS. Back at our old billet. Had a pleasant social evening, with the help of French beer and Vin Rouge.

AWAY from the fighting, what a change takes place in us. The knowledge that with a bit of luck we may be out on rest for almost a month makes us carefree and happy. The days pass pleasantly enough. Back in the same village we left so hurriedly, billeted in the same barn with the smelly midden adjoining, we try to cloak ourselves in a mantle of peace and contentment.

Already we have inspected the stream from which we procured our last meal of eels, and hope to have another eel supper before long.

The trees in the orchard are as heavily laden as ever, so we shall visit them later when it is dark.

The farm-yard itself provides plenty of amusement during the day. It is a stud farm, and the services of its animal occupants are constantly in demand, while my knowledge of life in its most crude form is greatly added to. Yesterday we helped a cow to calf, my first experience of the intimate workings of nature. It all seemed rather brutal, but Mac assures me it is quite customary to assist a cow to bring a calf into the world with the help of a rope and a dozen willing hands. This morning we were amused onlookers while the farmer made a litter of male pigs sterile, a sharp knife and his fingers being the only tools used.

Later, in the afternoon, a girl from a neighbouring farm brought a cow to be served by the bull which lords it about the yard here. To see a girl in charge shocked me badly, but she seemed quite unmoved and very workmanlike as she manoeuvred her end of the business into position, then stood by and approved. Strange people, these Frenchies, when judged by our own standard of morals.

The comedy of the day is provided by a sow who evidently doesn't approve of our gentleman boar, and to see her unladylike antics all over the yard and midden, with her farm-hand escort holding grimly to the rope attached to her leg, provides endless amusement for us. The boar at first entered into the sport, but finally, realising his attentions are unwelcome, does the only thing a gentleman could do under the circumstances, and goes to sleep—in the centre of the dirt heap—while the farm-hand, disdaining all our advice, both good and bad, goes off in disgust with his sow.

Then, finding there are no more amorous callers on the books, we sit around and swop yarns, mostly of women and wine.

One of our fellows has been informed by a Belgian youth in the village that the ma'm'selle at our farm is any soldier's meat, as he puts it, for a price, and I can well believe it by the bold glances she casts in our direction as she goes in and out of the numerous barns, but it gives me a feeling of pride in my comrades when I notice that none of them is eager to accept her obvious invitations. Our regiment may have a reputation for gallantry out of the line as well as in, but I can vouch that out of the trenches it isn't just so gallant as rumour would have it.

Then there is the young lady we have christened the "cow girl." She is a flapper of eighteen years or so who looks after a herd of cattle in a near-by field. Rather a pretty girl; she was pointed out to us as being willing to teach any soldier the art of love-making for a matter of a paltry five francs. We have noticed that her shapely legs are always on view whenever we happen to pass her field, and a few men in our battalion are already praising her as being a proper artist in her profession, but, as Webster says, her brush must be well tarred, as three of them, including the colonel's groom, have been sent down to a base hospital, and mademoiselle with the neat ankles has been removed by the military police this morning.

"I can hardly believe it of a kid like that, can you, Streaky?" enquires Mac.

"Me," Streaky answers in surprise. "I'd believe anything of her sex. What I can't believe, though, is that any man would be mug enough to pay five francs for what those fellows have got; they make me vomit."

"Tea up, A Company" is heard coming from our cook's quarters, and we stroll over to the barn for our mess-tins and continue the topic all through our meal. I am beginning to think that this customary talk of women at breakfast, dinner and tea is the secret of the magnificent digestive abilities of our war-time army.

To-night we are going to celebrate the success of our last attack in the line with funds kindly gifted by a generous company officer, the only survivor in our commissioned ranks. After much argument as to the best method of disposing of this gift, we have decided to rule out all charitable suggestions, and give the nearest estaminet the benefit of our newly-acquired wealth. Madam, the owner, is at first a little suspicious, but the bundle of notes proudly exhibited by Webster soon reassures her, and from cold indifference she thaws to embarrassing friendliness. We are all *bonne soldats* and *mes enfants*, such is the power of money. Smiling benevolently upon us and the notes Webster places in front of him on the table, madam takes our order for the first round of drinks, and with shrill calls for Suzanne and monsieur, clatters away along the tiled passage.

"What about a song?" someone suggests.

"What about a drink first?" Webster retorts.

"Where's the damn' music-barrel, anyway? Haven't they got one in this bloody pub? Hi, Streaky, go and parles madam, and tell her we want some music on the subject."

Five minutes later Streaky appears with Suzanne, pushing along the most antiquated piano I have ever seen. We greet its appearance with loud cheers and many calls for Taffy, our musician.

Anxiously we watch Taffy fingering away at the innards of the piano, then, apparently satisfied, he sits down and lets his fingers run lightly over the keys. A bar or two, then he nods approvingly and the party is on.

Ragtimes are the favourites, and as the drinks disappear the lustier we sing them. I think we all have a sneaking desire to get a little drunk if possible and forget the war for an hour or two.

This is the first time I have tasted French wine, and I'm rather surprised at its impotence and disgusted at its flavour, but I gradually discover that by drinking it in sufficient quantities and ignoring the taste, one can become a little merry, and that is my ambition to-night.

When the fun is at its height we are honoured by a visit from the orderly sergeant and the donor of our funds, whom we cheer as only we know how, and to our repeated requests for a song he obliges. Fortunately Taffy knows the music of his fancy. It is a sentimental song. "My Dream" I think, and he possesses a magnificent tenor voice. We are in the proper mood for a little sentiment, and as he finishes our applause brings the whole village to the windows and door of the estaminet. We refuse to let him go without an encore and he smilingly accedes to our wishes with a song we all know : "Some night, some waltz, some girl." Immediately he finishes, Mac whispers something to Taffy and jumps up on a table.

"Now then, altogether, boys." And as Taffy strikes up we all burst into "He's a jolly good fellow." That finished, we have drinks all round, including our officer, all strictly against army regulations, but it is these little acts which endear an officer to his men, and to-night this last surviving officer of our company, at present our captain, is indeed a hero. We'd follow him to hell and back for the asking—madam's wine is having its effect. It is also depleting our stock of five-franc notes, and shortly after the departure of our company officer and sergeant, we hand over the last of our cash and try to make our glasses last out as long as possible, while Taffy, with a farewell rattle, runs through all the old favourites from "Tipperary" to "If you were the only girl in the world;" then with many Bonjours to madam and monsieur and a hug or two from the bolder spirits for Suzanne, we stroll out, a little unsteadily in some cases, into the quiet country lane.

It is a beautiful August evening, calm and peaceful. The night smells of the countryside act more vibrantly on our senses than all the wine we have consumed, and I feel it is great to be alive as our steps become a little more unsteady and our singing more boisterous.

Away to our left searchlights flicker up, and we hear the

distant droning of powerful engines. Flashes are followed by explosions as the bombs are dropped on the dumps at Audricque, then the bark of "Archies" accompany the rattle of machine-guns. The noise subsides a little, then becomes spasmodic until only the ominous droning is left, gradually becoming louder as the planes approach in our direction. To the front-line soldier bombing raids by enemy planes are only minor incidents and this one doesn't even hold our attention. It may seem hopeless trying to forget there is a war, but to-night, with the help of madam's wine, war for us doesn't mean a tinker's curse.

Chapter Ten

THE PRISONER

August 24th, The Barn (between Calais and Audricque). *Weather glorious. Very few parades. Divided up a parcel that arrived for Streaky to-day.*

Poor old Streaky, couldn't help wondering how he got on and what became of the Jerry who helped to bring him in.

Lying in the long grass of the meadows, the sun beating down on our already tanned features, we idly smoke and yarn away the hours between parades.

My thoughts seem to come and go as quickly as the tunes from Webster's mouth-organ, until, as he slips into a longer piece than usual, they take definite shape and focus on a pale, surprised face under a German steel helmet. I should like to meet the owner again, in happier times perhaps. He may have been a Jerry but he was a thorough sport and a brave man, shrewd, I should think, and certainly calculating. I am once again in spirit going over the whole episode.

The raid from the start was doomed. We had barely got clear of our own wire, when a playful Jerry machine-gunner rattled off a few stray rounds. His fun cost us our officer and a corporal, both very likeable fellows, and also was a reminder to us that a stray shot can often find a billet. The sergeant now in charge of the raid held a hurried consultation in which we all shared, and as it was imperative that we should get a prisoner of some kind to please corps headquarters, it was decided to carry on and at least make a show.

Deviating from our pre-arranged route to keep out of the way of the playful gunner was a sensible precaution but not a time saver, and we were already minutes behind with the time programme. On we crawled in single file with a scout out on each flank, myself bringing up the rear. My heart thumping and my breath rasping like a steam engine, I could just make out the man in front of me five paces away, a darker blot than the rest of the landscape. When he crawled forward, I crawled; when he stopped, so did I. Alternately I tried to keep my eye on him and the rear. There was always something moving behind me. I began to get windy. It would be so easy to laze a little behind until the others were out of sight, then slip into a shell-hole until the show was over, and invent some yarn after to justify my action. The thought kept recurring in my mind, but still I crawled after that hazy shadow in front. The very fear of being left alone forced me onwards.

Suddenly there was a commotion ahead of me, more sensed than heard, and I took a firmer grip of the loaded stick I carried, and waited. Revolvers were only to be used in self-defence, a rather vague instruction. The shadow in front of me appeared to be joined by another shadow, then it came backwards towards me.

"What's up?" I found myself whispering.

"Get back, a Jerry patrol in front. Keep in touch, and don't make a noise."

Something definite at last. Anything was better than that mysterious quiet crawling towards the unknown. I was fed up with the business anyway. It might have been wiser if I had bolstered myself up with that generous rum ration instead of handing it over to Webster. However, this would just about put "finis" to the whole thing. We had lost too much time and couldn't possibly keep up with the artillery arrangements. These were my thoughts as I scuttled backwards.

A stifled cry at my back made me face about and peer into the darkness. Nothing could be seen. My windiness having disappeared at the first sign of action, I hurriedly crawled forward again; all thought of retreat had gone. Voices cursing and shouting broke the silence. A bomb burst ahead of me, then pandemonium. Instantly I was on my feet and experienced that strange feeling of elation devoid of fear which seems to be Nature's own drug for the nerves when death, swift and sure, can only be beaten back by one's own exertions. A figure loomed up out of the darkness with the familiar Jerry helmet so easily distinguished from the cap comforters our party wore. I fired away at it until I saw it drop, then recognising Mac's voice I ran in that direction until something tripped me up and I fell headlong into a shell-hole. Before I could rise somebody was on me. Every second I expected to feel the hot searing bullet burn into my flesh, but instead clawing fingers grappled at my throat. My revolver lay useless from its cord somewhere at my back, but all thought of my weapons had gone as I tore at the fingers encircling my neck and kicked at the huge bulk on top of me. Strive as I might, I could not loosen the grip on my throat. The pressure on my windpipe and the nearness of death, instead of befogging my senses, only cleared my head, and I no longer kicked and tore at random. Ever move became calculated as I waited to get in the blow I had so often practised with Mac and Webster for just such an occasion.

I could feel my tongue being forced through my teeth, steel bands seemed to be drawing round my eyeballs, but I had a confidence which my position hardly justified and waited a little longer until I was sure there could be no mistake. My life depended on it. I could see the pale face above me with its heavy moustache and snarling teeth as through a mist, but still I waited until I had his legs astride me and raised him bodily with my left knee—the moment had come. As one knee relaxed my other crashed home with all the power I could muster against his privates, and with a groan he rolled to one side and doubled up, while my yearning lungs filled themselves greedily with huge gulps of air.

For minutes I lay beside the writhing, groaning figure as the machine-guns, regardless of friend or foe, swept the ground, the bullets flying over the lip of the shell-hole like a stream of bees. I was so intent on trying to rub away the pain in my swollen neck that I hadn't noticed the other occupant had ceased his groaning, until an ominous movement and the metallic click of a revolver being cocked, drove my nervous body into instant action, and I smashed the loaded cane, still strapped to my wrist, against the white face turned towards me. Again and again I struck until the white became red, and the figure lay limp and sagging at the bottom of the shell-hole. I grasped the revolver he had dropped and flung it clear of the shell-hole, then tried to gather my scattered senses.

The firing had died down, so cautiously I lifted my head above the crater, but darkness obscured all signs of the other raiders. Later I imagined I saw a huddled-up figure or two, but a Verey light made me duck down with nervous eagerness. For a while I lay beside the motionless Jerry and watched the blood stream over his moustache and down his tunic, and listened to the snorting and bubbling of his laboured breathing through the broken, splintered nose. Carefully I crawled a little nearer and peered at the battered face. My handiwork filled me with loathing, and in an endeavour to ease my conscience I nervously applied my field dressing to his wounds, which I somehow felt would atone for my viciousness. That finished, I just had to get away fearing he might die there beside me, so regardless of duty and the need of a prisoner for information, I scrambled out of the shell-hole and crawled in the direction I thought our trenches lay. My progress was slow. I had no idea where I was or which direction to take. When a flare went up I disdained all caution in my desire to recognise a familiar landmark or the rat-tat-tat. of a friendly machine-gun.

A movement in front flattened me out, and with heart thumping the ground, I lay and listened. I could see nothing in the darkness, still I waited, every nerve taut and strained, the thumping going on inside me more vibrant than ever. Again I seemed to sense a movement, this time a little to my right. I was afraid to move. By this time I was certain there were other prowlers about, and fancied I heard a groan but could not be sure. A flare shot up almost on top of me, curved down in an arc of green light, sizzled and spluttered out a few yards behind me, then darkness more acute than ever.

On I wriggled towards the spot from which I fancied the groan had come, until I saw figures disappear into a shell-hole. Minutes dragged by, but no sign of life emerged from the hole. Instead I heard subdued voices and strained my ears to find out if they were British or Jerry, and never did such vehement though whispered cursing sound so sweet. Warily I crawled a little nearer until I could even make out the words, and recognised Mac's voice telling somebody to go to hell.

My call stopped the flow of cursing which followed. There was dead silence, then as I called his name again I heard:

"Let's have a squint at you."

Cautiously I moved forward, knowing how easy it is to excite that little extra pressure on a trigger by making too sudden an appearance. I looked down into the crater and upon Mac's revolver pointed straight at my temple, then to the frightened face of a Jerry, and towards a curled-up figure in khaki. Mac nodded towards the khaki heap in answer to my dumb enquiry:

"Streaky—a hand grenade. We've got to get him in, Jock, he's stopped a bad one. Do you know where we are?"

"No, I'm lost. I've been roaming about for hours. Don't you know?"

"I'm damned if I do, but this blighter says he does," and Mac gave a tug at the belt round the Jerry's waist.

I had quite forgotten him and looked suspiciously in his direction.

"Oh, he's all right," Mac assured me. "He's going in with me. The blighter nearly startled the life out of me when he spoke up in English. What do you make of it, Jock; he says he knows which are our trenches and which are his?"

"I do, I do," chimed in the Jerry.

"Well, if he knows our side of the street, let's hop it, Mac," I advised.

"That's the damn' trouble; he won't act as guide unless I promise to let him go when he lands us at our wire."

"I make a proposition, good proposition," the Jerry anxiously informs us, but is silenced with another tug at his belt.

"What do you think, Jock? Shall I knock him daft, or let him carry on?"

Unsuccessfully we tried various ways to make the Jerry give us the information we wanted, but the need for silence hampered us greatly. Without the wounded Streaky we could have taken a chance, but with him the odds were too great, especially if the German spoke the truth, and at last we reluctantly fell in with his proposition. He was to lead us to our wire, and if everything was in order, he returned. If not, well, Mac would see to that.

That decided, we turned our attention to poor Streaky. Never again would he look at this world with those smiling eyes of his. The bomb which had so badly disfigured his face had also obliterated the one charm that was Streaky's —a nature as sunny as his life had been sordid, reflected through a pair of humorous twinkling eyes. Blind—never to be able to see again, to have known green fields and blue skies, to have watched the sun sinking like a golden ball in the west, to have seen the simple beauties of nature which are our birthright, and then—a sudden blinding flash and darkness, complete and impenetrable.

Tenderly the Jerry and I carried him over the uneven ground, while Mac brought up the rear keeping a watchful eye on our guide. His careful handling of Streaky made me wonder why this youth in the field grey should be an enemy and not a comrade, and once when our eyes met, he smiled and whispered "Poor Kamerad." I could only repeat "Poor Kamerad."

This was war, yet I felt no enmity towards that young German. In the short time I had rather grown to like him, he was so sincere in his desire to help Streaky. He could be a good pal, I fancied, just like Mac or Webster, and yet he might easily have been that other German I'd left behind in the shell-hole.

In spite of all our care Streaky's wound started to bleed afresh. I felt his heart; it was beating faintly. The German produced a rather soiled handkerchief and with its help we stopped the flow a little, then on we struggled until we came to wire entanglements, when Mac joined us.

"I'll give a shout, Jock, and if everything is cigarro Jerry can beat it; if not, well, I'm keeping this handy"—and his revolver was poked into our erstwhile comrade's ribs.

"You'd better take Streaky back a bit, just in case things don't turn out right."

A moan or two escaped from Streaky's lips as we lifted him to the safety of a shell-hole, and breathlessly I waited as Mac with his revolver still tickling the Jerry's ribs, advanced with him towards the wire again.

His first shout was unanswered. He yelled again and the sentry's challenge rang out. Our troubles for the time being were over.

A second later a grey-clad figure slipped into the shell-hole beside me.

"Good-bye, Kamerad"—and our hands met.

"Good-bye, Jerry, and good luck." Then he was gone.

With difficulty we managed to get Streaky through our wire with as few cuts as possible and into our front-line trench, where we waited for a stretcher to take him down. His cries, as returning consciousness revealed nothing but darkness to him, still ring in my ears.

"I can't see, I can't see, everything's dark. Is that you, Jock? What have they done to me? My eyes, oh, my eyes."

"It's all right, Streaky," I tried to comfort him, "the doctor will soon put you right. You're going home. You've got a blighty, just think of it."

"But my eyes, Jock, I can't see. Oh, God, I'm not blinded, am I?"

"Don't talk rot," I remember replying. "You've got a cushy blighty if you wangle it properly. If you don't you'll get no further than the base, then you'll be back here within a couple of months. Don't be a bloody fool, play up to them and it will be all aboard for Blighty for six months."

But I could not pacify him. He knew he was blind, and his heart-breaking sobbing followed me as I walked round the traverse with Mac on our way to headquarters to report.

We had barely covered a hundred yards of trench when a shout in German from our wire brought us to a halt. Hugging the side of the trench, Mac drew a bomb out of his pocket and slipped the pin, while I gripped my loaded cane nervously and waited. There was another shout, this time directly above us. A sandbag fell from the parapet, and into the trench flopped a German whom we naturally took to be the first of a raiding party, but before I could strike home with my cane he was on his feet and grasping my arm, while in a surprised tone came the one word, "Kamerad." He was bareheaded and I recognised him instantly.

"Well, I'll be damned," I heard Mac's amazed exclamation, "Jerry back again."

Mystified, he was at first unable to answer our many questions, then as he realised the position his shoulders drooped and his hands went up. His explanation was quite simple to we who knew the conditions. A fall into a shell-hole, a nasty knock on the head, a scramble up on the wrong side and Mac's one-time prisoner had returned to him.

He looked so pathetic standing there, and such a wan smile crossed his handsome features as he shrugged his shoulders and blurted out the one word "Kismet," that we forgot all about penalties for our subsequent actions. After all, he was hardly an enemy of ours. Had he not helped us to bring in Streaky?

"Beat it, Jerry, go on, over you go."

At first he didn't seem to understand us until we tried to hoist him bodily over the parapet. His foot slipped, however, and down he came. He had just secured another foothold when around the traverse appeared an officer with his orderly—it was too late, just "Kismet."

I wonder where you are now, Kamerad. You are better off than I am, anyhow. You are away from it all. Fate certainly is a strange thing.

From a distance I seem to be aware of someone yelling :

"Wake up, Jock, it's tea-time; wake up, you lazy blighter, the sun's scorching your eyeballs." My musing comes to a sudden end.

"Eh, what's that, Mac?" I drowsily exclaim. "Oh, tea-time; don't worry, I'll be there, I've never missed a cook-house yet."

I rub the sleep out of my eyes and am again back in the present. Webster's mouth-organ is still going, a grasshopper clicks noisily somewhere near my ear, a couple of butterflies flit to and fro above my head, while as far as the eye can see runs the straight poplar-lined road. A peasant trundles along it leading a horse and cart. Time to him seems to be of no importance. The very atmosphere breathes peace.

I try to shut out the past and forget there is a future. If only this could last for ever. That is all I ask. A quiet countryside unknown to war, with green trees instead of splintered stumps, clean earth that hasn't been tortured and poisoned by explosives, a task like that peasant's to justify my existence—and peace.

But that is not for me. Too soon I shall have to go back to it all—I feel as if I am doomed.

Chapter Eleven

TRAINING BEHIND THE LINES

August 28th, 1917, The Barn. A great holiday this, marred by the thought of going back.

Field training to-day and an inspection by the "All Highest." A clatter of hoofs, a flash of gold braid and red tabs and he was gone.

Heated discussions to-night on "Après la guerre."

FIELD days and intensive training are now the forerunners of another spell at the front, and each morning finds us on the march to some rendezvous.

The new drafts, oblivious to what is in store for them, treat these outings like a picnic and their good spirits certainly are infectious. We thoroughly enjoy playing at war.

On arrival at the appointed spot we find the whole

division assembling, and with much banter and good-natured chaff, are directed by a guide to a farm-house commandeered as our headquarters for the occasion. The battalion is halted outside, and the signallers and staff noisily take possession of the two front rooms, while the plans are briefly outlined to us by platoon sergeants.

Our trenches are the ditch at the side of the road, our objective the second or Jerry black line, the battalion objective a strong point in the shape of a quarry, a thousand yards in front.

Flag-waggers denote the barrage, and woe betide the man who treats the scheme as a joke and sits down instead of flinging himself flat at the sound of the whistle.

Our officer emphasises the fact that this training must be taken seriously. Every man must take advantage of cover wherever possible as if actually at the front, and we must deport ourselves like seasoned troops of a storm division going into action, not like a host of schoolboys at a Sunday-school treat. A hint is also dropped regarding the likelihood of an honoured visit by the Commander-in-Chief, who is desirous of personally thanking our division for splendid work done in the last attack. I have the feeling that we are expected to swoon from sheer delight at this piece of news, but strange to say it seems to leave us older soldiers, at least, quite cold and unmoved.

We take up our position in the ditch and wait for the flags to start waving, then over we go, and move forward to the attack. The flag-wagging comes to a stop in front, the barrage is stationary, whistles blow, and down we flop. This is the first imaginary strong point. Our phantom guns will no doubt put it out of action in a few minutes, leaving no time for a snooze.

"Something like a war this. I could stick it for duration."

"So could I. Oh, damn that whistle."

Up we get and advance into a field of ripe corn. In the centre the stalks stand so high that we are completely hidden, and certain unpopular sergeants and corporals are bombarded with tufts and lumps of earth. Much shouting ensues but the corn is thick and friendly, and nobody knows from which direction the missiles came. A hare springs up and threatens to stampede the whole formation, but authority at last brings us back into line, and our chances of hare soup for dinner are gone.

When we emerge from the cornfield, it is a sorry mess, with dozens of beautifully trampled paths running right through it, but Monsieur Le Farmer stands by and smiles —the English pay good compensation.

Once again in the open we are under the critical eye of the headquarters staff, and the business develops into a well-drilled field day. The rests during the gunners' shoots are very acceptable, and allow Mac to take pot shots with a catapult at the opposing troops, composed of men of our own brigade made up for the occasion as Jerries with white bands round their hats.

The sound of beating hoofs draws our attention to the field we have just left, and an exceedingly smart cavalcade, glittering with gold braid and red tabs, with lancers in front and behind, canters past—the Commander-in-Chief has honoured us.

"Don't think he noticed us, Jock. Won't he be annoyed when he finds out"—and Mac lazily stifles a yawn.

"Some say 'Good old General'."

The rest of Mac's observations are lost in the general noise that accompanies the rush to our last objective, the quarry. This we capture in grand style, yelling ourselves hoarse and putting the fear of death into its occupants, who begin to wonder if we really have gone mad, and not realising we are just making the best show we can while the General is about.

Imaginary counter-attacks are repulsed with ease, and having won this bit of the war we return to the field-kitchens in the rear for our midday meal of stew.

A practice battle may be good training for those in authority, but to the ordinary private soldier like myself, who receives the minimum of information as to what it's all about, it means merely another outing to be made as enjoyable as possible.

Afternoons are spent in a newly rigged up "Bull Ring," where we are drilled in the art of killing, the culture of the bayonet and the meaning of the all powerful word "hate." This part of our training is no picnic. A sandy stretch ringed in with wire, it is the nursery of the house of hell. Brotherhood, goodwill and Christianity are words unknown within its environment. Thrust, lunge, stab, curse and hate——these are its teachings. Leather-lunged sergeants, the finest of men gone mad with the lust for blood, experts at their fearsome trade, instil into us the surest and quickest methods of drawing the life-blood from a fellow creature. Their raucous voices are heard all over the drill ground as they bellow out their commands.

"Charge them, and let them know you are coming, put the fear of death into them by cursing and snarling, kill them, *kill them*, and above all remember the kill-de-luxe is always accomplished by cold steel. The bayonet is the weapon for aggressive warfare. Get your weight behind it, and it slides into their innards as easy as my missus, and Heaven knows she's easy enough. Watch them squirm as you draw it out, and never forget to smash the butt against their privates; they may recover from a bayonet wound, so make sure they can't go home and put their wives in the family way.

"Now then, let me see you charge these dummies, and look as if you meant it. You've got-lungs; well, use them; you may frighten your best girl, but you won't frighten me."

Backwards and forwards we charge, thrusting and stabbing, sweating and cursing, while dominating everything is the rasping voice of our instructor.

As the long summer afternoon draws to a close we are marched out of the ring, feeling as if we have come safely through some terrific ordeal, and passed unscathed the hot fetid portals of a hell. Inside its wired-off space the air is vibrant with a current of fierce vindictive militarism, which finds a channel into our beings under the false names of Morale and Courage. It is a relief to see its hot dusty ground disappearing behind us.

Leisurely we stroll along the country road back to our billet, making a stop at each orchard on the way and cramming our pockets with apples to our hearts' content. A day's work behind us, a peaceful evening ahead.

Night, with the full moon shedding a soft light through the barn, the hooting of an owl outside, the rustling of leaves and the sound of restless cattle—these are the things we can appreciate while we puff contentedly at our pipes and cigarettes as we argue far into the night.

When will the war end? What will happen to us? Questions we can never agree on.

The first we can find no definite answer for; it is something only to be dreamed about, something that, deep down in our hearts, we doubt if we'll ever live to see. Nevertheless that does not prevent us from speculating and surmising on just what will happen to us when the miracle takes place.

Mac is of the opinion that there has been such a wastage of men that something will have to be done to increase the diminished population. Dear Mac, how enthusiastic he can become over his pet argument.

"I tell you, boys, there will be stud farms, the nicest and finest of girls housed in luxury and fed on the best, one he-man to a hundred of the dear ladies, nothing to do but eat, love and sleep, with plenty of each—just think of it, boys—paradise; and take it from me, I'm going to lord it over one of these dovecots—my oath I am."

"Rot, a lot of bloody rot," breaks in Webster. "I'll tell you what will happen to you duration soldiers. You'll have the time of your lives, you'll be hugged and kissed, treated and petted, they'll have banners strung across the streets : 'Welcome Home, Our Heroic Tommies,' you'll be received with open arms, they'll let you mess on their doorstep and thank you for doing it, you'll be the heaven and earth and all that therein is for just one month, then some morning they'll wake up and realise the war is over, and that's when you fellows will have to start using your own toilet paper. You'll get the cold shoulder, as they'll have no more use for a penniless, out-of-work, fighting man who stinks of trench manners and speech. Hell, the very people who have fattened and prospered on your blood and sweat will be the first to denounce you; you'll be shunned like a lot of sewer rats.

"Ah, you can laugh, boys; you're little tin gods just now, but when it's all over you'll find you've not only had to fight the war but you'll have to fight the peace as well, and a damned sight harder too, if you're going to win through, so get it out of your thick heads that you're in for a cushy time, and put all that in your pipe and smoke it."

As Webster proceeds to light his pipe, he waits with an amused twinkle in his eye for the storm of abuse he knows will follow his shattering of our dream, and he hasn't long to wait :

"Let's ram this sock in his mouth"; "Smother him, somebody, he's too cheerful"; "Kick him, he's still breathing"; "Let's bump him, boys," comes from different corners of the barn, but we are all too sleepy to take their advice and become involved in a rough house with the doughty Webster.

When the noise subsides, Taffy attempts to carry on the argument. With his head to one side and his pointing index finger wagging away in tune with his ideas, it is evident he has given the subject some thought :

"It is difficult to know what will happen to you fellows," he commences, and is instantly stopped by a great clearing of throats, intermingled with helpful hints on speech etiquette :

"My lords, ladies and gentlemen"; "Comrades and fellow workmen"; while above all booms Mac's voice, telling the world :

"Shut the pubs, open the breweries and give the fighting man a chance."

Unabashed by this good-humoured hostility, Taffy carries on until we are all listening intently :

"It's useless trying to prophesy what will really happen when the war is over, boys. All I know is that there will be a couple of million men suddenly thrust back into civil life, many of whom war has stripped of their thin veneer of civilisation, men accustomed to look on life cheaply, all of them coarsened in different degrees by the exacting life they have been forced to live. As in war, so it will be in peace, and anything might happen.

"Some of you, of course, have jobs to return to. For you, the war will merely have been an episode, but there are others like Mac, Duggan, Barham and a few more who had just started an apprenticeship. To them the war will have been more than an interruption; the most valuable years of their lives have been wasted here; they'll have to start all over again, handicapped by age. Then there are the babes, like Jock there."

"Hold on, Taffy," I interrupt.

"It's quite true, Jock, there are dozens like you out here, straight from school into this, men before you were youths, the only trade you know—that of killing. Yes, unless the old country can dig up a Solomon, peace is going to bring one glorious mess, an unequal fight against a public who will soon forget our sacrifices, and new generations who will know nothing of the war and what it meant to those who served.

"That is what peace is going to mean for us, boys. It makes me wonder if those who return are going to be so fortunate as they think they will be."

"And here endeth the third lesson," interposes Mac.

"Good old Taffy; one of these days you'll be nodding your head in a pulpit, but hang it all, if peace is going to be like that, I'm all for the jolly old war."

"Hell, look at the time," Webster exclaims in astonishment. "Damn' near two o'clock. Some of you blasted blighters would spout all night. I'm getting down to it, so shut that bloody door somebody, it's getting chilly enough in here to freeze the brass knick-knacks off a cast-iron monkey."

Snuggled into our blankets and greatcoats, the majority of us are soon fast asleep, but for a while I toss restlessly, thinking of the different opinions. Mac's, of course, I dismiss as fantastic; Webster's, well, like all old soldiers he dearly loves a grouse. Taffy now, he has evidently given the subject serious thought and his words keep returning to my mind, but, after all, what does it matter, any sort of life is better than war! I'd exchange places to-morrow with the most humble and lowliest tramp at home to get away from here.

A few short months ago and this was the height of my ambition—to fight for king and country. War, glorious war, with its bands and marching feet, its uniforms and air of recklessness, its heroes and glittering decorations, the war of our history books.

From the cradle up we have been fed on battles and heroic deeds, nurtured on bloody episodes in our country's history; war was always glorious, something manly, never sordid, uncivilised, foolish or base.

The untimely deaths and disfigurements, the filthiness and unnatural inhuman aspects of war nobody ever seems to have thought about, and if, perchance, one should be killed, is it not glorious to die for king and country?

What idiotic piffle is expressed by those few words. The man who first phrased them must have been the prince of buffoons. What fool wants to die for king and country? Is it not a finer and more sensible thing to live for them? That's what our historians want to teach us—to live for king and country and our fellow men.

That would be a life worth living, embodying just that touch of comradeship which we out here could appreciate, the life of a true Christian civilisation. That is the ideal which keeps most of us going, now the novelty of war has worn off, and if by chance we should fall by the way, may our sacrifice not be in vain.

Chapter Twelve

A DAY IN CALAIS

September 2nd, BILLET BETWEEN CALAIS AND AUD-RICQUE. One glorious day in Calais. I'd almost forgotten what civilisation was like.

Don't know if I should mention this, but here goes—I've seen the inside of a "red lamp."

"PRIVATE PURVES has permission to be absent from his quarters from 8 a.m. till 12 midnight for the purpose of proceeding to Calais."

I scan over the slip of paper, then fold it carefully and stow it away in one of my bulging pockets. With Mac and Webster I am going on a day's holiday, and this is my "Pass Friend" for all inquisitive redcaps. Already rumours are floating around that we return shortly to the front, so we are determined to make the trip a real birthday.

It is a glorious morning, and with bicycles borrowed from the signal sergeant we start off with twenty francs each in our pockets, an insatiable appetite for civilised excitement, and a day of our own to do with as we like, our first since coming here—who could wish for more?

Gaily we pedal along singing snatches of army songs and making sorry attempts at harmonising, occasionally breaking off to greet all and sundry with cheerful *Bonne jours.*

The long military road to Calais stretches in front of us white and poplar-lined, and we pass by fields of every description, stretches of beet, waving corn, cabbage and potato, while over some of the hedges we get momentary glimpses of orchard trees laden with fruit. To-day, however, our acquired scrounging instincts lie dormant. We have no eyes for the beauties of the countryside; we are on holiday, we are going to mix with human beings dressed in civilian clothes, we are going to see shops, theatres, taxis, we are even going to sit on a beach and gaze on the sea, we'll hear music, eat chocolate and rub shoulders with women— decent women.

Faster we pedal and still faster, singing and shouting to each other, we know not what and care less. Just three happy fighting men with money in our pockets and a day's enjoyment ahead—we want the world to know.

Towards midday, although we still have a good hour's journey before us, we call a halt at one of the larger villages and enter the first estaminet. Cycling on the hot dusty road creates a thirst, but the only refreshment we can procure is beer—French beer and very warm at that. I gulp it down; it clears the dust from my throat but leaves me thirstier than ever.

"This stuff is no good," I exclaim in disgust. "Let's see if we can get a lemon. What do you say, Mac?"

"Yes, come on Webby, we don't want to hang on here all day, and you look as if you were becoming anchored."

"Not me, boys," retorts Webster. "Lemons ain't in my line for a drink, but they'll be better than this maiden's piss. Let's hop it."

We tour the village for a fruit shop, but it doesn't seem

to boast one as up and down its main street we saunter, followed by four or five young boys touting for their sisters. Their innocent-looking faces make me wonder if they have the least idea of what they are doing or saying.

"I take you to my sister Ecossais, she veree good, veree cheap, veree clean. *Bonne* jig-a-jigg."

"Alleh," I yell at them, but still they persevere and hang around the door of a shop we enter, which looks as if it might unearth a lemon. We try our limited stock of French on the buxom madam behind the counter, all to no good, then as a last resource we hit on a one-act drama depicting our hero hot and bothered, he sucks his fingers and lo, he is revived and finds eternal life!

Madam's face glows, it positively beams as she bends down and rummages in a bag behind the counter, eventually fishing out two cucumbers.

"Hell," ejaculates Mac, "let's give it up, either she's hopeless or we are."

"*Combienne, madam?*" I enquire and stare as intelligently as possible as she rattles off the price in quick French. I am none the wiser, so fall back on the old expedient of handing over a note or two and waiting for change.

Out in the street we are once again bombarded with :
"I take you to my sister, jig-a-jigg, *tres bonne.*"

Webster asks me for one of the cucumbers, gazes at it—
"Some lemon," he remarks—and flings it towards the youngsters, who surprised at his generosity, forget all about their sisters and scramble and fight for possession of it, while we mount our cycles and soon leave the village behind.

Nearing Calais the atmosphere of peace disappears, and entrenchments, overgrown with grass behind belts of barbed wire red with rust, begin to appear on either side of the road, while at every bridge and railway crossing blue-clad sentries stroll backwards and forwards or lounge against any support that will bear their weight as they smoke away the hours of sentry-go. The Poilu may be and doubtless is a good soldier, but one thing is evident : he has the privilege, and possesses the knack, of making a war as comfortable as possible, which is a glaring contrast to our own regulations and training.

In the town itself everything is jolly and "Business as Usual" looking, while soldiers of almost every nationality throng its streets: French Poilus, French Colonials, Belgians, Portuguese, Indians, our own Colonials and home troops, with a few American engineers.

The French have an air of boredom and carelessness of military detail, which contrasts unfavourably with the smartness of our own troops. The Belgians are a replica of the French, only a little more so. The Portuguese are a dirty, scruffy-looking lot, and the base seems quite a good place to let them fight their war in. The Indians are rather detached and regal looking, just a little too slim in the shanks to make really smart-looking soldiers afoot. Our own men are the pick of the bunch; whether home regiment or Colonial they are, on the whole, a soldierly-looking lot, varied perhaps as regards physique, but universally clean and dependable looking, intriguing maidenly hearts with an occasional glimpse of the gay manly swagger of a kilt or the saucy devil-may-care tilt of an Australian slouch hat.

The Americans have a colonial look about them similar to our own Anzacs and Canadians, and seem likely enough fellows, but have taken too long to think about coming out here to earn our admiration.

The civilians at this hour seem to be either going or coming from business. The male population is composed of either extreme youth or age, the happy medium being seldom seen outside a uniform.

The girls with their silken-clad ankles and summer frocks are like angels to us, they are all so charming. It is only now, when we are once again mixing in feminine society, that I realise how much we have missed them lately, and how much we owe to their presence. We become more particular with our talk, and actually forget to curse, while our behaviour becomes less boisterous; in fact we act like thorough gentlemen and hardly recognise ourselves, and all because there are females about. I'm beginning to believe they are the real backbone of our modern civilisation.

On second thoughts, however, I realise they are not such

angels after all, but merely girls, as I notice them admiring whole-heartedly the athletic figures of Mac and Webster. I feel rather insignificant beside these two handsome specimens, and grudgingly admit to myself that the fact I am considered a fairly smart soldier and an expert in nearly every branch of training the army can offer, besides being the holder of three boxing championships, must be scant compensation in female eyes for my lack of inches—with much stretching and racking of muscles I can just scale, and no more, five feet five inches; not much to look at when sandwiched between Mac and Webster. That doesn't worry me much, however, and I regain all my confidence before we reach the Y.M.C.A. hut. Our bicycles we store in an outhouse, then enter the hut to see what we can scrounge in the way of dinner. Subtle enquiries reveal there are no free meals to be had in the town. Calais is certainly becoming war-weary.

We have just decided that if we intend to eat we'll have to dip our hands in our pockets, when Webster stops us with :

"Hold your hosses, boys, hold your hosses, look who's behind the counter—Mike, of all people."

And before we know what it is all about, he is shaking the hand of a fellow serving behind the counter as if his life depended on it.

In a few minutes he rejoins us looking as happy as a pig among dirt.

"What a stroke of luck, boys; that's Mike, my half-section in the old crush in 1914. Fancy coming across him here. He's got a cushy job, but Mike never forgets an old pal. Everything's velvet, boys, the grub's on the house. Listen, we'll go up one at a time and order from Mike what we want. He will see us right. You go first, Jock."

Accordingly I approach the counter, and, after a look round, order a couple of pies, a few buns and the inevitable cup of tea, handing over a five-franc note. My meal is brought and the change returned to me with a wink from Webby's pal. It feels rather a fistful of money, but I just grab it and take my pies and tea over to the table we have commandeered.

As soon as I am seated I obey Webster's instructions to

have a squint at my change, and I find I have exactly ten francs. I chuckle with pleasure as I cram the money into my pocket, thinking at the same time, I'm afraid, that army life hasn't improved my sense of right and wrong. Mac and Webster in turn repeat this little performance, and return to the table the richer by ten francs, a plate of buns and a mug of tea.

We have little enough time to spare, so hurry over our meal, and on the way out, go once again to the counter in turn and buy cigarettes. This time I hand over a franc note and receive a twenty box of Turf cigarettes and five francs in exchange. I now have a comfortably filled inside; twenty-nine francs in my pocket and cigarettes to spare. Calais is a great place.

Outside in the sunshine we join the throng in the street, and have barely gone fifty yards when a young girl with a charming smile hands each of us a card on which is the printed information that Madame Antoine's "Palace of Pleasure" is situated in a street near the prom, and that she has twelve beautiful girls from London and Paris waiting to entertain lonely Tommies like ourselves, while on the back of the card is a photo of one "Yvonne" posed in her birthday suit, plus silk stockings and garters.

"Is this a red lamp?" Mac and I enquire simultaneously of Webster.

"Of course it is, you mugs. What d'you think it is—a bloody confirmation class?"

We laugh excitedly. We have heard a lot about these brothels. They are a constant topic of conversation in trenches and billets, but the opportunity to visit one has never before presented itself to us, and now that it has we are torn between a desire to satisfy our curiosity and the natural loathing we feel towards something we have been taught is shameful and degrading.

Webster decides the matter for us.

"Damn it, you're men, aren't you?" he enquires. "Let's be merry while we can; who knows, the next time up the line we may all go sky-high! Hell, what you chumps are afraid of beats me; you don't realise what you've missed."

"Oh, we're going all right," I hasten to reply, "but only for a dekko, we're not going upstairs with any of these old tabs."

"You'll change your mind when you get there," retaliates Webster.

I feel so excited at visiting the place I hardly notice the crowds in the street, until we are hailed from across the road by some of our machine-gunners :

"Ahoy there, you Highland blighters, don't you know pals when you see them?"

We cross the street and find they have already visited the "Palace of Pleasure," so get instructions from them as to the direction to take, and with cheeros and a promise to meet them later to see the leave boat depart, we make tracks for the twelve beautiful girls.

"And if you want a good thing," one of the gunners yells after us, "take the small one in the blue garters, she's a peach."

After taking one or two wrong turnings we eventually find Madame Antoine's place, just an ordinary looking estaminet in a rather dingy street. Inside we pass along a narrow passage and through a swing door into an ordinary sized bar-room with tables and chairs alongside both walls, and at the far end the bar counter. We are no sooner through the door than three females approach us, their complete outfit a silk shawl, barely covering their supposed charms, high-heeled shoes, silk stockings and the inevitable garters.

"Me good jig-a-jigg, Tommee."

Their arms encircle our necks, their hot breath fans our cheeks, and the smell of scent from their mercenary bodies greets our nostrils. My face blushes a deep red as I follow Mac and Webster with their females to a table. So far I have had no dealings with women outside my own family, and girls to me are a sacred sex composing all that's good and clean. The stories regarding the women of the army brothels I have never wholly believed, and now that I am in contact with the real thing I have no method of dealing with it.

Shamefacedly I try to dislodge her arm from my neck, my one desire not to hurt her feelings and yet make it quite clear that I am only here out of curiosity. Back her arm comes as she presses her thinly-clad body against mine whispering : "Me give you good time, Tommee," but I

can only blurt out: "No money, ma'm'selle, no money."
Instantly her arm falls from my neck as she splutters away
in French, and rises to make for another likely customer.
Thinking I have offended her, and in an endeavour to
show that it is only the lack of the necessary cash which
prevents me from being friendly, and also in an exaggerated
attempt at bravado, I playfully give her a tap as she passes
on the generous expanse of almost exposed behind. She
whirls round, and snaps out: "No money, no damned
good," accompanied with a resounding smack as her hand
comes in contact with my jaw.

Amidst laughter from the surrounding tables, and with
neck and face for the second time blushing a vivid scarlet,
I sink down on my seat, and try to take cover behind
Webster.

"This beats the band," remarks Mac.

"I thought we were going to see twelve beautiful girls,
and there's nothing here but a bunch of painted hags hawk-
ing their wares."

Webster looks at him in feigned surprise:

"Hell, what do you want for five francs? Cleopatra?
Damn it, they're all clean and that's about as much as a
good soldier should want."

Mac shrugs his shoulders:

"I've a different opinion, Webby, of what constitutes
the word clean. However, we shan't argue about that. Let's
have a drink."

We order the usual beer. It is weak liquid refreshment
but suits our pocket. We sip it slowly and look around us.

The amusement I derive at first from seeing the women
trying to entice men upstairs with them, gradually turns
into disgust. I count eight women ranging in age from
seventeen to twenty-seven, clad only in a wrap of some thin
pale coloured material, each one sporting a different colour
with garters to match. Some sit on men's knees and drink
out of their glasses, or encourage the men to paw them, and
follow it up with an invitation to go upstairs, and if their
efforts to incite a lustful interest are fruitless, they leave
their would-be victim without any attempt to hide their
disgust at the spineless thing of a man who has withstood
their blandishments.

I really believe they are disgusted with us who refuse their invitations. To them it is just a trade, a profession. They have goods to sell and we are the potential buyers who haven't the guts to clinch a bargain. They are immoral themselves, either through choice or circumstances, but, in any case, professionals in their calling, and seem to detest any poor amateur who cannot appreciate their art.

Soldiers are constantly coming and going, each new arrival being confronted by one of the damsels and bombarded with invitations. There is, apparently, a code of honour amongst them not to poach on another's preserves, but as soon as one realises her charms are not bringing results, she sidles off and her place is immediately taken by another. Every now and then one goes arm-in-arm with a man up to the bar. Money is passed over the counter, and they disappear upstairs to the bedrooms.

A slip of a girl in a pale green wrap seems to be doing a roaring trade. Already she has had three customers since we arrived and seems likely to get a fourth. I feel rather sorry for her. She is young, not much older than myself, her eyes are bright and her face flushed, but her nervous gestures and bodily lassitude betray the pretence of gaiety she adopts.

And these are women, the delicate, modest, virginal creatures we have been taught to revere. I am no prude. Army life has knocked all that out of me, but the utter abandonment in this brothel positively stinks.

Wherever there are soldiers, there are women. I have seen them in the camps at home, in the villages in which we have bivouacked out here, but always speaking their part in innuendoes, revealing themselves only under the cloak of darkness, or in the seclusion of strict privacy, but in this place all is different. To a hesitating customer they display their full bosoms and bulging thighs, or press their bodies against his, until he either capitulates or transfers his affections elsewhere. There is no concealment of their trade. This is a brothel and they are harlots, willing to sell their bodies to any man who pays the price, and ready to use every trick and artifice in view of a hundred eyes to obtain a customer. Modest people who are easily shocked have no business to be here where they pander to the desires of the lustful only. Outside the red lamp is above the door, the symbol of women and wine.

My attention has been so focused on what is going on around me that I have failed to notice that Webster has picked his fancy.

His cheery : "Well, soldiers, see you when I come down, just going to give ma'm'selle a treat," draws my attention to my comrade. Mac and I watch him walk up to the bar with his ma'm'selle hanging on to his arm and looking up into his face as if to her he was the only man in the world. Notes are handed over to a fat greasy old woman behind the counter, then they disappear through the door leading upstairs.

"I hope he enjoys himself with that little two-faced blighter," I remark. "Did you see the way she looked at him, Mac? Just as if he was the one and only, and I'll bet she has been with a dozen men already to-day. Some place this, what do you think of it, Mac?"

"Hellish, Jock, it's enough to put me off women altogether. Still, I wouldn't have missed it for anything."

"Neither would I. It's an experience, but not one I'd like the folks at home to know of. Just look at the hungry lustful expression on some of those fellows' faces; pathetic, isn't it?"

"Damnable," Mac replies, "but after all I don't suppose you can blame them. They are alive to-day, to-morrow— well, who knows! They aren't all the same though. Look at that couple there."

I look and see a big hefty girl with a truly terrific spread of behind doing her best to entice an Australian to go upstairs with her. She tries every trick of her stock-in-trade, but to no purpose, until, disgusted, he turns and strides out.

The British soldier may not be a saint but he can still claim to be morally sound. It is surprising, under the conditions we live and the temptations flung in our way, that any of us are morally clean.

There are many sitting around the tables whose expressions only denote contempt, sight-seers like ourselves who are already wishing they hadn't come. We are not all like plaster saints, however, and there are a few who, once away from military restrictions, allow themselves the luxury of excess, but if they capture a little pleasure or forgetfulness from it, who can blame them? Life is so very uncertain out here. Even so, I have not yet seen those mythical queues lined up outside a red lamp, neither have I seen a really drunk soldier. Perhaps that is because I have little experience of the back areas, or have never been in a part of the line where such things are possible, or I may just be fortunate in my choice of pals. We front-line men either have the money and not the opportunity, or the opportunity and not the money, or both and not the inclination, which results, amongst my circle of friends anyway, in a standard of morality and sobriety worthy of a better cause.

I am just watching one of the girls for the sixth time displaying a shrapnel wound, or it may be an old abscess, on her thigh to an admiring group of Tommies, when Mac nudges me and points to the bar, and I notice Webby ordering a drink. He gulps it down and comes towards our table.

"Well," I enquire, "got it all over?"

"You bet, she was the goods; come on, let me put you on to her Jock, I'll explain matters to her."

"Not for me, thanks, you old ramrod," I burst out.

"Come on, Mac, it's time we were clearing out of here now that Webby has got the dirty water off his chest."

Outside the air feels much cleaner, and we take all Webster's gibes and hints regarding our manliness as good jokes.

The day passes all too quickly and night-time finds us once more on the road, poorer in pocket but richer in memories.

We have sadly watched a leave boat slink out of harbour, forgotten our troubles as we played with youngsters on the sands, filled our insides with eggs and chips, laughed outrageously at a comic picture in a French theatre, gazed at the immodest postcards displayed in the shops, wondered in amazement at their street lavatories, wherein a man can go and do what he wants and exchange pleasantries with his female acquaintance in the street, and last of all visited a British canteen and shared in a little tussle with two over-zealous military policemen. Verily our day has been complete.

Towards midnight we arrive back at our billets tired but happy.

"Here the wanderers come," I hear somebody shout.

"Hello, Jock, how did you get on, meet any nice girls?" Then in feigned surprise:

"Heavens, I do believe they've brought Webby back sober. Tell us all about it, Mac."

"You got your holiday just in time, you lucky blighters," someone else remarks; "we go up the line to-morrow."

"What's that?" the three of us enquire together.

"We're in for it again, it's on company orders, parade 8.15 a.m., destination unknown."

Slowly we climb into the barn; our good spirits have become sadly dampened, the shadow has once more fallen.

Chapter Thirteen

ZERO

September 17th, WIELTJE. Quite a strafe going on, but we are safe in this dug-out.

Taking over from the front line companies at Gallipoli Farm, I think, to-morrow, and "go over" on the 20th.

Trying not to think of what is before us.

THREE-QUARTERS of an hour before zero! The steady drip, drip of water from the roof of our cubicle has almost lulled me to sleep. Half our battalion are packed away in this dug-out, a typical British one, damp, stuffy and cramped. It has only one thing in its favour—depth, and that to us means safety.

The thud of the searching shells above can be heard, the dug-out trembles with their violence, but we are too far down for them, they cannot touch us here. What matters it that the walls are thick with slime, or that the roof leaks like a sieve and we sit huddled together on a floor of thick, sticky mud. Down in this burrow we know we can live and that truly is heaven. A few more minutes of time and we'll have to leave this sanctuary and then——— Those who can, stop thinking, and like myself try to find respite in fitful oblivion.

The rum ration is brought round, a spoonful to a man, and as usual Mac and I give ours to Webster. So far, I have never taken it, as personally I can't see what good a spoonful is going to do me, but, on the other hand, neither can I see the harm, for, as Mac often says, it isn't enough to keep one's stomach from turning; but I have been brought up in a temperate home, and have no desire to break the old faith even to help win the war. French beer and wine I have learned to place in a different category to alcohol, but army rum is to me strong drink, a belief which Webby stoutly encourages.

After much swearing and good-humoured chaff, the sergeant with his orderly, jar and spoon departs to the next cubicle, and we are left alone with our thoughts. My own I try to make a blank, as it is the easiest way. I know what is before me and am fast becoming a confirmed fatalist. I look round at my comrades; Webster and Taffy are talking in low tones, both very serious looking. Mac is lying across my feet; his eyes are closed, but by this time, like myself, he is very much awake. Two of the others are scribbling on a field postcard and exchanging confidences, while yet another, a new recruit, is reading a letter, evidently his last from home, and appears to be the most unconcerned of the lot.

Try as I like, however, my mind will dwell on the folks at home, and I wonder if I will ever see them again. Such morbid ideas are foolish, however, and I try to concentrate on other things, but home seems to be uppermost in my mind and I recall with tender thoughts the day my brother and I crawled into the dog kennel to smoke our first cigarette, mother's surprise at seeing what she thought was the kennel on fire and the smoke escaping from every join in the woodwork, the pail of water which came splashing in on top of us as she attempted to extinguish the flames, then the sorry spectacle we made as dejectedly we crawled out, sick and wet, and——— "Fall in on top at the double" brings me back to the present and makes home seem very far away.

Outside it is pitch black, but all is bustle, while innumerable figures flit to and fro like ghostly shadows. On our side it is fairly quiet for this part of the line, but the Boche seems a bit restless and is searching with his heavier guns. Verey lights sweeping up reveal us to each other as moving silhouettes marching over the uneven ground to our assembly trench.

The fifteen minutes before "going over" have a peculiar eeriness all their own. One's heart seems to thump a little louder, while a pulse in the throat keeps beating in unison with it. There is a subtle air of expectancy. Everywhere is activity, a muffled ghostly activity. Orders are given and passed on in a whisper, thousands of troops to right and left of us must be on the move, but our vision is connected to the back of the man in front of us, the sides of the trench and a slice of cloudy, almost obscured moonlight.

We arrive at our assembly point, a hastily dug trench in rear of our front line from which we go over with the third wave, just in time to get across no-man's-land before the Boche recovers from his surprise, providing the attack is the surprise packet we trust it will be, and nicely placed to catch all that comes our way if he is expecting us.

The ten minutes pass slowly. The trench is supposed to be free of traffic, but carrying parties keep stumbling along it. A company of a neighbouring battalion come next, and there is some discussion as to who are the rightful owners, but possession is more than nine-tenths of the law out here, and they eventually about-turn and depart. Confusion in our little stretch of trench becomes more acute, but as the zero hour approaches, it disappears altogether, and we are left with nothing to take our minds off the dragging minutes.

I find myself wondering if the others are as much afraid as I am. It is the waiting that unnerves a fellow, the waiting and the uncertainty of it all. If only I could escape from it I'd willingly do cook-house and latrine fatigues for the rest of my life, nothing would be too menial, I'd give my soul into bondage to live my life in peace. I have one trump card—my age, but I can't summon sufficient courage to make use of it. I am torn between my natural fears and my anxiety to play the game like Webster and Mac. Thoughts and excuses vie with each other to obtain mastery over my faltering resolutions.

The others are in a different position altogether. They must go on; illness even, feigned or otherwise, would avail them little now. They are doomed as far as seeing this attack through is concerned, and they know it. When the door behind us is locked it is easy enough to go forward, there is nothing else to do, but I, holding the key to safety shrink from exposing my fear to my comrades, by opening it, although every nerve and fibre in my body is crying out to me to avail myself of this opportunity to preserve my life, a natural instinct, but one which I strive to overcome. I took on the job, and with God's help I'll see it through. It comes easy to pray at a time like this; little matter the words; they are all centred on this miserable life of mine, and somehow, when I am finished, my fears disappear and I become quite calm. Strange how we all look to our Maker in times of stress, and gain courage and strength in doing so. Even Webster admits he prays every time he goes "over the top."

Once again I begin to take an interest in my surroundings. A machine-gun rattles away to our left, while an occasional shell whistles over our heads and bursts in front or rear. A Verey light shows me Mac on one side chewing away at a piece of gum, for all the world like a cow contentedly chewing the cud, and Webster on the other calmly fixing his equipment, while over all hangs a vibrant stillness as if the very atmosphere was charged with the overwhelming activity shortly to be released. I can't help wondering if the Boche, two hundred yards away, cannot sense the tension.

Five minutes to go—our platoon officer slithers along the trench repeating as he goes:

"Wait for the whistle now, boys, and keep in touch."

The waiting is over; our hearts thump away as loudly as ever, but our mental fears have vanished. Unconsciously we make sure our bayonets are properly fixed, sling our rifles over our shoulders, and with a shrug to settle our equipment more comfortably, file towards the opening in our trench. For a full minute not a sound can be heard, and then, as if by the wave of a wizard's wand, the air is

rent by a million screaming, hissing devils of death. It
is zero.

Out of the trench we scramble and form into some semblance of order, then move forward rather anxiously knowing that if we can reach and cross no-man's-land before
the Boche counter-barrage drops, we are in comparative
safety for the time being. Our own wire holds us up for a
second or two, but at last we are all through the prepared
gaps. Here we re-form, and after watches have been consulted, advance again. Everything is done to time. We
advance so many yards in so many minutes. We take cover
for so many more minutes while the artillery deal with a
machine-gun nest, then we advance again, providing the
guns have done their work in the approved manner.

The Boche wire is crossed before we see any of our own
dead or wounded, while evidence that our gunners have
done their job well is apparent. The "Jerry" front line is no
more. In its place there is a jumble of ploughed-up earth
interlaced with timber and iron sheets, and an occasional
concrete emplacement still standing, battered but indomit-
able. These constitute our greatest source of worry.

Now we meet up with our first and second waves who
are digging in, and we carry on through them. Webster and
Mac are still on either side of me. So far, we have been
very fortunate, but the machine-guns begin to take toll,
while shells commence dropping amongst us. Our own barrage in front forms a wall of spouting earth and death
between us and the Boche. The din is terrific.

A machine-gun suddenly spurts out right in front of us,
and automatically we drop flat. Some I notice drop clumsily
and lie still; others clutch frantically at limbs. Our casualties have commenced.

The gun rattles again and is easily located in the semi-
darkness by its flashes streaming from a concrete pill-box
still defiant. There is no doubting the gameness of these
Jerry machine-gunners. We take pot shots at the aperture
in the concrete wall, while a Lewis gun rattles a tattoo all
round the loophole. but fails to stop the spouting stream
of death it exhales. One of our bombers suddenly rushes
forward, but half-way across he seems to take a left turn.
His body from the waist up bends over and slithers on the

ground as his legs patter on for a pace or two before he drops. We continue our fruitless fire on the emplacement, but are now being plastered with the latest war invention on this front—oil drums, we call them. They burst above us like shrapnel and spew forth burning oil. To our left three fellows have caught the full force of these shells, and are rolling on the ground trying to extinguish the flames. They are just like torches. Their screams are terrifying, but those accursed maching-guns prevent us from going to their aid.

Another bomber makes a dash towards the emplacement, and we almost raise a cheer as he crosses the intervening space and crouches down below one of the apertures. Suddenly his helmet seems to be knocked off by an unseen hand. We wait to see his arm swing up and deposit its messenger through the little slit; instead it sags limply while blood commences spouting from his neck. His face has disappeared, leaving him practically headless in a kneeling position, one hand resting on the concrete wall, the other hanging down still clutching the bomb—so near and yet so far.

The shrill sound of a whistle is heard above the noise of bursting shells and machine-gun fire, and our company officers sign for us to work round to the flanks and rear of the pill-box. We crawl on our stomachs from shell-hole to shell-hole, as our Lewis gunners engage the Jerry garrison and keep their attention fixed to their front. At last we have wormed our way round, and are now to the rear of the emplacement where we form in a semicircle with bombers a few yards in front. There is a sudden rush, and it is all over. Regardless of uplifted hands three of the occupants are bayoneted as they emerge from the narrow entrance, before we realise what we are doing. It is not that we are brutalised, but we are so keyed up to killing, that our minds can't relax quickly enough. We rush forward with the one intention of beating down all resistance; we must, to save our own lives. Little wonder then that when men surrender, they are sometimes too late to stay our hand. The slightest movement in the heat of close combat can often be misrepresented. It becomes natural to make sure first.

The delay has left our wings in the air, but we soon regain touch with our right and left companies, and plod on behind the protecting screen of our barrage.

Prisoners emerge from dug-outs, their hands in the air, fear and bewilderment expressed on their faces. Still dazed from the terrific bombardment which has passed over them like a scourge, they are almost childish in their desire to show friendliness, dreading the unknown future, yet eager to leave behind the hell from which they are escaping. We pass them by; they are safe enough, and our moppers up will herd them together and escort them to the cages in the rear.

When we come into line with the rest of our brigade, we dig in for fifteen minutes, while our guns pound away at the final objective. All the guns the Boche can muster seem to be slamming away at us. The earth is in a state of continuous tremors, but we have one consolation: our opposition are getting it twice as hot as we are.

In frantic haste we "dig in." The closer we are to the earth, the happier we feel. How we have learned to love it in all its aspects, the clean dry loam into which we nestle, the hard chalky soil which defies our entrenching tools— we curse its stubbornness and bless its solid covering in the same breath—even the muddy slimy mixture in which we flop and flounder. To us who live and die in its embrace, it provides comfort and security—dear mother earth.

After much scraping and scooping, I have a hole just large enough to give my head some protection. It resembles a very shallow grave which tapers away and leaves my feet fully exposed above ground. I lie in it face downward and watch Webster, who is patting the heaped-up earth in front of his head like a youngster building a sand-castle. Noticing my eyes on him he shouts across at me, but I can't make out for the noise what he is trying to say, so, as it is evidently meant to be a joke, I answer with a grin and a nod. We haven't spoken a dozen words to each other since we started. Signs seem to be all that are necessary, with an occasional cuss word flung in.

An order is passed down by a corporal crawling from man to man that we advance half-left here, and must, on no account, bunch together. I nod mechanically, and he passes on to Webster. When the whistles blow shortly after, we leave our shallow holes and go forward at a jog-trot with our company officers setting the pace. It is the nearest approach to an infantry charge I have ever taken part in, but the rough going soon slows us down, until, as we near our objective, it has deteriorated into the usual steady but slow gait of the overburdened fighting man.

The sight of Jerry machine-gunners hastily trying to assemble their guns brought up from the shelter of dug-outs, fans the flame already smouldering in our breasts—we must kill or be killed. The desire for personal safety blots out all that is going on around us, our minds and actions become centred on those figures in front. A bursting shell lifts me clean off my feet and hurls Mac on top of me. Each thinks the other hurt.

"Hit?" shouts Mac.

"Hit, be damned," I reply as we pick ourselves up and skirt the newly-made crater. Falling debris clatters on our tin hats and shoulders unnoticed. We have eyes and senses for nothing but those machine-guns and the necessity to kill. We almost muster up a rush over the last fifty yards, and we are not a moment too soon. The first few shots from the guns account for five of our platoon, but they are too late to stop us; we stab and thrust.

A gunner appears in front of me. I have no knowledge of singling him out. To me it just appears that he is there in my road. His revolver is already pointed at my chest as I lunge viciously, miss my mark and graze his side. A bullet crackles past my head as I step in and kick brutally at his shins while somebody else drives a bayonet into his side. As he falls I lose interest in him, my attention being drawn to a Boche trying to withdraw his bayonet from the chest of a khaki-clad figure. With each tug he lifts the moaning fellow a foot off the ground, giving a more vigorous tug as he observes my approach. Too late, however, he drops his grip of the rifle, and I almost derive pleasure in the groan that greets my ears as my own bayonet slides into his stomach.

On looking down at his victim, I find the weight of the rifle has lifted him to a sitting position, so carefully I take the weight off the bayonet and unlock it, then as gently as I can I withdraw it, his hands grasping the steel as I do so, as if in protest, and with a final groan consciousness leaves him—it is much better so.

When I rise from the side of the unconscious figure, the guns and strong point are ours; we have captured our objective. Sentries are posted, while the remainder of us start consolidating our position and try to get the captured machine-guns into action, ready for the counter-attack, under the instructions of our company commander who leans up against some sandbags and supervises our work. He is deathly pale and haggard looking. I am surprised at his listlessness, he is usually so full of beans on an occasion like this, then I notice the reason—his left hand is shattered and hangs dangling from the wrist by a sinew. Fascinated, I watch him calmly level his revolver and shoot off the hanging member, then instruct his orderly to bind it up. That done, he becomes his usual self again—the work of consolidation goes on.

In this war it is becoming a simple matter, if given the necessary artillery support, to capture a limited space of ground. Our guns concentrate on the objectives and pound away at them until they are reduced to powder, then we go over, and if the gunners have been proficient in their work, we despatch or take prisoners the dazed remnant of the garrison. The new positions are strengthened and fortified, and it is our turn to be pounded and blown to hell. When the Boche artillery lifts, what is left of us man the hastily-dug trenches, usually a mere succession of linked up shell-holes, and stem the advancing infantry. If he fails to regain his lost ground at the first attempt, he will try again and again until utter exhaustion or lack of reserves compel him to call a halt. And so this war drags on, a test of endurance and man power.

Gradually we get the captured position into some semblance of the strong point it is supposed to be. Each man has two sandbags with him, and these are filled and placed as a parapet. The gun positions we strengthen with corrugated-iron and wood supports. The battered dug-outs we try to bolster up until our pioneers arrive. The wounded are collected and placed near the largest dug-out to await the darkness and stretcher bearers. Walking wounded are left to take care of themselves.

We clean up the mess and place the dead in shell-holes to our rear, then start on a communication trench to our headquarters behind.

We are all exhilarated with the sense of victory, especially our new drafts, who seem to derive new life from the source, but the bad luck in the shape of weather which always accompanies our offensives, is still with us, and as if to dampen our ardour the rain starts, first as a slight drizzle, then as if mocking us, and with a desire to accentuate our own impotence, settles into a spirit-destroying downpour. Our ground-sheet capes become a playground for it as, alighting on our shoulders, it slides down our capes and finds a haven by steady streams in our trousers, putties and boots. Capes are useless things anyhow, especially when there is work to be done, so eventually we fling them off with a curse. When boots are squelching water and mud, putties and trouser legs like soaking dishcloths, we become a little careless of our comfort, although those who can, tie sandbags round their legs and obtain some measure of dryness.

The shell-holes we are trying to connect together fast become quagmires, and we ourselves are caked in wet mud while our rifles are choked and useless. Machine-guns continually enfilade our position, and although the heavier Boche guns are silent, his aeroplanes come nosing around above our shallow trench and engage in a little bombing practice, or, in a fit of defiance, dive down with Lewis guns belching lead.

It is impossible to evacuate the badly wounded, so we encourage as many as we can to look after themselves, and get them started on their crawl towards the rear, while the mud gradually takes on a reddish bloody tinge. Finding the journey too much for their failing strength, many crawl into shell-holes, only to realise that water-logged holes can be as dangerous as bullets or shells. Their cries for help become nerve-racking. They are so widely scattered and the area so pock-marked with holes that we have great difficulty in locating them. Cries and groans in the general din seem to come from a dozen different directions at once, and though there are many we find in time, there are others for whom we are too late.

In this part of the line we have a splendid variety of deaths. One can be shot cleanly, mangled, blown to nothing, burnt to a cinder, have your innards eaten away by gas, or drowned, sufficient to satisfy the most morbid instincts in any of us, but drowning as we find it here seems to be the most cruel. To be wounded in a shell-hole and gradually feel oneself slowly sliding and sinking into the muddy liquid, too weak to hold a battered body above the surface, comrades within hearing distance and a throat that evokes a whisper in place of a lusty shout—truly that is torment.

Chapter Fourteen

WOUNDS AND BATTLEFIELDS

September 24th or 25th, POPERINGHE. Still alive, but more sick of it than ever.

I've seen enough of killings and battlefields to last me all my days.

Flanders certainly takes first prize for the stickiest, slimiest, stinkiest mud in the universe.

ANOTHER relief completed and another spell of a few days' rest ahead of us. Once again we have gone through the routine of handing over signal wires, and pointing out suggested spots for visual stations, given our most candid views of the war on this accursed front, and departed, leaving the new signallers in possession.

Clear of the communication trenches we get an uninterrupted view of the countryside, and can see that the shells are falling mostly on the main road which leads to our assembly quarters in the ruined town of Ypres ahead of us, so with true old soldier's instinct and the peculiar windiness which accompanies coming out on rest in a shelled area, we leave the road as a natural course and make our way over the muddy morass of waterlogged shell-holes which constitutes Flanders as we know it. Bursts of shrapnel worry us little, but the heavy going as we slither and slide in the thick gluey mud soon has us puffing. It is impossible to walk in a straight line, so continuous are the craters. Shells have fallen all over this front like rain-drops in a thunderstorm, and have left behind this torn and battered surface.

In the slimy water which fills each crater we get glimpses of grisly derelicts of the battlefield. A khaki-clad leg, three heads in a row, the rest of the bodies submerged, giving one the idea that they had used their last ounce of strength to keep their heads above the rising water. In another miniature pond, a hand still gripping a rifle is all that is visible, while its next-door neighbour is occupied by a steel helmet and half a head, the staring eyes glaring icily at the green slime which floats on the surface almost at their level. Further on, a poor horse lies on its side, its innards protruding from its hindquarters. The other objects of war's art I have passed by with a shrug, but beside the remains of this faithful friend I pause. Its muzzle is drawn back showing its clenched teeth, giving it in death a vicious cruel look, so contrasting to the placid gentleness of his kind.

The short pause has allowed the others to get ahead of me and I go squelching after them. In my haste I slip on the edge of a crater and go sliding down almost on top of a pair of army boots sticking out just above the water. Mac returns and gives me a hand to free myself from the clutches of this sucking, stinking pot-hole which reveals a morbid fancy to trick me into its vile contents. With a tug I free one foot only to slither down again nearer those upturned boots.

"What price a bath, Jock?" Webster jokingly enquires, as he returns to see what the fuss is about.

"Come on, give me a hand, you blighters," I reply.

"Catch hold of my rifle, Webby. Now then, altogether." And with a mighty pull Mac and Webster haul me up the side of the crater to the top, where I land on my hands and knees, covered in mud from the waist down.

Uncomfortably I trudge after the others along a duck-board track, until black bursts of shrapnel overhead drive us off it.

"How about a breather?" Mac suggests.

"There's no need to hurry, and I'd just hate to stop a packet going out."

"Them's my sentiments," I reply in support of Mac.

"What about the ruin over there? Wherever there's a rubble heap there's a cellar. I can smell it."

"There's lots of things besides cellars that I can smell," Webster adds as he steps gingerly over a kilted figure black and putrefying. "Hell, don't he stink?"

We approach the ruin, and find it is being used as a dressing station. On the German's blind side it is surrounded by hundreds of stretcher cases and walking wounded, while in rows, covered with a blanket in most cases, lie those Tommies who had found their sanctuary at last in Flanders mud.

"Looks like this is the vet's," says Mac with a grin.

"Aye, and there's the mortuary, they are usually close together"—and Webster nods to the rows laid out so orderly in comparison with the sitting and lounging figures scattered in a semicircle round the door of the dug-out which serves as consulting-room, surgery and funeral office combined.

"Somehow I always feel happier near a dressing station," Webster confides. "There's no fear of them burying you alive."

Then in the same breath: "Who's got all the fags? I'm rooked."

After much raking at the bottom of pockets we unearth amongst the three of us a solitary badly battered stub of a cigarette. Mac, with an air of ownership, tries to straighten out the creased stump as he ruefully informs us it will just have to go the rounds—two draws apiece to start off with.

Between the draws we have an opportunity of studying the ground and the wounded men around us. Here we have one side of war which is seldom revealed, its innocent victims, its tragedy. The side which those at home know so little about, which those fire-eaters whose speeches we read in the papers seem to be so totally ignorant of, otherwise they could never talk such drivel. What a pleasure it would be to enlighten them; just one afternoon, that's all I'd ask, to conduct those stay-at-homes round this corner of Flanders. How would I do it? Something like this, I fancy, and I let my mind wander :

"Just a few of the casualties, gentlemen, regrettable but unavoidable, and considering the great gains we have made, a matter of a thousand yards, it is unquestionably worth it. The men themselves, you will notice, are quite cheerful and in excellent spirits. Some are already chafing at the delay which will occur before their wounds are healed and they are once more in the firing line. (I would, of course, omit to relate that these are the walking cases, who, with a cushy flesh wound and visions of Blighty, are at the top of their form.)

"I think you will agree, gentlemen, that the cases are all rather interesting. We have a splendid variety in this part of the line, and, I may add, we are always fully equipped to portray to the best advantage just how frail the human form is when brought in violent contact with explosive metal, poison gas or liquid fire.

"Take this case in front of us. Now, gentlemen, you will notice the scalp is cut right off, the work of a thin splinter of shell, ever such a thin splinter, keen as a razor blade. An eighth of an inch lower and we could do nothing for him. As it is, you will see his brain is horribly exposed. Yes, that's it there, pulsing with every heart-beat, looks like the milt of a herring, only darker in colour. Will he live? Oh, most assuredly, providing he survives the journey and consequent dangers down to the base. They'll patch him up all right. His brain may be affected afterwards, but they will certainly do their best for him, have no fear on that score, gentlemen.

"We'll pass on to the next. Ah, yes, the work of a shell again. You will observe a piece of metal has splintered the thigh bone. The force of impact has almost torn the leg off. Just a simple matter of amputation. Our surgeons are very expert in that particular branch. We'll pass on, gentlemen.

"This, now, is a case I should particularly like to draw your attention to. No, no, it isn't a piece of steak. That gentlemen, was once the head and shoulders of a young man. He had been caught by a flame-thrower; beastly things, they burn the flesh and leave it red and raw. Doubtless he has lost his sight, just as well perhaps, but it really is marvellous the steps that are being made in perfecting skin grafting. Luckily, of course, this young soldier has merely been flicked by the flame, otherwise the result, as you can readily understand, would be a matter of ashes.

"These others, gentlemen, are rather commonplace. Their only interest lies in the manner in which they portray the several ways shells have of tearing the body, all more or less similar, I'm afraid.

"Leg and arm off here, both legs in this case, a shattered side, spine broken, pretty hopeless, and this one another thigh wound with gangrene setting in; all very messy and ugly looking. Accept my apologies, gentlemen; this way, please.

"Ah, this is different; yes, just as I thought, machinegun casualty, gentlemen. You will notice the five perforations at the foot of the abdomen, a nasty wound; but then, the machine-gun is a nasty weapon. One gun can hold up the advance of a brigade; essentially a weapon for defence. If properly handled it can play havoc amongst attacking troops. Elevation should always be low, unless for barrage purposes. A gunner, to be an expert, should be able to cut daisies. To hit below the waist should be his ambition, no living object could pass such a deadline.

"But, ah, I'm transgressing, gentlemen. Sorry if I've wearied you, it's a favourite subject of mine.

"As I was saying, you will notice the five perforations here at the foot of the abdomen; they don't look so deadly as a shell wound, but they are vital, nevertheless. As a man he is now useless to the community, and stomach wounds out here are usually fatal.

"Step this way, gentlemen. Here we have the effects of gas. Rather sickening, I admit, but if you will be so kind as to give me your attention for just a second or two, I'll explain the major points. The worst cases, you will notice, are continually vomiting a green fluid. Their lungs are being slowly burned away. Asthma, did you say, sir? Well, yes, I suppose it is similar in a small way, as far as the wheezy difficult intake of breath is concerned, but oh, much more painful and deadlier, a bad business, a bad business.

"And these—no, we shall not disturb them, gentlemen. They sleep soundly—too soundly. They came here to uphold an ideal, but discovered it to be a mask cloaking all that's repugnant to civilised Christian manhood, but in the unmasking they discovered a nobler ideal, a war to end wars, and with that end in view, and like the true men they were, gave of their best generously, ungrudgingly, even to this. Gentlemen, these are our dead. One experiences an uncomfortable feeling amongst these brave souls who have passed beyond, as if they had attained something to which we can never respond. We feel unworthy of their very presence, but, gentlemen, I do not wish to mar this very instructive afternoon with an air of despondency. After all, there are thousands of young men dying daily out here. That is our privilege, and although you, yourselves, cannot be with us, we know how deeply you regret it. Gentlemen, I wish you a very good day."

Yes, it would be something like that, I fancy, only much nastier, and I turn my attention to the work of the orderlies which goes on like clockwork. Stretchers are carried in to the dug-out, and others brought out, while a number of Red Cross men attend to the needs of those waiting their turn, sorting out the urgent cases and occasionally lifting a stretcher with its load and placing it beside the still figures on our left. Life may still flicker away in the torn body, but to their expert eyes it is only a matter of time, and time to them means everything.

"The doc's earning his rations to-day." Mac speaks his thoughts aloud, and we notice that as fast as a stretcher comes out, another goes in, while a steady stream of walking wounded go to and from the dug-out. There must be between four and five hundred badly wounded men lying about, and they'll all have to be evacuated to-night. Each man will have to be carried to the road over three hundred yards of shell-pocked bog which no motor ambulance could hope to cross, and all to be accomplished during the few hours of darkness when the road will be getting its share of attention from the Jerry gunners.

"Thank Heaven we're not in the R.A.M.C.," Webster remarks as he rises and gives himself a stretch.

"Come on, let's beat it, things have quietened down a bit."

We pick up our packs and make another start towards our assembly quarters.

Battlefields have always fascinated me. To the initiated they hold a special interest of their own, especially when the actual fighting has advanced sufficiently to leave the old battle area practically safe for loitering, and as the dressing station and danger are left behind, I begin to take a more vivid interest in the signs of battle which surround us.

That tank there—a direct hit has put it out of action, and the crew, or what was left of them, have dismantled their machine-guns and brought them out to the open. There they lie as they died. A corporal, quite a youngster, has either staggered back to the tank after being hit, or has been blown there by an explosion. There he stands and has stiffened in a spread-eagle attitude. His trousers have disappeared, and his belly has been ripped open up to the chest. His bowels trail down to his feet, where they lie mixed up with shreds of grey army shirt. Another who has obviously gone to his assistance lies huddled at his feet. He has just crumpled up. One hand still holds a field dressing, and the other lies in the grey mass of his pal's inside. The clutching fingers have encircled the tube-like bowels in such a fierce grip that the nails have cut into the skin, and through the perforations there is still oozing out the corporal's last undigested meal. I turn away with a shudder. I can picture them as pals, the one unhesitatingly going to the assistance of the other, comradeship, something beautiful and fine, then this obscene ending.

I go over to the shell-hole where one of the guns has been placed. The gunner is still in position behind his gun with the top of his head ripped off, leaving his shoulders and part of the gun draped in congealed blood. Alongside of him are two others, one lying face downwards with no visible sign of a wound, while the other is a bit of a puzzle. He is just a mangled mass of flesh and bone. His wounds are horrible. One would almost think he had been battered to death. I cannot understand it. A shell could have done it, but would almost certainly have blown his limbs apart, and it is too messy a death for bullets. It might be the result of a bomb, but then the wounds would be more localised. The more I try to puzzle it out the stranger it seems—just one of the many mysterious deaths with which this war abounds.

Lying about in all attitudes are these heaps of rain-soaked khaki. A strange feeling this, walking amongst the unburied dead, one which I have long since become hardened to, but which always makes me oddly uncomfortable.

Webster, I notice, is unconcernedly going through the pockets of one of these huddled heaps, an act which we don't look upon as robbing the dead, just a matter of souvenir hunting. If we don't do it some back area wallah will, and it is much better that a front-line soldier should have the little odds and ends a dead comrade has no further need of than some soldier who perhaps has never been within shelling distance of the front.

I am not particularly fond of that sort of scrounging myself. I always feel I am being watched, as if unseen eyes are keeping tally on my movements. Even as I walk round them I can sense the presence of something I cannot see.

The majority have, I believe, died peacefully. That bunch of five have been caught by a shell. There were evidently more of them, for I can see three legs and an arm lying ten yards away, those two, victims of machine-gun bullets, while a little to the left I count eleven practically in a row. The same gun has caught them all.

The cast-off equipment and rifles denote where men have been wounded and have been stripped of all superfluous gear. Later the battlefield will be cleaned up, the equipment reissued and the dead buried. There will be nothing to show that it has been a field of death.

We come to the old Jerry second line of trenches, and here, as we know, some fierce isolated hand-to-hand struggles took place. Round the first traverse we begin to get signs of them. Three Germans and a Tommy all huddled together in a heap which we have to step over, then over a solitary German with his head battered to pulp, followed by four of our own fellows and three Jerries, significant of close combat, and, a little further on, a Jock on top of a Boche, his fingers round the German's throat and a bayonet sticking out of his back. It has gone right through him and pierced the German beneath him, killing both.

Round the next traverse we come across one of our own officers, headless, his pockets turned inside out, one hand still grasping a revolver and the other a cane. A few yards further on, by the side of a dug-out, we find a Boche pinned to the wall of the trench by a rifle and bayonet. His hands have stiffened round the bayonet as he vainly tried to withdraw it. The rifle stretches with an upward slant across the trench and we have to push it upwards a little more to get past. The corpse moves as I squeeze by and a queer grunt comes from its mouth. Just wind which the movement has forced from its lungs, but it gives me a fright and I am glad to hasten on.

All along the trench we meet these sprawling figures, friend and foe. Some are in comfortable positions and look as if they are just asleep and may wake up any minute, but others have not had an easy death, and their twisted bodies and contorted features give evidence of their last struggle. In one case at least gangrene has set in. His skin is already a dark grey and has a puffed-up jelly-like appearance. Another twenty-four hours and he will be as black as a nigger, and the white maggots will be visible as they crawl underneath the surface. The spot reeks with the foully penetrating stench of decaying flesh.

Part of the trench near a small dug-out has evidently been used as an advanced dressing station, and the dead completely block the way. Friend and foe are piled on top of each other in such a galaxy of bloody bandages, clotted blood and shattered limbs that even we have had enough, and climb out of the trench, glad to get away from it.

Battlefields, I suppose, will always interest me, but I prefer them after they have been cleaned up, where the only signs are the shell-holes, the derelict guns and powdered emplacements, with a stray rifle or helmet here and there.

It is easy then to find romance and adventure in every little pile of empty cartridge-cases, in the broken limber and the shell-holes which surround it, the battered strong point and the solitary rifle with the bayonet buried in the ground. There is scope for the imagination in these things. They may hint at violence but do not exhibit the effect on human flesh. The background is there, and I can paint in the central figures to suit my fancy, and strangely enough they are never like those we have just left behind. The glamour of a battlefield lies only in the imagination.

Chapter Fifteen

THE SOMME

October, date unknown, HONNECOURT—EPEHY, SOMME. *War isn't so bad after all.*

In comparison to Ypres and Passchendaele this part of the line is a picnic.

Saw our gunners send a Jerry transport sky-high—great work. Thought afterwards about the poor Jerries—not such great work.

WAR has its varying degrees of frightfulness, and after our long sojourn in the north, with its continual bombardments, attacks and counter-attacks, mud and death, our new front on the Somme is a veritable haven of rest.

The countryside, although gone to seed, is clean to look at. There are woodlands in abundance, a contrast to the churned-up mud and stricken stumps of the north. Everything is overgrown and uncared for, but the mark of the slayer is absent. The ground lacks that tortured look we have been so accustomed to; in its place we get little glimpses of another phase of war.

A cart only half loaded stands in a field, with a pitchfork stuck in the ground near-by, just where the labourer left it at the first hint of danger, and his jacket, sodden and tattered, still hangs on a stanchion near the gate, as if his departure had been sudden and left no time for delay.

Evidence of these hurried departures are scattered all

over. A perambulator with buckled wheels nobly strives, with the aid of its broken spokes and rusty framework, to defeat the attempts of its load of children's underclothing to flutter away on every friendly breeze after their youthful owners. A dilapidated harmonium is visible, miserably exposing its innards to all who pass the gable-end of the little parlour in which it had once been the pampered, well-dusted hallmark of snobbish village respectability. A more gruesome object, a kennel, with long rusty chain and rain-washed skeleton of a dog, the neck bones encircled by a sodden leather collar. As I gaze on it I inwardly hope the faithful animal was killed before its master fled, or, if not, that his bones lie rotting the same as his dog's.

A litter of tattered ledgers and account books proves to the sceptical that commerce of a kind at one time did flourish in this now abandoned village. Optimistically we kick the books aside, and, strange to say, actually do unearth a lidless cash-box, but too many troops have already passed this way for it to contain anything more valuable than dirty rain-water, and the slimy, sluggy things that stick tenaciously to its sides. Hardly a brick has been left standing in any of the little towns and hamlets, as the Boche in his retreat through this country early in the year razed everything which possessed a roof. Likewise every orchard has been ruined, and the trees methodically cut down near the ground. One cannot help but admire Jerry for his thoroughness. When our troops followed fast on his retreating heels not a roof was left standing to shelter them, not a grain of food or unpoisoned water left to feed them. Like everything else the Boche does, he carried out his retreat well, regardless of outside criticisms. War to him is just war, no more, no less.

Our trenches in this sector in front of Cambrai are wonderful affairs, cut out of solid chalk, ten feet deep, wide and well kept, with an absence of funk-holes and dug-outs that tells plainly of a life of ease and peacefulness by their former occupants. As a storm division we can hardly believe our good luck, and are not greatly surprised that when in reserve positions we are taken by platoons and given lectures on aggressive warfare. To the younger soldiers these little talks convey nothing, but we old-timers can read between the lines. We are not going to enjoy for long a happy state of warfare.

Patrolling, working parties and carrying fatigues make up our twenty-one days in the line, and the war takes on an aspect of navvying which we thoroughly detest. At the beck and call of every arm of the service, we do sentry and patrol work in the front line, in support we dig and carry day and night, and while in reserve supply the navvies for any corps that likes to ask for them. Digging, toiling, sweating, awakened from our sleep to repair barbed wire or dig some new trench, back again at dawn we are requisitioned by tunnellers or artillery—work, work, work, with little time to sleep or think, while ever around us hovers death in the shape of snipers, machine-gun fire, shelling at cross-roads and the dozen other deaths that accompany trench warfare in a quiet sector. Never prominent, but never absent, it picks its victims singly and in pairs, quietly and unobtrusively, but nevertheless deadly and sure.

Our only respite, the ten days out of every thirty-one, we spend back at billets in Tincourt and Hamel as divisional reserve. There we get a chance to sleep and rest, intermingled with drill and sports, with an occasional concert party or a makeshift cinema erected and run by the A.S.C.

These ten days seem to slip in quicker than any of the others, and before we realise it we are on the road back to the front-line trenches, convinced that life is still worth living.

There isn't the constant fear of concentrated bombardment or of attack here. The country, to our eyes, is good to look at, and at certain times we can walk in the open without being sniped by artillery.

Occasionally the Boche will lob shells over at a single soldier foolish enough to expose himself, but we soon get to know his varying degrees of vigilance and time our promenades accordingly. It is strictly against rules to walk in the open, but after traversing a mile or so of narrow, twisting communication trench, there are few amongst us who can resist the temptation of a walk above ground. It is not done, however, without a certain amount of risk, and after having half a dozen shells aimed at you, one begins to realise how cheap shells are in comparison with the life of a man.

This seeming waste of shells is a source of wonderment to Webster, who can remember when shells were more precious than the lives of a dozen men and were husbanded like bars of gold. Now shells don't count, only dead men.

Three miles back in the village of Epehy we have a wonderful observation post. It is built behind the remains of the red brick gable of the last house directly facing the Jerry lines. It is a beauty, a cylindrical tower fifteen feet high, made of iron and concrete. A spiral stair leads up to a trap-door and a little chamber, in which we dump our equipment. The stair continues upwards to another trap-door, which opens to the observation chamber. A row of bricks has been unobtrusively removed from the gable wall, and through the slot we gaze behind the enemy lines. There in comfort with our maps and telescopes we spend pleasant hours watching the enemy movements.

The artillery have a similar but more spacious post in the gable of the adjoining house.

I can find only one fault with our little nest. Looking back from the front line towards the village and seeing it as the enemy must, our red brick gable stands out in such relief from the grey background of rubble and masonry, that it is just asking for attention from enemy gunners. It is so obvious that we might as well put up a notice board in front and label it "Observation Post."

That, I find, is a common fault with our people. They make things too easy for the Boche gunners, while he on his part is more subtle, more cunning, and puts his observation posts and strong points in the most unlikely places. No doubt, in time, we'll learn a wrinkle or two from Jerry and take war for the codeless, unsentimental thing it is.

Thought of what might happen, however, if the Jerry gunners become curious, doesn't bother us much once we are within the friendly concrete walls of our little post, and from behind its shelter we tranquilly keep watch-dog on the comings and goings in the opposite lines.

It is exciting sport to watch an enemy transport come lazily over the brow of a hill, the mule idling along, the driver contentedly puffing a pipe, oblivious of a score of inquisitive eyes; to see an officer of apparently high rank striding through a meadow, a gun under his arm and a dog at his heels. Nearer the lines, a head that appears above a parapet for a second or two gazing curiously towards our trenches, or a stooping running figure that unbuttons its pants as it bolts towards a trench latrine. In a reserve line a party digging an emplacement. The diggers themselves cannot be seen, the only sign of activity being the small eruptions of earth they fling over the parapet.

All these things give us a thrill which can only be experienced by watching the movements of an enemy who is unaware of our attentions. They also make us realise that the Boche is just an ordinary fellow going about his work or pleasure with the same hopes, the same fears as ourselves.

Each night our reports are sent in to the brigade intelligence staff, and there the day's work ends so far as we are concerned. Not so the artillery observers next door. They are in direct communication with their guns, which are ever ready to act under their instructions.

At dusk, far behind the enemy lines, a transport of some twenty horse-drawn wagons and four motor lorries can just be seen halted beside a wood. They are waiting until it is a little darker before venturing nearer the front trenches. The spot is well chosen. The background completely swallows them up except in one place, where a chalk pit accentuates the outline of a solitary wagon.

I have swept over the wagon with my telescope a dozen times within the last five minutes. Officially I am supposed to be content with happenings in and around the Jerry front trench, but at dusk, after I have been relieved from duty, I've always had a liking for roving around the back areas with a spare telescope.

Again the wagon comes into view. This time I focus a little longer on it. Wagons don't usually hang around the same spot longer than is necessary. I can clearly make out the driver rubbing away at some part of his harness, while the mule team relieve the monotony by muzzling each other. Idly I follow the road with my telescope. There is a slight movement to the far side, and I notice another wagon with a group of drivers sitting on a bank. I study the ground more carefully and notice a loop track which curves round the edge of a wood and then regains the main road. At intervals of ten yards, I judge it to be, the transport is halted.

What an opportunity for the artillery. Hurriedly we send over a note, giving the map reading and size of the transport to their observers, but discover they are as watchful as we are and already are in touch with their batteries.

With my eye at the end of the telescope I watch and wait. My heart commences thumping unnaturally, my breathing a little sharper, and a feeling in my body as if my blood flowed a little faster at the prospect of what awaits that unlucky transport. A few seconds and a shell bursts to the rear of the column just inside the wood, then another a hundred yards or so in front. I notice the drivers get to their feet, then walk towards their wagons. Another shell bursts this time right on the edge of the wood. The black fan-shaped upheaval gracefully subsides and the smoke leisurely disperses. For a second or two everything looks normal again, then, as if urged by some strange, playful demon, the earth commences to spout up on all sides, making a box walled in by death. Inside the box the heavier shells fall, flinging up mountains of earth, while floating above the tornado are the dark cloudy puffs of shrapnel smoke. The road for three hundred yards becomes screened off from the rest of the landscape by smoke and flying debris.

Three minutes and the guns stop as suddenly as they started. The smoke and dust gradually settle and disappear, leaving a strip of torn earth, wrecked and splintered wagons and mangled flesh, while down the road towards the front a team of frightened mules tear madly. I follow their wild gallop through the telescope until a curve in the ground obscures them from my view.

Mechanically I sweep over the ground. It is almost dark now. Just a quiet countryside, almost too quiet, I think, until I hear the rat-tat-tat of an alert machine-gunner, and the crack of a solitary rifle. In the distance I hear the rumble of wheels over cobble-stones, and see the first Verey light shoot up, a sign that the front is settling down for the night.

We pack away our telescopes and maps, descend through the trap-doors and down the spiral stair to the rubble heap that was once a country villa, then through a littered and weed-grown back garden and along a country lane, where the glow-worms are like hundreds of little pin-points of phosphorescent light blazing the trail to the railway embankment and our dug-out billets.

That we have just witnessed the slaughtering of over fifty men and horses doesn't give us a second's thought. We look upon it as rather a smart piece of work on the part of our artillery. Our thoughts never centre on the men and animals who now lie stiffening on the edge of that little woodland. Fathers, sons, brothers, what matters it? We never think of them as such. To us they are just Boches, our enemies.

And yet, the only two unarmed Germans I have come in close contact with could so easily have been my friends. One was the prisoner taken by Mac, the other was a young Bavarian, who, after an attack, lay wounded not far from the little shelter I was using as a signalling relay post. My glance often fell in his direction, and I was struck by the hopeless pained look on his face when nobody was about, and the pathetic shadow of a smile he mustered up for any passing Tommy.

When I left my shelter to patrol the line I offered him a cigarette and tried to convey by signs that he should make an attempt to get back to a dressing station. He in turn managed to convey to me that his leg was broken and useless, so I left him and carried on.

At night when I returned he was still lying there in the rain, and I helped him over to my funk-hole where we shared between us his great-coat and my last cigarette. With signs and broken French we swopped our family history, exchanged addresses, and in the cramped quarters of the muddy hole, soaked to the skin and with shells threatening every second to find out our hiding-place, realised that though wearing different uniforms we had very much in common.

The rest of that miserable night we spent more like

brothers than enemies. An hour after dawn stretcher bearers arrived and I saw him on his way to the casualty station, then thoughtfully made another start with the business of war. The incident had left its impression on me, and shown just how little enmity actually did exist between us. Once we got to know each other and realised the other meant no harm, all thought of fighting disappeared and we became merely a couple of human beings glad of each other's society.

The majority of us out here, however, never have an opportunity of finding out what manner of man the khaki or field-grey uniform clothes; the colour is all we are sure of.

Killing has become our job; wounds and death are of everyday occurrence, and if at times we wonder if the result will justify the sacrifice, it makes little difference— the war still goes on.

Chapter Sixteen

A COURT-MARTIAL

October 14th, TINCOURT, SOMME. *We are going to right a wrong. Unfortunately Mac and I are off on a signalling course, so won't see the fun.*

Just our luck to be sent on a course when we are out on rest at billets.

A DEPUTATION from a Lancashire battalion has just paid us a visit, and we have allied ourselves to a little scheme, which, if it became known to the higher command, would no doubt land us all in front of a firing party.

A young soldier of a neighbouring battalion is being court-martialled for sleeping at his post and desertion in face of the enemy. It sounds rather a serious crime, but when the whole facts are revealed, it has quite a different aspect.

For fifteen days during an attack, the accused soldier, a youngster of nineteen, had no regular sleep, and for the last forty-eight hours had been on continuous duty. He had been found asleep while acting sentry at a post. Many have been found doing the same thing, only a decent, understanding officer hasn't reported them.

Lack of sleep numbs the senses and it becomes a physical impossibility to keep the eyes open. Danger, safety, even death, become minor considerations. Sleep is all that matters. When a sentry reaches that stage it is best to call the sergeant on duty and explain matters, or, if forced, to demand to see the platoon commander, who, if he is a soldier and an intelligent one, will understand and put on a relief if possible. In this way a sentry is doing his duty far more zealously than attempting to defy nature. It is the wiser way, but is seldom resorted to as it takes a lot more courage to explain matters to a harassed sergeant or officer in the middle of the night, than to try and stick it out and, if the worst happens, rely on not being caught.

The army expects the impossible from human nature. It defies every known law, and in the majority of cases, through the medium of branding a man a coward and shooting him at dawn, gets away with it.

At home things are different. They can only go a certain length. Soldiers have friends near at hand and can incite public opinion, but once abroad, the mailed fist descends, the army becomes a soldier's master, it owns him, his time, his body—it doesn't give a damn about his soul. At home he may be his mother's darling, but there are four or five million of his kind out here. He is just a number who has got to do as he is told, whether it be cleaning out somebody's latrine or digging his own grave—he is a soldier.

The officer who stumbled on this sentry who couldn't do as he was told, removed his rifle and put him under arrest. The soldier, thoroughly frightened at the prospect before him, bolted from his escort on the way down to battalion headquarters and was missing for fourteen days, being eventually found roaming about the divisional area.

He had broken two of the King's sacred rules and Regulations, the penalty in each case being death. What the army is inclined to overlook is the fact that they have tried to force a frail human being to break one of Nature's most rigid rules and regulations without any penalty. Consequently he is to be court-martialled in about six days' time, and his comrades are soliciting the help of all battalions in the area to carry out their little scheme.

Briefly it is, if he is sentenced to be shot, will we, in the event of being selected to supply a firing party, refuse to carry it out and do all in our power to stop it? Their chief-spokesman, a banker in civil life, is an intelligent, well-educated fellow, and there is nothing mutinous about his speech. It is just an attempt by sane men to overcome the harshness of the war machine and prevent the murder of a comrade for failing to do an impossibility.

We all heartily agree, and the procedure is then explained to us.

The members of the firing party will carry out all orders, until they are actually on the spot, then they will unload and pile arms. An attempt will be made by a ruse to abstract the cartridges from the revolver of the officer in charge, but in any case our job is merely to refuse to carry out orders at the last minute. Comrades from his own company will be there to prevent the officer or the Provost-Marshal from carrying out the sentence. That will be the moment of danger and every attempt will be made to manage this without the aid of firearms. They already have a man who has guaranteed to lasso both these officers and make them ineffective in exactly ten seconds. The rest of the battalion will stay off all parades until their comrades of the firing party return. Each battalion will support the other.

A note stating the grievance will be handed by each battalion to its commanding officer. Violence on no account will be resorted to, other than by special friends of the prisoners, and if things do not progress favourably, there will be a special parade of all battalions concerned to ground arms.

Watch will be kept on the Provost-Marshal's head-quarters in case a firing party of military police should be detailed. Information regarding this will be obtained from an inside source at least the night before, giving ample time for each battalion to be warned and instructed as to the course they should adopt.

Arrangements have even been made for receiving information regarding the actual court-martial while it is sitting.

To safeguard ourselves the story of the whole affair, giving the accused soldier's name, the truth of his offence, the names of the battalions supporting the demonstrations and the arrangements they have made to ensure that the death penalty will not be carried out, will be in England the following night. Copies will be taken by another soldier on leave two days hence. These will be held in readiness to send to the local papers of each battalion's home town if the finding of the court is one of death. In that case copies will also be sent to the leading daily papers, also *John Bull*. Civilian aid has been recruited for the sending of wires so that no time will be lost in putting these copies into circulation.

The prisoner's brother, a company sergeant-major in the same battalion, will lead this passive resistance. His orders are to be obeyed implicitly. The whole affair shows. an organising ability worthy of a very efficient and intelligent sergeant-major. Even minor details have been carefully thought out, and rallying places have been fixed, an intelligence staff appointed and code signals made up. Signallers and runners even are provided.

Zero day will be the day of the court-martial.

We are asked to appoint our own commanders and spokesmen, and advised to prevent intimidation by getting the battalion to act automatically and in unison. There will be a pow-wow the following evening for the commanders and their assistants at a spot yet to be appointed. That is all.

When the delegation has departed, we enthusiastically commence choosing by vote our own leaders, and issuing our own brand of threats to all faint hearts and suspected tale carriers. They are surprisingly few. The younger soldiers are game for any form of excitement, and the older ones we try to win over by telling them that for once we are going to prove that putting a soldier in the family way isn't the only thing the army can't do to him. To those we fail to convince of the righteousness of the cause, we use other methods. Veiled hints of the next time up the line and bullets in the back, is one of the favourites, and the very few we can't win over and who will have nothing to do with the scheme, we fling out. Any leakage of information will be tacked on to them, and they know our way of dealing with that form of louse.

It is well on in the night before we have visited the other companies and made our arrangements with them, but towards midnight we arrive back at our barn, tired and excited.

Webster is our company commander, and I have been chosen as the spokesman for the battalion. Not a very enviable job, but then I have special qualifications, as I am the only man in the battalion who, in the shape of a birth certificate, holds not only a sure passport to Blighty but a ticket that will walk me right out of the army; in other words, as Webster aptly puts it, I don't need to give a damn.

We chatter and argue till early morning, telling the others of the various arrangements we have made. There is a touch of excitement about this little business which is manifest in our veiled secrecy and the crusader-like feeling we have of being the champions of an innocent victim.

Discipline we can understand. It is undoubtedly a necessity, but let it be sensible discipline tempered with understanding and not blind to the deficiencies of human nature.

At last we settle down for the night, and I slip under my blanket and lie thinking for what seems hours. Will the battalion hold together if it comes to a show-down? Will the other battalions stand by us? They are all keen just now, but there are always the timid ones ready to cower under the rule of authority. There's one thing certain : our company at least under Webster will stand fast, there's no doubt of that. I dream that night of leading the battalion— or is it the whole British army !—on a forlorn hope, riding at its head on a prancing white horse, banners fluttering and bands blazing away. It is a glorious feeling, and I am anything but pleased when our own band, playing its reveille of popular songs through the street of the village, wakes me up.

Breakfast over, and we learn from an orderly that my name and Mac's are on the battalion orders to report at the orderly room for special duty. Hurriedly we make our way to the other end of the village where the orders are posted outside the house which serves as headquarters, and sure enough there are our names with instructions to report in full kit at the orderly room by nine o'clock for special duty.

We return to our billet trying to surmise what "special duty" might mean. Sergeants and corporals are waylaid for information, and we get different ideas from each one.

We are going back to Blighty to work on munitions.

We are to be sent over the lines dressed as Jerries for espionage purposes.

A new arm of the service has been born, a cross between a tank and an aeroplane, and we are to be the personnel for the first experiments.

One corporal, at least, is truthful and admits unashamedly that he doesn't know.

Webster reckons it will be a course of some kind—bombing or Lewis gun.

Sharp on nine we are both at the orderly room in full war-paint, wondering a little but not caring very much. I believe if we were told to proceed immediately to Timbuctoo, we would merely say "Very good sir," without flickering an eyelash.

Inside the orderly room, which is simply the kitchen of a cottage rigged up with a trestle table, a chair or two, piles of forms and a typewriter to give it the office atmosphere, our minds are soon set at rest.

The sergeant-major reads out our instructions from a paper. We shall receive passports to proceed by rail from such-and-such a place to some equally unknown other place, where we shall report to some unheard-of aerodrome and receive instruction in signalling from the ground to aeroplanes in flight. The adjutant then enters and gives us his blessing and views on the vital necessity for complete co-operation between the infantry and the air force, a harangue to which we pay little heed. We stand at attention trying to look as interested as possible, while all the time our minds are soaring skywards, high above the clouds in an aeroplane.

Outside again we meet Webster who is obviously disappointed that we are not going to Blighty, and yet can hardly hide his pleasure in the knowledge that we are only going away for a few days and not leaving him out here for good. He pals us to the end of the village where we board a lorry leaving for the railhead, and as we top the first rise, Webster, the billets and the road to the front disappear from the landscape, when we can think more easily of the pleasant interlude from the trenches which lies ahead of us.

It is only a matter of an hour's run, and the time soon slips in swopping gossip with the lorry driver and his mate. On arrival we find we have two hours to wait before the train departs, so go on the scrounge to the Y.M.C.A. The hut is crowded with leave men and fellows like ourselves going on various training courses. A crown-and-anchor board is in full swing in a quiet corner, but we are not tempted. It is a jolly throng who are all going away from the front, and that in itself has a cheering effect. Then there isn't the feeling of apprehension which usually surrounds a leave train crowd.

In other parts of the line Jerry has a bad habit of bombing railheads when a leave train is about, and his long-range guns can be very disturbing to a fellow with fourteen days' holiday ahead of him, but here there isn't a sign of a Boche plane, and as for shelling, it just doesn't happen.

The train, after many false alarms, steams slowly in, and we gulp down our hot tea and make a rush for the nearest truck. There is much shepherding by an overworked R.T.O. and an exasperated corporal, but everybody is happy and contented, and when at last we actually do begin to move in the proper direction, we show our appreciation by lusty cheers and shouts—we are off.

Our route at first lies through the old battlefields of a year ago; a desolate area of rusty belts of wire, old trenches, shell-holes and ruined villages, but Nature has done her best to obliterate the signs of war, and although the scars are still evident, the festering wounds are hidden beneath a mantle of green.

Occasionally in the distance we see the marquees and tents of a field hospital, or pass a huge service dump, but for miles on end it is just a lonely expanse of uninhabited waste land.

We have just sighted our first civilians, and what is more,

interesting to the majority of the khaki crowd, our first female working in a field, when the train stops with a rattle and grunt at our destination.

There is a hurried look at our typed instructions which we have some difficulty in finding amongst the miscellaneous collection of papers and photographs which help to form our manly chests; then satisfied that this is the right spot, we jump down on to the wooden platform, while willing hands deposit our baggage on top of us, and the train rumbles on as we sort ourselves out.

At the R.T.O.'s hut we find another six infantrymen on the same job as ourselves and, what comes as a real surprise item, an Air Force tender waiting to convey us to the aerodrome, a welcome and consideration which we have long since ceased to expect. At last we are beginning to taste the luxuries of soldiering in the back areas.

The camp has never played host to infantrymen before, and we are accorded the respect we deserve. No longer are we poor miserable foot-sloggers, but to the mechanics and others who haunt the drome, something in the way of heroes, a reputation which perhaps we hardly merit, but one which we find rather pleasant and do our best to encourage by tall tales of our prowess. The two ribbons that Mac sports lend a tinge of truth to our colourful yarns. They like to hear them and we love to tell them, so everybody is happy.

The food is splendid and the quarters luxurious. There is even a canteen with a reading-room where we can play games or read in comfort after duty.

The spirit of comradeship which pervades the camp is infectious, and we soon find ourselves sacrificing our sleep to watch the dawn patrol take off, and anxiously counting the returning machines as eagerly as the most enthusiastic airman.

Discipline, as we know it, between officers and men comes a poor second to the job on hand in this camp. A pilot's life may depend on the condition of his machine and guns. He has to rely on his mechanics to see him through, and they never let him down. Around their beloved planes army discipline fades away, and they become ordinary mortals extending to one another whole-heartedly support for the sake of self-preservation.

The average life of a pilot is a short-lived affair. Death to him is always just round the next cloud. He knows it and makes the best of things, but for the ground staff, war, in our opinion can be a very pleasant affair, and yet they have their grouse. The long hours they work, the absence of leave, the lack of variety in their diet, and the loss of the little luxuries and comforts they had been accustomed to in civilian life. It is all good-natured grousing, but we listen in amazement. We poor mortals would give ten years of our lives to be in their shoes and think ourselves fortunate. War has its own particular brand of humour.

Our course of instruction proves to be nothing more difficult than signalling in morse from the ground to aeroplanes in flight. It is done with the aid of a gigantic shutter-disc pegged down flat. The shutters open and close by the pulling of cords on the same principle as the ones we use in the trenches, the only difference being the size and position from which we signal.

After four days' instruction we finish our course by going aloft and viewing our efforts from the airman's point of view. I can't say that I am desperately keen to go up. I'd much rather stay on the ground; still, if the others can do it, so can I. There can't be much chance of the plane going wrong, otherwise the pilot wouldn't look so unconcerned about it. Nevertheless they go a long way up and that means a long way to come down if there should be a mishap.

When my turn comes I try to look as indifferent as possible as I give the name and address of my next-of-kin, and display the identity disc hanging round my neck. A fleece-lined coat is handed to me along with a helmet and goggles, and with them slung over my arm I walk as jauntily as possible to the plane, while inwardly I feel as if I had signed my death-warrant and am walking to my execution.

I salute with my disengaged hand as I approach the pilot standing by the machine.

"You the man I'm taking up?"

"Yes, sir."

"Good, we'll be up about half an hour, three different

altitudes. Each time I'm ready, I'll wave like this"—and he describes a semicircle and back with his left arm.

"That will be your signal to commence unravelling the dot-dashing business—understand?"

"Yes, sir."

He moves towards the machine, then turns and gives me another look.

"What part of Scotland do you come from?"

I tell him.

"Splendid, then we are townies."

"Yes, sir."

"What's the name?" is his next query.

"Purves."

"Well, I'll be damned; not the paper people?"

"The same, sir," I answer proudly. "My grandfather's business."

The awkwardness I usually feel in front of a strange officer begins to disappear, and I become more talkative.

"And which Purves are you now?" is his next enquiry, and I try to elucidate my exact position on the family tree.

"Then it will be your brother I know. Willie, isn't it?"

"Yes, it will be."

"A fag"—and he holds out a gold cigarette-case. "We've just time for one before we get going."

That's what I admire about these pilots. Their rank hangs very lightly on their shoulders. They are quite ready to talk on equal terms with a humble Tommy. Our own officers are on the whole good fellows, but there is always the barrier of rank.

"Let me see now, it must be four years since I last saw Bill"; then, as a foregone conclusion: "He's out here, of course."

"Oh, yes," I answer with some pride. "He's been out almost since the beginning. I had a note from him this morning. His brigade's out on rest about sixty miles from here."

"Sixty miles, eh? What did you say the name of the place was?"

I tell him, then as an afterthought: "At least that's the way it is spelt."

"Well, well."

"Say"—I feel myself becoming quite excited over the very thought—"is there any chance, sir, of going round that way when we are up and perhaps having a little engine trouble or something?"

"Who knows!" he replies thoughtfully. "I should like to see Bill and have a chat with him. Straying from the straight and narrow is against the rules on this sort of job, but we might take a chance. We'll see. Come on, we'll get going."

I climb into the rear seat of the plane directly behind the pilot and find it is roomier than I expected. The floor is of wood and looks quite solid, so are the sides. Evidently not such a fragile thing an aeroplane after all. I had been half afraid that if I stood up and put my full weight on the floor, I'd go right through it, but this floor looks strong enough to hold my ten stone.

Somebody climbs up and shouts something to me, but I can't make out what he says for the roar of the engine, and before I get a chance to enquire, a rush of wind like a gale strikes my face as the propellers commence whirling. Mechanics run clear of the wings, and we are off.

I lean over and watch the ground rushing past, then gradually leave us. So far I haven't felt any sensation, but we are certainly flying. Over some trees we skim and start climbing in circles round the drome, while the whole panorama is laid out before me. The earth, I notice, takes on a different aspect altogether. Roads become narrow winding strips of grey, fields just squares and oblongs of various shades of brown and green, woodlands are rugged patches of a darker hue, while the aerodrome, with its camouflaged hangars and huts, blends into the surrounding countryside and is almost indiscernible but for tell-tale specks of khaki moving like ants around the buildings and the planes lying on the green runway like small birds with their wings outspread. It is a new world to me.

The solidity of my little cockpit gives me a sense of security I had never anticipated, and I know I am going to enjoy the trip. The air is clearer and more bracing up here. A feeling of utter joy of living takes hold of me, and I discard my helmet, letting the wind run through my hair.

I look down again and pick out the drome beneath me,

and locate the series of red and white dashes which is the signalling shutter. Huge as it is, from this height it is only a tiny square of changing colour amongst the mixture of greens and browns.

We have stopped climbing now. The pilot gives me the agreed signal, drops a green flare for the benefit of those on the ground, and I focus all my attention on the square of red. It starts to send its message, quite readable to trained eyes, and I write it down blindly on the pad attached to my thigh by straps. It is just the usual practice message which the army signaller enjoys sending when no officer is about:

"To O.C. Sleeping-Out Passes.

"Sir, You would do me a ripping favour by granting Private John Thomas a permanent sleeping-out pass.

"Yours in anticipation,

"LUCY TIGHTBOTTOM."

The message is repeated as a check, then I give the agreed sign to the pilot and we commence climbing again.

Once more we start circling, and repeat the performance of message reading. The shutter is now a mere pin-point, but I manage to get the complete message down. It is more official this time, and clearly informs me that someone in authority is about down below.

For a third time we start climbing, then flatten out and circle, but this time I find the distance too great. Small fluffy balls of cloud float into my line of vision and I lose sight of the disc for seconds on end. The rush of air tends to make my eyes water, so I give it up as hopeless and write my report down on the pad:

"Distance too great for reading with naked eye, also climatic conditions tend to be unfavourable at this altitude."

I read it over and feel quite proud of my effort. I sign it and leave it at that.

The pilot turns his head, smiles, and swings his arm forward. I know what he means and nod my approval. Thrilled with the idea, I settle myself comfortably and let my thoughts forge ahead so as to appreciate this joy ride to the full. Won't Bill be surprised? It's three years since I last saw him, and fancy visiting him this way. What a tale to tell the folks at home next time I write. That reminds me I'm due them a long letter. I've sent nothing but field postcards for the last fortnight.

We pass through a cloud, nothing but white fluffiness all around, damp too. I can feel it on my face, then out into the bright sunshine again. I look down, but the earth is hidden for the moment by low-lying clouds. The pilot draws my attention to some white balls of smoke to our right and shouts "Boche." I strain my eyes, but the shells are bursting miles away and no sign of a plane is visible; some marauding Jerry running the gauntlet of our "Archies."

On we go, now bathed in warm sunshine, then almost chilled as we pass through a cold clammy cloud. This is romance, the whole heavens to ourselves, not a thing in sight but patches of clouds. Queer things clouds, so thin and transparent at the edges, and so dense and cold in the centre. What an adventure; it's so vast, endless, away from everything. I'd like to go on like this for ever. Peaceful and quiet too, I'll bet, if it wasn't for those powerful engines, but strangely enough I seem to have become accustomed to their din. How warm it is! The sun's rays at this height are so hot that it is difficult to realise it is November. Hello, what's that? Something dark seems to rush past at my back, and at the same instant I recognise, above the noise of the engine, the sharp continuous rattle of a machine-gun, then our own gun commences spitting away, and the earth looms up on my left. A second later I am gazing at blue sky, while a plane with the black crosses of a Boche machine streaks across my vision. Once again the earth comes into line, followed by blue sky, and I feel the blood rushing to my head as I get a glimpse of green fields which appear to be far above me and racing immediately we right ourselves and fly straight, for which I breathe a prayer of thankfulness.

We seem to have been flying sideways, upside down and vertically all in a matter of seconds, and my inside has a rather unsettled feeling, but I forget that as I see the Jerry machine again a little in front and above us. There is another rattle from our gun, and I follow the course of the tracer bullets right into the plane above. For a second or two it seems to waver, but I lose sight of it as I am flung heavily backwards and feel the rear of my seat pressing hard against my shoulder-blades as we head for heaven. The other machine is forgotten, and I grip the sides of the plane, wondering what is going to happen next and just how far away that blue sky is. Two almost vertical side turns have me gripping the sides fiercer than ever, and I am somewhat relieved when we get on a more even keel and enter a thick bank of cloud. We turn this way and that way, but only fog surrounds us. We've either lost the Boche or he has lost us, and after minutes of blind flying at last emerge into the sunshine, but the plane with the black crosses has completely vanished. We explore two more patches of cloud, then give it up as a bad job, and now I notice our nose is turned towards the drome. Our little visiting party is evidently off.

But what a tale to tell Bill, and what a yarn to relate to Mac and the boys when we get down! It's disappointing not being able to make our visit; still, I've had a thrill so I suppose I should be satisfied. We come below the clouds, and in the distance I recognise the hangars of the aerodrome. In a few minutes we are spiralling down and taxi to a standstill beside a little group of pilots and mechanics. Questions are hurled at my pilot. Everybody seems to have forgotten that such a person as myself exists, until one or two of the mechanics come nosing around for news, and with them I inspect the machine for bullet holes. Our Jerry friends evidently got in a good burst when he first appeared and we count five altogether in the structure of the rear cockpit. It seems impossible that anyone could have been sitting in such a small space without being hit, yet here I am.

The pilot, I notice, is having a spot of bother in explaining matters, but as he appears to have the situation well in hand, I discreetly slip away towards the store hut and hand in my overalls, and with them, all connection with His Majesty's Royal Air Force.

Twelve hours later finds us reporting our return at battalion headquarters, and it is only when on the way to our billet that we remember the court-martial, and the preparations that had been made to frustrate it before we left.

Eagerly we hunt up Webster for all the details. The court have sentenced the prisoner to ten years' imprisonment, and his brother, who had been the organising brains behind our little demonstration movement, decided to let sleeping dogs lie. He reckoned the war could hardly last another ten years and that his brother would be much safer in a prison in England than a front-line trench in France.

The hungry appetite of King's rules and Regulations has been appeased by a sentence which is decidedly one of life instead of death, and the occasion has unearthed a company sergeant-major with the ability of a brigadier.

Chapter Seventeen

CAPTURE AND ESCAPE

October 22nd (I think), CAMBRAI SECTOR. I'm well up on the list for leave, in fact I'm "sweating on the top line."

It can't come too soon for me. As windy as hell.

Had a most unpleasant experience. Trying to treat it as a joke, but it has left its mark on my nerves.

Just discovered, too, what a beautiful colour khaki really is.

THERE are always certain things in modern warfare which, to the ordinary fighting soldier, seem senseless and of no account, duties which do not justify the risk they entail, unnecessary fatigues with their labour and discomfort, and a host of other trivial annoyances.

I can understand the purpose of a signal cable buried in a six-feet trench running almost up to our front line. It is a very handy thing to have and one that Jerry doesn't often let us accomplish. Decidedly an asset, it ensures perfect communication between the front line and headquarters under almost any condition other than the heaviest of bombardments, and requires a direct hit to break the cable.

But why it should be necessary to keep me cooped up in a hole barely six feet square, midway between two of the strong points which form our defensive system in this sector, with only an unmanned trench and belts of wire in front, keeps me guessing. If I had my way I'd run the cable to one of the strong points where it would be of some use, and not, as at present, a useless piece of junk serving no purpose. No doubt it was originally laid to conform with our usual trench system, but since that has been discarded for a line of posts and strong points, the cable lies forgotten by everyone but our immediate commander.

After all, why should I worry? It's a cushy job to a certain extent. The hole I live in, though small, is large enough for my requirements. It is well roofed with thick beams and a layer of sandbags turfed over. From outside it wouldn't be discernible, only the covered-in cable trench ends abruptly, and the grass has not yet fully overgrown the turned earth.

The entrance is only large enough to allow me to scramble in and out, and is cunningly screened with two green-coloured sandbags. Inside, two-thirds of the room is taken up with the usual two-storey wire-netting bunks, while a couple of biscuit-tins occupy half of the space left, and serve as table or arm-chairs as required. At the entrance end there is a field telephone exchange and buzzer, to which are attached the ends of the entrenched cable.

My job officially is to maintain the lines of communication, which consists of phoning up Webster each morning, who, with another signaller, is installed in a similar dugout about five hundred yards further back. The usual conversation after calling the code signal in morse on the buzzer is: "Cock o' the morning, Webby. How's things?"

To which salutation I get:

"Bloody fine. What's doing at the war?"

Then follows the front-line gossip about mythical reliefs and long rests, rats and lice, or a gramophone from battalion headquarters which Webster intends smuggling up to his abode, with promises to allow me to share the concerts over the phone; finishing off with the cheerful grousing which is our one and only unchallenged privilege.

At midday the cable is tested again, then, if there are no Boche observation balloons up, I stroll down to Webster's post. A rise in the ground screens this part of the line from frontal observation, and although in sight from the Jerry trenches to the left, the stroll, though strictly forbidden in the daytime, is worth the risk. There I collect my rations for the following day, play cards or visit the "bird-cage," a strong point garrisoned by one of our companies. In case of a visit by authority we have a splendid system of understanding with the signallers at the headquarters end of the cable, and always get ample warning which enables us to get back to our posts long before any red tabs appear on the scene.

The days pass cheerfully enough. It is a quiet sector; the countryside is pleasant and almost unmarked by aggressive warfare, and my job frees me from fatigues and working parties. There is little else to do but eat, smoke and sleep if possible.

It is the nights I dread. Things are different then. I am alone with my thoughts and fancies.

The one-time occupant of the top bunk in my post, a young soldier, Sarney by name, went out for a breath of air before turning in. That was a week ago, and I am still awaiting his return.

Webster and myself, with a corporal, spent two nights roaming about no-man's-land and the patrolled ground between our posts hunting for him or what was left, but to no purpose. Battalion headquarters have now dismissed the matter by posting him as missing and have not yet sent another man up to take his place. That doesn't matter so far as the work is concerned; it is the loneliness at nights which makes a pal desirable.

As darkness gathers I close the sandbag entrance, light the candle and try to read. I struggle through a chapter or two without knowing what I am reading, finding it impossible to concentrate when every noise draws my attention elsewhere. At each sound—the scuttle of a rat or the wind flapping the sandbag entrance—I expect to see Sarney's ghost come sliding down beside me. Disgusted with myself, I throw down the book, blow out the candle, and, lifting one of the sandbags, sit by the entrance with my head just above the level of the ground.

I watch the scudding clouds and the moon behind them struggling valiantly to pierce their gloom. With long tentative beams of light it searches out the weak spots in their cloak of fluffy obscurity, and as they thin and taper away it gradually penetrates their armour until it is proudly shedding its full brilliance over all. A thin wisp of white comes stealing across its arc, developing slowly but defiantly into a thick blanket of darkness, against which its rays fight gallantly but hopelessly; and so the incessant battle goes on.

At home, hundreds of miles away, they will be looking at this same moon, these same clouds, watching the same battle of light against darkness, but under such different conditions. And so my thoughts wander until they are brought to an abrupt end by a machine-gun from our side which rattles out a gay "pom-tiddly-om-pom," to which a Jerry gun replies "pom-pom." A minute later from Jerry's side comes "Pom-tiddly-om-pom," completed by our gunner's "pom-pom," then silence.

It's a funny war, this. I suppose now that they have exchanged greetings they'll close up for the night, but no, once again from our side comes "pom-tiddly-pom-tiddly-om-pom." Jerry, however, knows that one too, and sharp on its tail comes his "pom-pom." A draw, so far, I reckon to myself, and wait for the next turn, but they have evidently recognised each other as old opponents and don't waste any more shots. What a life, ready to play with each other and equally ready to fight!

A faint stifled squeal at my back makes me start nervously and twist round, but nothing is to be seen, then I fancy I hear the scuffling of tiny bodies in the long grass, and fling a stone in that direction—silence—some poor rabbit gone to his doom, I imagine, just another life extinguished.

Hell, but how jumpy I'm becoming. If only they would send up that half-section of mine and give me some company. How can they expect anybody to live alone in the middle of a waste like this without becoming a bundle of fears and fancies.

I am beginning to jump at every sound. If I had a pal with me or even knew there was somebody else in front I wouldn't be so windy, but I can't forget those yards of unmanned trench over which a Jerry patrol could so easily come unopposed. I keep telling myself I am quite safe; no Jerry could get through our two thick belts of wire without being discovered by our listening posts, but still my nerves keep playing tricks, and I live at night in a continual state of expectancy, ears and senses always on the alert until, in desperation, I lie down in my bunk and pray for sleep.

And how marvellous nature is. For endless minutes I lie listening and waiting. It seems impossible that I can ever find oblivion in this state. I become afraid to turn, and must always keep the opening to my hiding-place in sight, until nervous exhaustion makes me bolder and I turn and face the wall. If only I can sleep, whatever happens will come upon me suddenly, and I will be saved that soul-destroying waiting for the unknown. At this state sleep mercifully comes, and I know no more until a streak of daylight appears through the sandbag-covered entrance—another night has passed.

But how slowly the time drags until I reach that state. For the last four nights I've told myself I'll turn in early and forget the war, yet here I am, letting my thoughts develop into prowling Jerries and returning Sarnies. What a fool I was to let Sarney go for that stroll, and a bigger fool he was to take the risk. However, he was big enough and ugly enough to take care of himself; it was his own funeral. Nevertheless, I'd feel more at ease if I knew what had happened to him. Maybe he's a prisoner getting a free trip to Germany, or lying wounded in some out-of-the-way copse or shell-hole, or perhaps—ah, well, better not think of it. That's the idea, I'll forget all about it.

Sliding back into the dug-out, I carefully close the entrance and relight the candle, then glancing at my wrist-watch I am surprised to see it is past midnight. The evening has passed quicker than I thought. It's time to get down to it, so as usual I go over to the field telephone and ring up Webster. A minute elapses before I hear his cheery voice:

"Hello, that you, Jock?"

"Yep. I'm dossing now, Webby. How's things?"

"All cigarro. We've got a couple of trench-mortar boys keeping us company. They're just back from leave and still got some dough left. Yours truly is holding the bank and fifteen francs to the good. How does that sound? Come down early in the morning, Jock, and we'll slip over to the artillery canteen and bust it."

"I'll be there, you old card sharper. Well, cheero."

"Say, Jock," comes Webby's voice, "are you lonely there?"

"Not me, I've got a couple of fine rats that are quite sociable."

"Look here, Jock," Webster persists, "as soon as I've cleaned out these two rookies I'll hop along and keep you company."

"Not a bit of it, Webby, I'm all right. I'll see you in the morning. Cheero."

And with that I put down the earphones, rather annoyed with myself at the thought that my windiness had been apparent to Webster.

I give a last look round the small dug-out, place my rifle handy, then slip into the bottom bunk, fully clothed, and blow out the candle. Twice I am almost asleep when the clammy cold feet of a rat on my face brings me back to wakefulness, and I have to start all over again, but eventually I must have fallen off as the next thing I remember is finding myself fully awake, my breath coming in short gasps as I raise myself on my elbow and listen. I can feel the sweat breaking out all over me and subconsciously have that knowledge that there is someone near me. I lie motionless, but can detect nothing that might induce this feeling of danger, yet almost wihout any thought on my part I find myself groping in the dark for my rifle, and feel more comfortable as I grip its friendly barrel. With my thumb on the safety catch and my fingers encircling the trigger, I keep my eyes on the sandbags at the entrance, and watch.

I can distinguish nothing unusual from the night sounds of the front, and am inwardly cursing myself for a windy fool, when my ears catch the sound of heavy feet on loose, stony soil. Instantly I am on my feet and cautiously peering through a join in the sandbag covering. At first I see nothing, then two figures come into view and halt in a crouching attitude ten yards away. I am on the point of hailing them when something suspicious in their manner makes me strain my eyes to get a better look at them. They rise and move forward again, but a Verey light brings them to a sudden standstill, and with the help of its subdued light I recognise the familiar Jerry helmet.

So great is the shock that for minutes I don't seem to breathe but can only stand and gaze, until suddenly I realise there are other moving figures, and I count fourteen. Immediately my thoughts fly to the bombs I have so neatly placed on the shelf near at hand, but that is hopeless. I'd have to get out on top to throw them, and I'd be knocked over in no time if I showed above ground. First I'd better try and warn Webster, so with thumping heart and eyes riveted on the entrance, I buzz away at the morse call of Webster's post for what seems an age before I get a reply. The sound of the buzzer to my ears grows louder each time I press the knob, and I am forced to waste valuable seconds getting hold of a blanket to cover the instrument and smother the noise.

At last I get Webster's answering call, and hear him enquiring over the phone:

"What the bloody hell's the matter, Jock?"

I am afraid to answer back into the telephone in case my voice should carry to those outside, but in desperation, at Webby's repeated demands, I am forced to whisper hoarsely into it:

"Jerry's about, use the buzzer." Then feverishly I dot-dash the message: "German patrol going in direction of bird-cage, have counted fourteen."

There is a sudden commotion on the roof of my dug-out and the message finishes in a long buzz as I make a grab for my rifle, but remember too late that I left it in the opposite corner when I picked up the blanket. Blindly I dash over for it and kick one of the biscuit-tins. Immediately the sandbag covering is torn aside, the ray from a flash-lamp alights on me and guttural commands are shouted in. I don't understand the words, but well I comprehend the tone of voice and the meaning of the stick bombs held in the hands of the two Jerries now looking down on me.

By this time I have a fair grip on my rifle, and in the three seconds that elapse before I scramble through the opening with my hands up, I make and reject several decisions, yet I have no recollection of thinking. Everything seemed to happen spontaneously after I made that grab for the rifle that wasn't there.

And to think I had always told myself I'd never be captured as long as I had a rifle in my hands, that I'd go out fighting no matter what the odds, yet here I am trying to get on my feet, holding my hands as high in the air as possible, and somehow feeling relieved at still being alive. Truly the urge of self-preservation knows no pride.

I am roughly shoved and pushed over to an officer, who, in a semi-whisper, hurls some words at me to which I answer "no compré." He grasps me by the shoulder with one hand and shakes me like a madman, while he flourishes a revolver in front of my face. I feel sure my end is near and expect every second to feel a bullet smack into me. A great dread of death comes over me, but strange to say, now that I think it so near, all signs of funk disappears, and my one regret is that I didn't fight it out when I had the chance. I keep mumbling automatically "no compré," "no compré," which seems to enrage the officer, and eventually in his disgust he pushes me violently against one of his men standing behind, who butts me malignantly with his knee.

A few short commands and I am being marched off with a couple of bayonets prodding my back, and so passes an eternity, although it must only be three or four minutes since I gave the biscuit-tin that fatal kick.

My escort halts when we arrive at the first belt of our wire entanglements, and it is then I realise that our machine-guns are barking away from the bird-cage and quarry redoubts. Webster has managed to pass the word on, that is one consolation; their raid will be a wash-out.

Some delay occurs before a pathway through the wire is found, and the bullets by now are singing around us, causing my captors to get mixed up amongst the barbs in their haste. This rather tries their tempers, and after being roughly handled I retaliate by shoving one of them over an upright support which blocks our path. I try to cover it up by assisting him to his feet, but receive a nasty kick on the shins for my pains and a dig between the shoulder-blades from the butt of his comrade's rifle which, fortunately, knocks some sense into me and helps to cool my rising temper. For the rest of the journey through the wire I take all the pushing and prodding as gracefully as I can, and keep my hands well above my head.

When at last we leave the wire behind, I am minus half my nether garments and bleeding from deep gashes in my legs and thighs, but I am still alive.

All the yarns I have heard of prisoners being killed by their escort come uppermost in my mind. The darkness only adds to my dread of the future, and I have a helpless, hopeless feeling which the rough handling by my escort only makes the keener.

Our field guns have now become roused, and as we penetrate the thin barrage they put down our progress develops into a pulling and shoving from shell-hole to shell-hole. My captors begin to take a greater interest in their own skins as the shelling increases, and twice, if only for a second or two, my wrist becomes free and there is only the bayonet of the fellow behind me to be reckoned with, but my senses are too dulled by the explosion and my experience of the last quarter of an hour, to take action before it is too late.

A third time we fall in a heap at the bottom of a shell-hole, and this time I am on my feet first and tugging desperately to free my arm. The fellow has a good grip and tries to pull me on top of him, but I stamp my foot in his middle and kick viciously with the other. He shouts something to his comrade who is trying to struggle from underneath him, at the same time grabbing me with his other hand. I tug furiously but can't get free, then in changing my position to get a kick at the white face of the Jerry underneath, I seem to stamp all the wind out of the fellow who holds me. There is a grunt, my arm is free and in the same second I am out of the shell-hole and running deeper into the upheaval of the barrage. Fear urges me on and brings me new courage; shells lose their frightfulness. I can only think of the two Jerries behind me, and on I stagger. Once an explosion lifts me into the air and I land on my back, but as soon as I have gathered my dazed senses, I am up and off again. How long or how far I ran I have no idea. I have a vague recollection of the shelling abating a little, of crouching near a narrow path in the wire and watching the sparks fly as if from a smithy's anvil as machine-gun bullets lash the entanglements and make of it a pathway of death for the retreating Boche. On I go again, but in the darkness I cannot find any other openings, and in desperation make four futile attempts to get through the maze of wire. The last effort almost imprisons me, and I lie in a shell-hole until I can summon up courage for another attempt. Dawn begins to break and I am still on the wrong side of the wire. This is the seventh time, and with the help of the grey light I make better progress. Still five yards to go. Excitement almost overwhelms me. Picking my way is too slow, so I throw discretion to the winds and struggle and fight blindly against the clutching lacerating barbs.

Half an hour after, with the tears welling up in my eyes and mingling with the blood on my face, I fall head downwards, exhausted, but clear of the wire. Approaching daylight hastens my tottering steps. What remains of my uniform hangs in shreds, while blood trickles and dries from dozens of cuts on legs, face and arms.

I know I am walking like a man intoxicated and try to steady myself. When I reach a shallow trench I have just sufficient interest left in my well-being to take a hasty look before I topple down into it. My senses are too paralysed to realise that if it had been garrisoned I should have been spotted approaching minutes ago. Along it I stagger, and some of the tiredness leaves me as I notice visible signs of British occupation, then suddenly round a bend appears a khaki figure. I notice the quick movement of his rifle and shout out hurriedly. He calls out over his shoulder and advances. Another figure appears and I am soon telling my story in short, disconnected sentences. Then an officer arrives and hands me a flask from which I drink. The spirit makes me cough and splutter, but gives me a warm comfortable feeling inside. More khaki-clad figures appear —khaki, the most beautiful colour on earth.

Chapter Eighteen

MAC GOES WEST

October (don't know date), St. Emily, Cambrai. *Suppose it had to come. Mac killed.*
Must get exact date.

It is a lovely November morning, just sufficiently cold to make tramping a real pleasure, while the air has that sharp bracing effect on our bodies which makes it difficult to restrain the energy it rejuvenates within us. The sun is a red ball in the hazy sky, and there is just enough mist about to screen us from the eyes of an observant artillery-man or machine-gunner. It looks as if we are going to thoroughly enjoy our carrying fatigue.

We owe our morning jaunt to a Boche shell which landed on our signallers' dug-out during the night, and blew our gear, along with a signaller, sky-high. Brigade headquarters, on hearing of our misfortune, promptly came to the rescue by offering to supply the necessary wire and instruments from their surplus stock, providing we supplied the carrying party, so, scenting a cushy job, Webster made arrangements and with a little wangling we've been picked for the job.

Brigade area at St. Emily presents a splendid ground for scroungers such as we, and the fatigue, such as it is, will be a light one. The corporal in charge is easy-going, so life for an hour or two will be very happy.

Buttons have been polished for the occasion, and we have even succeeded in inducing a shine on our footwear. All the appearance of a "square-pushing" party has been successfully effected, and why not? There's no knowing who we might meet on a morning such as this.

'Each dug-out and funk-hole, as we walk down the trench, is greeted with our *Bonjour, messieurs.*'

"Cock o' the morning to ye, soldiers."

"Gangway for a naval officer."

The occupants look after us with amused expressions, and vocal retaliations naturally follow :

"Hell, look what's here."

"Blimey, if it ain't old Don Juan himself," and a score of more intimate epithets, which could only be heard in a front-line trench.

Gaily we swagger along until, getting tired of the monotonous zigzag of the communication trench, we climb out on top and enjoy the beauty of the countryside so far as the morning mist will allow.

A mole, taking his morning airing, darts off at our approach, and before we realise it we are after him. Backwards and forwards he dodges, escaping the swipes we make at him with our sticks, by a hair's-breadth. We are oblivious to everything else in the excitement of the chase after a poor frightened mole. A lucky stroke and I knock him over. Picking up the kicking animal I give him another tap over the head. The convulsive movements gradually stop, and the little furry body lies inert in my hand.

"Got you, my beauty," I exclaim breathlessly after my exertions.

"Look at his little piggy nose. Funny sort of creature a mole."

Mac comes over and looks at the body. A trickle of blood comes from its mouth and drops on my upturned palm, leaving a little crimson spot in the centre of my hand.

"Poor little blighter, such a soft silken coat"—and Mac softly strokes the tiny creature from which I have knocked out all the life.

"What're you going to do with it, Jock?" enquires Webby, "we can't eat moles. There's only one bite anyway."

"Oh, I think I'll start saving them up," I reply. "A hundred or so and I could have a nice fur cardigan."

It is the first mole I have ever seen, and I am rather taken with the idea of a fur jacket made from moleskins.

I tie the body by the tail to my stick and begin to wonder. After all, what can I do with it? Whatever prompted me to chase and kill it? I must be a bloodthirsty brute. If only I had thought before I made that fatal stroke. Poor little inoffensive mole, it's life was as precious to it as mine is to me.

Other things draw my attention, however, and in the enjoyment of the walk, the little body dangling head downwards from my stick is soon forgotten.

A shell bursts at the cross-roads in front of us and breaks the stillness of the morning more completely than a bombardment. Its single dull-toned crump is all the more shattering and accentuated because of the peaceful placidness which surrounds us, a peacefulness which we had found so hard to become accustomed to when we first arrived here, but which, now that our nerves have become tuned and adapted to, we find so restful yet commonplace that we can even take an interest in a solitary shell burst half a mile away.

Our road runs through what must have been a village in the days before the war. The main cobbled street is all that remains. It has been kept cleared and repaired, but the rest is just two parallel heaps of unrecognisable masonry. At the far end we come to the village cemetery overgrown with weeds, tombstones levelled, coffins unearthed and bones scattered in all directions. A huge crater in the centre exposes splintered wood, bedraggled shrouds, coffins lying in tiers of three and four, some whole, others cut cleanly in halves. From these still hang tattered rags and bleached skeletons, the rest being a medley of skull and shin bones.

In the family vaults the havoc is not so apparent, but here another kind of fiend has been at work. Holes have been made in the cemented-up vaults, by human hands this time, and the contents look as if they had been stirred up with a stick. The natives in this part of the country are commonly supposed to bury the jewels of their dead along with their remains, and rumour puts the blame of this sacrilege on the retreating Boche, but rumour, of course, can be a very convenient and accommodating thing. There is no doubt, however, that the vaults have been tampered with, and anything of value contained therein, removed.

As a souvenir I break off one or two pieces of the coloured beadwork which seems to be a popular French material for the making of artificial wreathes. Beaded on wire in natural colours and every conceivable design, they certainly are more pleasing to the eye and more enduring than our own pale, pasty, glass-covered product.

We stroll about aimlessly for a bit, then having had our

fill of gruesomeness, step gingerly over broken and fallen tombstones, and by way of a weed-covered path make our exit through a huge iron gate swinging on one hinge, and so on to the main street.

At the cross-roads we stop to admire a wayside shrine. The figure of the crucified Christ only excites our curiosity because of its undamaged state; its symbolic significance is lost on our imagination. This is something we don't see at home, a bit of a curio, that's all. There is nothing in our phlegmatic nature to arouse visions of the supernatural in the imposing fact that in all the desolation we have just seen, this is the one and only piece of man's creative work which has successfully defied and escaped his destructive abilities.

With a shrug of our shoulders we pass on, wondering what sort of kick these country folk get out of erecting a statue like that at a lonely cross-road. We all have different ideas, and are just commencing an argument on religion, when our ears detect the wobbling, whistling sound of an approaching shell. It only takes a second for us to realise it is coming in the direction of the cross-roads, and with true front-line instinct, the four of us incline to the right of the road where the making of an embankment has left a shallow ditch, a foot deep. We stop to listen, and the same instinct that guided our feet now tells us the shell has overstepped the cross-road mark, and that approaching whistle, now becoming a terrifying shriek, denotes its downward curve.

I am flat, hugging the earth, as the rush of wind sweeps over me, and I feel the impact with the ground followed by a deafening "crump" that makes my ear-drums buzz, the hiss-hiss of flying steel and flint, and the thud of falling earth.

"Anybody hurt?" I hear Webster shouting as I lift my head up. The first thing I see is the body of the corporal lying face downwards, and know instantly, by the unnatural limpness of his limbs, that he has been hit and badly.

"Corp's hit!" I yell back, as I make towards the prostrate figure.

"Where've you got it, Corp?"

I am still a yard off the corporal's body, when Webster's voice calling Mac makes me turn round. Immediately the corporal is forgotten and I am kneeling with Webster alongside Mac:

"Mac, Mac, wake up old man, it's me, Jock."

"For Heaven's sake, Webby, let's get a dressing on him, here's mine," and I toss my field dressing over to Webster who is already tearing open the cloth cover of his own.

"Mac, can you hear me? It's Jock."

His eyes open a little. There is a gurgling sound in his throat:

"I'm bleeding freely, I'm bleeding freely."

Strange words, they come tortuously, but distinctly, followed by a string of curses, stranger still from Mac, which gradually turns into a choking gurgle, then silence, and I feel his body go tense, then limp, in my arms.

"Mac, liven up old man, we'll get you out of this," I blurt, as I cut away his blood-soaked tunic with my jack-knife. My anxiety to do the job quickly only makes me fumble all the more, and at last when I get his tunic and shirt cut away, the awfulness of the wound becomes apparent to me. Broad as Mac is, he isn't broad enough for the lump of metal which lies embedded in his chest. Almost frantic, I try to prise out the piece of steel with my fingers, but the splintered bone and already overlapping flesh hold it firmly in position.

"We've got to get him to a doc, Webby. Look at the way he's bleeding. How're we going to plug this hole?"

With our three field dressings, and parts of Webster's and my own shirt we cover the gaping wound, but cannot check the flow of blood.

"What do you think of him, Webby? Is he bad?"

"Pretty sick, just about all in, I fancy."

"If we can only get him to a dressing station they'll patch him up," I suggest. "He's bleeding like an ox. Come on, let's carry him. There's a station at brigade headquarters."

"What about the corp, did you look at him, Jock?" Webster enquires.

"No, damn it, I'd forgotten all about him; just a minute."

The corporal is lying twenty yards away, the upper half

of his head missing, and I notice it alongside his helmet five yards further on. We can do nothing for him, so I go through his pockets and relieve him of his field dressing.

To Webster's enquiring glance I give a shrug:

"Mutton, half his head gone. His brains are scattered all over the place. Never thought he had so many."

Unconsciously I have slipped back to the callous talk of the trenches.

"I've got his pay book and his stock of fags, two Ruby Queens. There's some dough as well," I add as I slip the lot into my own pocket to go halves with Webster later.

"Oh, and here's his dressing. Let's fix it on Mac before we move him. Poor old Mac, it's a hell of a war, Webby," I blubber as we adjust the last bandage and prepare to move him.

"Steady now, have you got him right?"—and with Mac supported on my heavy stick in a sitting position and an arm each crossed behind his back, we start on the mile and a half to the nearest casualty station. Our progress is necessarily slow and we are obliged to stop to tighten the bandages, then trundle on again as fast as we can manage, prompted by the ghastly hue that is turning Mac's once handsome sunburnt features into the yellowy grey mask of approaching death.

He breathes his last before we have covered half the distance, but still we carry on, telling ourselves we are mistaken, that he still lives and will be all right once the doctor fixes him up. I pray every yard of the way that my pal will live. Dear Mac, how could I face this life without your staunch comradeship and cheery smile? You must live—you can't leave me.

At last we lay our burden down inside the dug-out of the station. An orderly brings a Red Cross sergeant who looks at the blood-sodden bandages, feels Mac's pulse and lifts his eyelids. I stand beside Webby and watch until I can bear it no longer. Roughly pushing the sergeant aside I demand a doctor for my pal. I storm and rave and curse until a padre arrives, and with his arm around my shoulders, leads me outside. I shall always be grateful to him for the kindly way he conveys to me that Mac is no longer of this world. His sympathy and understanding is just what I require to offset my feeling of hostility towards Red Cross people to whom Mac is just another casualty, one of thousands.

It is difficult though to realise that I have seen the last of him. To have come through so much together, then this by a chance shell on a quiet front.

As I light a cigarette Webster emerges from the dugout with Mac's belongings and I blow my nose vigorously to try and hide my feelings, and as I do so, notice that my stick is still attached to my wrist by its string loop. I am surprised that I still retain possession of it, and at the same time I observe something else which dangles head downwards, a little dead furry creature—a mole. Its lifeless body brings regrets at my thoughtless action and some strange superstitious kink in my conscience links it up with Mac's death. I am filled with remorse, and untie the mole's body, then with the toe of my boot I dig a shallow grave, lay it gently in and stamp the earth down on top.

The morning which dawned so brightly for me has clouded over, and with the brightness has gone part of my existence.

With Webster I go in search of the headquarters and, without much difficulty, find the brigade signal office in dug-outs in the railway embankment. From there we get in touch with our company and make our report verbally, and at the same time I ask permission for both of us to stay until Mac is buried. This request is refused, and I am ordered to return immediately with Webster and bring as many of the instruments as we can carry.

The conversation over the phone I repeat to Webster and we decide to ignore it and remain until we have seen Mac decently buried. That settled, we hunt up the brigade cook, who is an old soldier of our own battalion. He sympathises with us and curses the army and everything connected with it, while politicians and civilians at home get the full blast of his vitriolic tongue; then to vindicate his outburst, he tells us he has just heard that his wife has given birth to twins and he hasn't been home for fourteen months. We add our own views on the waywardness of women as we open the tins of Maconachie rations he generously provides. Eating hasn't much pleasure for us and the talkative nature of our host gets on our nerves, so we hurry through the meal, each mentally occupied with his own thoughts.

Death is no stranger to us. It has been our daily companion for months, and Nature, ever thoughtful of our welfare, has born in us a callousness towards it, without which we could not withstand its hideous shock. We have seen it come quickly and mercifully, we have watched it slowly tear the soul out of a man before discarding the lifeless husk, lingering over its feast like some perverted monster, and have learned to treat it as an unpleasant but commonplace occurrence. This, however, is different. Mac's death has touched our own little trio.

Friendships are made quickly here. We learn to prize a man, not for the sort of citizen he was, but for the kind of comrade he can be. Social status means nothing in a front-line trench—a thief can be as good as a deacon. Mutual attractions or opposites draw us together, hardships shared strengthen the little circle formed, the shadow of death welds it together in unbreakable bonds, while comradeship imparts the touch of colour which enhances its beauty. When death invades one of these circles its presence becomes a family affair; the smaller the circle, the more personal it is. And so it is with us. We have come to know and love each other as brothers, jealous of the virtues, tolerant towards the little weaknesses each one possesses, and now that our own circle has been broken, death means something more than just another "gone west."

Nobody can tell us anything definite about when or where Mac will be buried. The padre, who is the most likely one to know, cannot be found, so we busy ourselves by collecting the gear we have to take back, then make ourselves scarce in the ruin of an old summer-house in a weed-grown garden.

Just before tea-time a breathless sergeant, accompanied by a signaller, ferrets us out, and with tales of courts martial informs us that battalion headquarters have been enquiring what time we left and the route we were taking. Not wishing to get us into trouble, he had spun the first yarn he could think of and he has now come to see us definitely on our way. Delay will now mean trouble for him as well as ourselves, so with a grudge and the usual cursing against authority, we shoulder the instruments and start our journey back to the company.

It is dark when we arrive at our signallers' dug-out and dump our load, and, strange to say, despite the sergeant's fuss, nobody asks what has detained us, although our company has been without signalling instruments for almost twenty-four hours and have had to send all messages by runners. We hand over the chits showing the things we have signed for, and report ourselves at the company headquarters.

The commander, we find, is visiting the battalion, and we can only make our appeal to be allowed to return for Mac's burial to the sergeant-major. He is sympathetic enough but can do nothing. We have been detailed for duty to-night and must just carry on. Our request, however, he will duly put before the captain on his return, and with that assurance we have to be content.

The remaining hours drag slowly by until we are mustered for our turn of duty. There are twelve of us and we are detailed as a covering party for men working on the wire. Off we are marched in single file up the winding communication trench and into the actual firing line. There is a halt here until the working party arrive, then over the parapet we go and wait at the outer edge of our entanglements, while the corporal in charge goes on ahead. Shortly he returns, accompanied by an officer and a sergeant. There are some whispered instructions, and we are moved forward into the darkness. Verey lights go up and we remain motionless, a moving object being much easier seen than a stationary one; then as the darkness envelops us again we move forward until the next light goes up, and so on until about fifty yards in front of our wire, where we are posted ten paces apart. There we have to remain until the working party are finished. It is a job which I thoroughly detest. There is no friendly screen of wire in front, no sentry or listening post to give warning of a hostile raid, nothing but our own alertness and rifles between us and death should Jerry take it into his head to pay us a visit. Even the pride I felt, on my first turn of this duty many months ago, in the fact that my own bayonet was the only defence between Britain and her enemies, has long since ceased to stimulate me; memory of those early inexperienced thoughts now only make me smile.

The weather is dry and that is one thing in our favour, although, to offset that, the nights are extremely cold, with a touch of frost. Still, I prefer that to some of the wet filthy nights I have spent in no-man's-land on the same job. To my right and left I can just distinguish the dark outline of the silent watchers on each side of me. The grass grows long in no-man's-land, and, experienced as I am, each rustle is a creeping Boche, every clump of bush takes shape and becomes a Jerry helmet, then when a Verey light with its artificial brightness lights up the whole expanse, I see nothing but waving grass, the sharp, jagged outline of the rim of a shell-hole and a few broken stumps of trees, all sharply defined against the background of darkness. There is a peculiar feeling between my shoulder-blades as I hear the Verey light commence its sizzling downward trail and I wonder just where it will fall. Tales of men who have received terrible burns from these falling lights come to my mind, and I am greatly relieved when the burning red-hot object comes into my vision a yard or two from the ground a little to my left, then follows a splutter, with darkness more acute than ever. The muffled tappings and clanging of wire behind us commence again, louder than ever it would seem because of their sudden stoppage.

Two hours pass and I begin to fidget nervously. My mind wanders off my job and I think of Mac. I just can't realise I shall never see him again. I keep repeating to myself: "Mac's gone, Mac's gone," but the full meaning of that fact doesn't seem to be able to penetrate. I am surprised I can be so composed over it.

A Verey light has just spluttered out in front of me, but I have hardly been aware of it, so engrossed am I with other thoughts, when the sharp rat-tat-tat of a machine-gun brings me abruptly back to the job on hand. Mechanically I crouch nearer the ground and curse under my breath the careless blighter behind who has drawn the fire of the Jerry gunners. The bullets ricochet and spark among the wire entanglements behind. There is a groan, then another, followed by a long-drawn stifled moan. The gunner fires another burst or two, then stops, and in a few minutes the tappings of the working party commence again.

I am fast reaching the stage where my hands and feet are becoming hopelessly numb, and my body stiff and cramped with cold, despite the numerous dodges I have learned to employ to keep my blood circulating by vigorous twitchings and kickings. The ground takes on a glistening whiteness as the frost gets heavier, and I begin to wonder how long it will be before I freeze altogether. The cold becomes so intense that I give up all attempts at trying to keep warmth in my body and just lie freezing until the corporal comes along the line of watchers telling us to fall back and line up at the wire. Movements so eagerly sought an hour ago is now more painful than lying still. My legs are useless, my feet just heavy lumps without any feeling. I try to walk, but can't tell whether I am putting my feet down or not, stumbling and falling so often that I finish the journey on my hands and knees.

I find the others in even a worse state than myself, but after vigorous stamping of feet, with swinging and thumping of arms, we at last get the blood moving in our veins sufficiently to enable us to stumble through our wire and into the trench.

Back at the company dug-out we get a ration of rum. Mine, as usual, I hand over to Webster, who, for the first time since I have known him, advises me to swallow the stuff myself, but I stubbornly refuse.

"Well, here's to what you're missing, Jock"—and it disappears down Webby's eager throat.

Being in the support line we have a mine dug-out thirty feet deep as our sleeping-quarters. It has innumerable steps with a rope for a hand-rail, which helps us to maintain our equilibrium when descending, and enables us to haul ourselves up when ascending. Down below, there are three compartments. The smallest is used by our signallers and specialists. The other two are our quarters. They might hold, with a crush, fifteen men each, but now provide accommodation for fifty men and their equipment. The air is foul with a mixture of stale tobacco smoke, smouldering candle wick, brews of Oxo cubes and strong tea, flavoured with the more human stinks of an overcrowded dug-out where manners and the finer instincts are at a minimum.

Every available yard of floor space is occupied by sitting or recumbent figures, equipment being utilised as seats or pillows. Some play cards, others boil water for tea or Oxo on little cookers sent out from home. There are the inevitable delousing parties and letter-writers, and at least one diehard reading. The remainder lie full length, or support their backs against the timbered walls and sleep. It seems incredible that anybody could sleep in such quarters with the continuous buzz of many voices, but I know from my own experience that it is quite easy if one is tired enough. What puzzles me is just how little sleep these card players can exist on. In support, reserve or back in billets, always the same little parties. They play cards and gamble whenever they have a minute off duty, snatching an occasional hour of sleep at odd times, mostly when they are broke. Lack of sleep seems to have little effect on them; they are a hardy lot.

From the foot of the stairs, in the flickering light of half a dozen candle stumps, it doesn't look as if an extra twelve could possibly find a resting-place, but we manage it. Our methods are anything but gentle. "Beg pardons" or "By your leave" are neither expected nor given. We merely choose a spot, fling down our equipment and sit on it, regardless of sprawling legs or other parts of anatomy which may be in the way. Nobody takes offence at our uncouthness. It is a hard life we live, and the ability to look after oneself and rough it with the roughest are assets which every soldier who values his peace of mind must strive to possess. Softness is played upon, firmness and rough handling when the occasion demands it being taken for granted.

There was a time when such a situation would have appalled me, when, raging inwardly, I would have held myself aloof, disgusted with the others for their lack of thought in not making room for me. But times have changed: I am as much entitled to sitting-down space as any of the others, and I am ready to out-swear or our-fight them to obtain it—just a matter of looking after one-self in the most exacting calling a man can follow.

After scrounging some tea from a pal, Webster and I decide to go to the company dug-out and make another request to be allowed to return to brigade to find out about Mac's burial.

We put on our equipment and ascend the steps. The gas blanket at the top shuts out all light, and as we push it aside and step into the trench, we enter another world. It is still frosty, but the clouds have disappeared, and expose a brilliant moon which makes the sky as bright as day in comparison with the darkness of the trench. Its dark walls, four feet apart, are too deep and narrow to allow the moonlight to penetrate, except for a few inches at the top which shows up like a narrow ribbon of light above the shadows of its depth.

At this hour it is deserted except for an occasional runner and sentry, one of whom stands outside the company head-quarters.

"Seen the sergeant-major knocking around?" we enquire of him.

"Just gone in a minute ago"—with a nod indicating the dug-out. "He'll be up in a jiffy."

Even as he speaks, a head and shoulders emerge round the side of the blanket, which acts as door and gas protection to the dug-out entrance.

"Hello, where have you two bees been? I've been looking for you all night."

It seems to have escaped his memory that we've been out freezing on a covering party, but we are used to the ways of sergeant-majors, so say nothing.

"You'd better look slippy if you want to attend that burial party, and remember, back by eight o'clock; report to me here."

"Right, major"—and off we go. I look at my watch—3.30 a.m. We've got three miles to cover to get to brigade. A good hour's tramp if we take the road. Slightly less across country.

"We'll chance the road," Webby suggests, "and with a bit of luck we might get a lift."

At the end of the communication trench we hear the

rattle of wheels on the rough road and put on a spurt. Our luck is in, and we jump up behind the driver of a belated regimental transport. Within half an hour we are in the vicinity of brigade and are soon trying to waken somebody up at the casualty station. A sleepy Red Cross man listens to all we have to say, then pokes his head inside the door again.

"Hi, Nobby, two blokes enquiring about a pal they brought in yesterday, name o' McDonald."

He turns to us again :

"What was he? Walking case or stretcher, 'cos it——"

"We want to know when he's being buried, that's all," Webster interrupts him irritably.

"Oh"—and he disappears inside the door, where we hear him conversing with Nobby. There is the rustle of paper, then :

"One o' those plantings last night, Nobby. Ah, there y'are—McDonald, that's 'im."

He returns again, gives Mac's name, number and regiment for verification, then :

"He was buried last night, end o' the village, last row, fifth from the right."

"How do we get there?" I enquire.

"Carry on to the cross-roads, turn left, the cemetery is on yer right a hundred yards along."

I look at Webby. "Too late, eh?"

"Yep, I thought we would be. They haven't enough to do here, it's too quiet. If things got busy they'd let you lie and rot for weeks. Anyhow, Mac's had a decent planting, that's one consolation."

Ten minutes' walk and on the right-hand side of the road we see the wooden crosses of the cemetery. We walk to the last row and count five from the end. There are only three beyond it. The ground, we can see in the moonlight, has just newly been turned. I step gingerly to the top and peer at the wooden cross.

"Yes, this is it, Webby"—and I read out Mac's name.

I am at a loss what to do or say. We just stand on either side of the mound near the head, and look down.

And this is Mac's last resting-place. His head will be about there, I think to myself. I can picture his red hair and his features, not as I last saw them but tanned and handsome; his broad shoulders here, yet the mound isn't any broader than the others. I look down its length and compare it with its neighbour. Exactly the same, nothing to denote Mac's individuality; it is just a grave.

We walk along the rows of mounds, then return to Mac's and stand together at the foot. Neither of us can find words to express our thoughts, we just stand in silence.

I find it difficult to visualise life out here without him, and yet I am more composed than I ever thought I could be at the grave of so dear a friend.

The silence becomes a little embarrassing, and with mutual understanding we take another stroll in the darkness around the cemetery. At first we are too engrossed and too deeply moved by our own thoughts to say much, but slowly become more talkative as we feel we can trust ourselves to speak, until we are pathetically recalling the happy times the three of us have had together, the things Mac has said and the things he has done, his little mannerisms and tricks of speech which so endeared him to us, his upright character, his splendid comradeship, and so back to the little mound again, over which we seem to have a feeling of mutual proprietorship. We are both loath to leave this spot which must hold the remains of our pal for all time.

The darkness of night gives place to the grey light of dawn, revealing more distinctly the crosses which surround us. I have an uncanny feeling that we are not alone, and imagine Mac's presence on my other side. The feeling persists until a creature scuttles amongst the undergrowth in front of us, and breaks the spell. Above we hear the drone of planes on their dawn patrol, while nearer us an early bird twitters away until his song is echoed by another and another, and gradually this field of dead becomes alive with our little feathered friends acclaiming the birth of a new day.

They will be "standing to" in the front line now. Mac and I have shivered together on that duty so often, but that is of the past. Mac lies here, and I am of another world.

It suddenly becomes very cold, and my teeth commence chattering as, fumbling in my tunic pocket, I bring out my battered pocket Testament, and from between its leaves take out the pressed petals of a wild rose, a memento of our last route march in Blighty. I drop them on the grave and walk away, surprised at my own emotions and a little ashamed at my display before Webby, who follows me silently on to the road. There I turn my head and take a last look at the resting-place of my best pal, at the same time vowing to return some day.

Chapter Nineteen

A LETTER

November 12th, 1917, Cambrai Sector. Letter from Mac's sister.
Answered it best I could.

A NEW battalion, a mixture of youth and age just arrived in France, has been attached to us for training in trench warfare. They come up to the line in companies, and we are supposed to put them through their paces. There are, I notice, a few old soldiers among them, men who have been out East, but the majority are either youngsters of nineteen, or, to my youthful eyes, old men of thirty-five roped in by conscription, soldiers of six months' service.

It is surprising how quickly they have adapted themselves to the new life, and now that they have become efficient at soldiering in Blighty, they have come out here to find that most of the rules they have been taught don't apply when up against the real thing.

The youngsters are as keen as mustard, and take to the new procedure as if it was some game they were being instructed in, but with the older men it is different. They have no enthusiasm, and give one the impression of being here much against their will, and so I suppose they are.

Each sentry has one of the new soldiers, and on my turn of duty I am accompanied by a fresh-faced youth of nineteen. He is a little excited at being actually in the front line, not a nervous excitement but more like that of a school-boy, all eagerness and expectancy.

I explain to him the lie of the land in front, point out the supposed machine-gun emplacements in the Jerry lines, our own posts in front of our wire, mostly inhabited at night, and a hundred other things a soldier should know about his particular part of the line. To all this I add my own pet theories and devices for cheating death. How to take a slanting look through the sandbagged loophole. One sees just as much and doesn't provide such a good target for a watchful sniper in the opposite lines. The spare cart-ridge stuck in the rifle sling. It is easier and quicker to insert than a new clip when one counts life by seconds. How to distinguish the different shells by their sound, and the necessity of judging accurately the interval bet-ween the bursts. The best way to approach a Jerry trench —erect and not bent double—then, if you are going to be unfortunate enough to be hit it will be on the legs and not in the stomach, and leg wounds aren't really dangerous while stomach wounds are. And above all, I impress upon him the necessity of taking advantage of every bit of cover. Ignoring it may look brave and impressive, but if you have a desire to live out here it is much easier accomplished by making use of all the natural safeguards. In that way only can you get the last laugh, as a dead man can't even grin.

He takes it all in and asks for more until my fund of information becomes exhausted and we lounge against the sides of the trench and swop happier experiences.

The noon heat has such a comforting, peaceful effect on us that death might be miles away, and for a minute or two we completely forget it.

Absent-mindedly I pluck a late rose growing on the parapet, and as I have never seen a rose flowering so late in the year before, take out my Testament and place it between the leaves.

"Have you one of these too," enquires my pupil.

"What?"

"A Testament."

"Oh, this, I've had it for two years now."

"I've one, I got it just before I came out."

"Well, I hope you are reading a chapter a day."

"Yes, I am. At least I have done so far."

"Why blush about it?" I enquire, noticing his embarrassment at his admission. "That's nothing to be ashamed of. I've read mine through twice, and jolly good reading it is."

"Yes, yours looks as if it has been well thumbed."

"Using it as a flower press hasn't improved it, I'll admit."

"Why do you keep those flowers and leaves and things?"

"Oh, I don't know. Seeing that rose just reminded me of when I was a kid. I used to walk miles to gather a bunch of them to bring home. This one here"—and I hold up for inspection one of my faded relics—"I got on my very first route march in the army, this one the day after I landed here, and the others just at odd times and places."

"How long have you been here?" he enquires next.

"Oh, about four months; it seems like four years though."

"You know, it's all so different to what I expected. I never thought it could ever be so quiet and so—so safe-like in the front line."

"Oh, I wouldn't call it safe," I correct him. "You never know what's going to happen the next minute. I've often thought the same myself in a trench like this with the sun shining, the blue sky above and the birds whistling, not a sound of war, and then in ten minutes it's been a shambles. You'll often get quiet spells like this down here; it's a quiet sector. Our crush is supposed to be here for a rest, and yet not a day passes without casualties. I suppose you expected to be scrapping all day and every day?" I ask in a desire to find out if his expectations are the same as my own were when I first arrived.

"Well yes, I did imagine it would be something like that. I never thought I'd be two months in France and actually five days in the trenches without firing my rifle. So far it hasn't turned out to be a very bloodthirsty war."

"No, we all think the same at first. I always pictured myself winning V.C.s, and was properly disgusted with the war for a whole fortnight, and then—well, I have changed my ideas. Now medals have lost all their attraction for me and I'd be quite happy if the war was like this always."

"Would you?" he asks rather surprised. "Not me, I'd love to have a shot at a German. Have you killed many?"

"Thousands."

"No, but really, have you?"

"Thousands, I tell you, and by the way, when did you last take a squint through that loop-hole? You're supposed to be a sentry."

"You've been looking."

"Sure, but you're on sentry-go too."

"All right"—and he takes a long interested look. "Not much to be seen, is there? How far is it to their trenches— about two hundred yards?"

"About that, two hundred and fifty to be correct," I reply.

"Thrilling, isn't it, when you think of it? Hello, what was that?"

We hear the report of a solitary rifle from across the way, followed by one from our side.

"A couple of snipers pot-shotting"; then, as voices are heard in the next bay: "Look out, here's the relief, and pick up your rifle, damn it, you're not supposed to let it leave your hands here. I told you that."

The relief comes round the bend of the traverse and we make our report; then, following the usual routine, we are dismissed and I give my new-found colleague my last piece of advice, the necessity of making himself as scarce as possible for the next four hours in the darkest corner he can find. With that, I leave him and disappear into the little dug-out cut in the side of the trench, which I occupy with Webster and two others. Nobody is at home, but I notice the mail has arrived, and in my corner is a much battered parcel from home, and a letter. The handwriting on the envelope I don't recognise, but that can wait until I've investigated the contents of the parcel. Eagerly I pull at the string and tear at the generous wrapping of paper, then comes more string round a cardboard box, but I am so impatient, I can't wait to untie it, and with one tug the string and lid of the box come away in my hand, exposing on top a note which I hurriedly scan through, then commence rummaging for the good things I'm told the parcel contains. One of mother's cakes—gorgeous—full of currants and raisins. I don't stop to consider the stinting and rationing which has gone on at home to provide the requisite number of eggs, sugar and fruit, so that this cake should be just the same as of old; I am too busy hauling out well-wrapped bars of chocolate, Oxo cubes, a box of cigarettes marked "From Dad"—all mixed up with tomatoes, a delicacy which I had specially asked for. The cigarettes are damp and red-looking, but as I put them in the sun to dry at the door of the dug-out, I consider they'll smoke none the worse for their tomato flavouring.

Then with a chunk of cake cut with my bayonet, I am ready for the letter.

"Dear Private Purves" (I read),

"I hardly know how to write you, and yet I don't feel that we are strangers. My dear brother, John, in his letters home told us such a lot about his pal, Jock, as he called you, that though I have never met you, I've known you for some time.

"We received a very sympathetic letter from your captain telling us how John met his death, but I just felt I had to write you, his friend.

"Mother has been in bed ever since we received the official intimation from the War Office. None of us can fully realise yet that we shall never see our brother again.

"Your officer told us he was hit by a shell fragment and died immediately. He wrote such a nice letter, and we all appreciate his kindness very much, yet how much more we would appreciate just a short note from one who perhaps was actually beside him when he passed away, one who was his pal.

"We would be ever so grateful to you if you could tell us the details of how it happened, whether he died peacefully or in pain.

"It seems a strange request, but what a relief it would be to us all at home, especially mother, just to know that even though he died far from home, he had a friend near him at the end who may have heard his last words.

"I cannot trust myself to write more, but will anxiously await your reply.

"This letter seems all disjointed, but we are so terribly upset at present.

"Trusting you will come safely through this horrible war,

"Yours very sincerely,
"Margaret McDonald."

I read the letter over a second time, then a third time, and am just commencing all over again when Webster's cheery countenance appears at the opening of our shelter:

"Come in and help yourself," I call out, nodding towards the cake. "I expect you knew all about this parcel long before I did, so don't look so damned surprised."

Stooping to avoid hitting his head on the corrugated-iron roof, Webster enters, all smiles, and picking up my bayonet he saws away at the cake, reciting to himself:

" 'Twas Christmas day in the workhouse."

As I eye the huge chunk he is cutting off, I tell him to take a big piece, there's plenty of it.

"That's all right, sonny, I'm just beginning. Don't like to be too greedy, you know. Oh, by the way how did you get on with the youngster?"

"All right," I answer, "quite a nice fellow and full of beans. He thinks the war is a picnic. It's just on the quiet side for him though, he's actually been here five whole days and hasn't fired a shot, and is absolutely dying to get at Jerry with his bayonet. Just the sort they want here, of course, but that talk makes me sick. You should have seen the disgust on his mug when I told him I wished it was always as quiet as this. I was less than a louse and a yellow one at that."

"They are good lads though," Webster cuts in. "They'll tone down a bit after their first show. That a letter from home?" he enquires with his mouth full of cake.

"No, not this time."

"From a skirt?"

"Yep."

"Um, I wouldn't be so damned talkative about it then."

"Oh, it isn't that," I make haste to assure him. "It's not private, you can have a squint at it." And I hand him the letter.

Webster reads and forgets to eat his cake. When at last he is finished he gravely hands it back.

"What're you going to do about it?"

"Answer it," I suppose."

"Hell, I know, but what're you going to say?"

"Damned if I know. What can I say? I can't tell her he got a lump of shell in his chest, that we plugged the wound with bits of our shirts, and that his last words were a lot of curses, can I? I've often thought of that, Webby. You know Mac wasn't a curser, at least not like—well, like you."

"No, it's an art with me. Still, that's away from the subject. You'll have to write something, so the sooner the quicker."

"How about doing it to-morrow?" I enquire eagerly. "That'll give us time to think about it."

"There you go, Jock, never do to-day what you can leave till to-morrow. No, that be damned for a tale, let's get the bloody thing off our chests and finished with."

"But what can we say?"

"We'll make up something. Have you got a pencil?"

I find the stub of a pencil and a piece of paper, write down, "Dear Miss McDonald," and there I stick.

Webster takes the letter and reads it over again, then puts it down in disgust:

"No, this ain't in my line, I give it up. 'Arf a mo' though. I'll tell you what we could do. How about spinning a yarn? We could say we were attacking. All the officers had gone west and Mac led us on but was killed by a shell just when we had captured the trench—you know the style of thing."

"That's useless," I answer irritably. "What if his folks should find out the truth afterwards? Besides, we don't know what the captain has told them."

"Oh, he won't have said much, just the usual. I know it off by heart: 'Your son was one of the most cheerful and reliable soldiers in my company, a gentleman in every sense. He will be greatly missed by all.'"

"That's all very well, but we can't be sure. Besides, Mac wouldn't want us to spin the tale to his old folks. No, we'll just have to tell the truth for once, Webby."

"Oh well, carry on, you're writing it."

Twice I have to tear up the paper, but at the third attempt I manage something that doesn't seem so bad. I hand it over to Webster:

"Here, read that out, Webby, and let's hear what it sounds like, and for Heaven's sake leave a bit of cake for to-morrow."

"Hell, what's a bit o' cake between pals," Webster retorts, cutting himself another slice.

"Here goes:

"DEAR MISS McDONALD,

"'Though I deeply regret the circumstances which necessitated your writing me, I cannot but say I was pleased to have your note.

"'It is doubtful, however, if I can add any further details of Mac's death to those you already know.

"'The part of the line we were in, and still occupy, is, in our experience, exceedingly quiet. That made it all the more distressing. It happened when we least expected it while going on a fatigue duty to brigade headquarters, a distance of about three to four miles from the front line, and we had almost completed the journey when a shell landed on the road almost on top of us. The corporal with us was killed outright; your brother was hit in the chest. We managed to stop the bleeding, and endeavoured to get him to a dressing station. He was unconscious and, I am sure, felt no pain.

"'On the way he seemed to regain consciousness, and evidently tried to talk, but the only words I could catch were Mother and Sis. He died with his hand in mine.

"'He is buried in a little military cemetery behind our lines. His grave is marked with a wooden cross giving his name, number, regiment and rank. I visited it three weeks ago.

"'It is very difficult to express one's feelings in a matter like this and to put words in the way one would like to, but I do hope my note doesn't seem abrupt.

"'If there is anything else you would like to know, or anything I can do, please do not hesitate to ask.

" 'I can only add : you have lost your brother, I have lost my pal.'

"Amen," Webster finishes, "and that's that."

"Will it do?" I enquire.

"It sounds all right, better than I could have done. All the same I'd have liked to have given him a better show than that."

"How can we? We haven't kept to the facts as it is; that would hurt too much; but if you have any decent suggestions——"

"Suggestions be damned, give the bloody thing to the post corporal and get done with it. What the hell folk want to send letters like that to us for, I don't know."

"He was her brother, wasn't he?" I retort.

"Aw, hell!"—and Webster rises and goes out into the trench, where I see him lighting a fag. I watch him as he angrily flings the match from him and inhales deeply. It is the first time I have seen Webster really rattled, and to think I was so conceited as to imagine I was the only one who had been affected by Mac's death.

I follow him into the trench and get a light from his fag.

"Sorry, Webby," I murmur.

"That's all right, Jock. Mac was such a decent spud."

"I know," is all I answer, and another link has been added to our friendship.

Chapter Twenty

THE RAID

November 18th, 1917, CAMBRAI SECTOR. Attended a church service, my first in France.

Strange thing religion.

In a blue funk. I'm detailed for a raid, a SUPPOSED volunteer and worth six pressed men.

Will be glad when it's over.

"We will now sing hymn No. 540—'Fight the good fight with all thy might.'"

The fellow at the harmonium strikes up the first few bars, the congregation of thirty turn over the leaves of their hymn-books and clear their throats. The accompanist stops and eyes the padre, there is a second or two of silence during which I can hear my next-door neighbour take in a deep breath, then the padre gives a nod to the organist and off we go at the pitch of our voices, at least everybody but myself. I'm just a little too shy to sing, or try to, among strangers.

I look around at these hefty artillerymen. They amuse me. There are so many different types. First the singers—the basses and the tenors, who with a village choir reputation, give the hymn big licks and harmonise like nothing on earth; then there are the real pillars of the kirk with eyes fixed on the heavens and their mouths opening and shutting like a trap-door as they bellow out the words of the hymn. No need for them to keep an eye on their books, they know the words by heart and are thoroughly in their element. Not so a few of the more timid ones, who are evidently ill at ease and quite out of their depth in this gathering. Church of any description doesn't seem to appeal to them, nor to those others who sing automatically with a rather vacant expression on their faces as if it was just another unpopular duty which had to be performed; and then myself, half serious, half amused, more of an onlooker than actually one of the congregation.

The tune of a well-known psalm prompted my footsteps in this direction, and the padre, seeing me halt on the extreme edge of his flock, came round and handed me a Prayer Book. His smile was so inviting. I just hadn't the heart to disappoint him, so joined his little band of the faithful.

And what a setting for a kirk. Above us the grey sky, in front the leafless trees of a small wood which screen us from the chilly November wind and the watchful eyes of the Boche. On one side a dump of shells and a canvas-screened latrine, on the other a battery of field guns lying snugly in their pits with sinister-looking muzzles pointing threateningly towards the enemy lines, silent at present while their personnel attend the service, but ready to deal out death immediately the last Amen has been sung. And the centre of all eyes, the grey-haired padre, wearing his white surplice with brown field-boots exposed below, standing placidly behind the altar of biscuit-tins covered for the occasion with a tablecloth, and looking quite pleased with himself as he fingers lovingly the huge Bible which gives his amateur altar the proper ecclesiastical appearance. A battered harmonium, salvaged from some odd corner, keeps the biscuit-tins company, and forming a semicircle round the padre and his paraphernalia, the congregation.

The strident notes of the harmonium fade away on the last bars of "Fight the good fight." There is a short pause then "Let us pray,". and we stand with bowed heads while the padre mumbles his way towards an Amen, in which everybody joins.

His address is short and interesting to an extent, but as usual there are certain bits of it rather dull and my mind begins to wander, but after the blessing, and when I am once more on my way, certain of his phrases make me think, and think deeply.

I seem to have got the hang of this religion stuff all wrong. I've been taught in Sunday School, and at home, that God is a super-being who sits on a throne in heaven, and now here's this padre giving that idea the lie. What did he say now? Oh yes, God is a spirit, and to substantiate that claim told a story of a driver in the artillery who, when his horse was shot under him, used his own field dressing to plug one of its wounds, ran the gauntlet of machine-gun fire to get water for it, and stayed by the wounded animal under shell fire until it expired.

"I see God in that action, my friends," I can still hear him saying as he thumped the Bible on top of the biscuit-tins :

"It was God. Never forget that God is a spirit, the spirit of friendship, the spirit of good comradeship, the spirit of kindness to dumb animals, the spirit of loving thy neighbour as thyself, the spirit of Christ."

Well, I can understand and have faith in that reasoning, but I'm damned if I could the other one. God isn't a being after all. He is the spirit that makes us help our fellow men, makes us feel kindly towards others, makes us tell the truth —in fact the spirit which, if it was universal, would make war impossible, the spirit that would make this world of ours worth while living in. Yes, I could get enthusiastic over that, but the story of thrones and living up in the sky leaves me cold.

And now, if I'm going to believe that lot, what about Jesus Christ, the son of God? That's a bit of a tickler. Strange how a fellow is left to ferret all this out for himself. I've attended church three times every Sunday for at least seven years getting spiritual nourishment, and it seems to me I've been fed on sops. I've had to come over to this little wood near the Somme and hear an unknown padre preach in the open air to a congregation of thirty, before I could get something to put my teeth into.

Now that I've got that something, where is it going to lead me? If God is a spirit, how could he have a son in human form, and strangest of all, born of a virgin. No, it can't stand the light of day, it's all a lot of bunk, and I suppose if I really believe it is bunk, then I can't believe in the Bible. H'm, seems there's no end to this conundrum. It beats me though how educated intelligent men can go on year in and year out, preaching that stuff and believe it. After all, what is the Bible? Just an inspired book which can be interpreted in about a dozen different ways.

I've no doubt there was a man named Jesus, but how could he be a son of God if God's a spirit? No, I'm inclined to think he has been some truly Christian gentleman who, believing and acting in the spirit of God, preached it to all mankind. In the story of his life we are told of the miracles he performed. It certainly makes colourful reading, but there are people who are cured by faith to this very day. Just as there are savages who can will themselves to die, so there are people who can will themselves back to health. The Bible and the Testaments were written hundreds of years ago. People were more superstitious in those days and more ready to believe in the supernatural, and we, centuries after, are asked to believe it too, without question.

Well, I'm hanged if I can, now that I've got hold of this "God is a spirit" idea.

The way I reckon it—God is the name of the real Christian civilised spirit, the spirit which we should all try to attain. Jesus of Nazareth was the man who first believed and preached it. The Bible is a story of the old world, and the Testaments the life of Christ. Tales of strange happenings and miracles should not be taken too literally.

If that is what I'm going to believe in future then I'm going to believe not in a supreme being, but in a supreme spirit, and the Bible—well, I can hardly take it to be the whole truth and nothing but the truth, unless with reservations, so it seems to me I'm going to be a bit of an atheist. I'd never thought of myself in that light before, and yet if one is going to think along sensible and modern lines, I see no other alternative.

And now, what was that other phrase the padre used?—something about "put your life and your trust in God's hands and he will carry you through." All metaphorically speaking, of course, but I see the point and think it's quite a good idea; a touch of the fatalist about it, but it suits me. I'll put my life in God's hands, anyway, and if I'm going to stop a packet, nothing can prevent it. If I'm not, I've nothing to fear, and that's quite a good faith for the next week or two.

These thoughts are too much of a brain fag though, and here I am anyhow at the bomb store; so I deliver my message and return to our temporary quarters at brigade, and the padre and his pet phrases are forgotten for the time being.

There are ten of us here at brigade, all volunteers, for the raid which takes place to-night. This is my third raid, and how I fear it! I detest raids, they're too much like suicide, and yet I'm a volunteer for it; but then one can be a volunteer before one realises it. Things like that just happen; that's all there is to it.

In this case the sergeant came into the billet, his note-book and pencil in his hand.

"I want names for a raiding party."

There is no response from the crowd in the billet.

"Come on, you fellows, one volunteer is worth six pressed men. What about you, Purves?"

"No thanks, sergeant," I reply.

"Windy?"

"Not me."

"Yeller, maybe?"

"Not me."

With a smile he starts writing:

"Not windy and not yeller; well, your name's going down."

"It's bloody well not," I yell back at him, rising to my feet.

"It's down," he remarks.

"Well, you can damned well score it off."

"Don't talk to me like that. Your name's down, it will be called out at nine o'clock parade"—and out of the billet he struts. Just a matter of minutes, but in that period I have graduated to Private Purves, a volunteer, worth six pressed men.

I wouldn't mind so much if Webster had kept out of it, but he, like the pal he is, on hearing that my name is down, has put in his, and we've both been detailed.

One thing, the enthusiasm that has been knocked into us by cunning instructors these three days out on special training, has chased some of the funk out of me. Still, I'm not looking forward to it. It's been a great three days, though, hard training with bayonet-fighting, bombing and practice raids on facsimile trenches to those we are going to attack, and at night gramophone music and sing-songs, while last night the captain sent along some beer, and the majority of the boys had a very mild souse. Just a happy family in perfect physical condition, inclined to be reckless and a little boisterous, but that is encouraged by instructors who have us worked up to the right pitch, and on our toes waiting for the curtain to go up.

Each one has his own reason for taking on the job, some because of their ignorance of raids and the desire for a little extra excitement, others because danger seems to draw them like a magnet. It is always the last time with them, but every call for volunteers finds them scrambling to the fore. Each battalion has them, and as they are killed off, others seem to get their fever. Then there's myself— bad luck and a sergeant with a strange sense of humour accounts for me, and I account for Webster. There may be a few like him who, finding their pal is going, refuse to stay behind.

Whatever the reason is for our being here and however much afraid of the raid we may be, nobody shows it; outwardly we are all fire-eaters.

Towards evening and just before moving off, we go over the details of the raid once again with the officer and sergeant who are leading us. Every man knows exactly what is expected of him, and on paper the raid appears a simple affair. We cross no-man's-land and lie in front of the Boche wire. There will be a diversion on our right while our wire-cutters get busy; then, as we go through the gap now cut for us, we kill every Jerry we meet—there won't be many we are told as his trenches are very lightly held—burst up his dug-outs and put up some sort of torpedo mine at a junction in his communication trench. The blowing up of the mine is our signal for home. All quite simple. It should be over in fifteen minutes. A box barrage will be put down to prevent any reinforcements reaching his front line, so we should have it all our own way.

After this recital there is an issue of rum and off we go. A lorry takes us part of the way towards the store where we collect our bombs, while the two who are looking after the mine business get their last instructions from a sapper officer. At battalion headquarters we hang about for a full half-hour before the colonel arrives and gives us his blessing. He knows how to talk to men and his words have just the right effect on us, only by the time we have moved up the communication trench and had another half-hour's wait at company headquarters, I feel I could do with a little more inspiration. Fortunately it arrives in the shape of another issue of rum which I don't hand over to Webster but gulp down myself. Damnable stuff, it takes my breath away, but once it has found rock bottom inside my tummy, what a life-saver; it gives me such a warm settled feeling, and helps me to enjoy this last fag we are allowed to smoke in the company dug-out. What luxuries these little things are, a spirit-warmed tummy, a glowing cigarette and perhaps only a few more minutes to live. Was life ever so sweet?

Am I afraid? No, I don't think so. Excitement has over-come any funk I did have, and in the small space of the dug-out the air is electrified. I can feel it. It seems as if the excitement created in one body could transfer its infection to another, the process involving the whole atmosphere. There's nothing like excitement for keying a man up; besides, I've just remembered that padre's injunction: "Put your trust in God, and he will carry you through." Well, I've done just that, and it's made all the difference. I feel I am coming back all right.

"Fags out, boys, file out on top." Our young officer, alert and efficient-looking, passes us out, and in less than ten minutes we are on the other side of our wire. Everything is so quiet and uncertain out here in no-man's-land. To me it is always the ideal spot for a violent end.

We split up into two parties with a man out on each flank, and commence our advance to Jerry's wire. The first hundred yards we walk bent almost double, then we get down on our hands and knees and go more cautiously. The last fifty yards we do on our stomach, and just as we reach Jerry's wire, the diversion on our right commences, timed to the very second. The wire pings away as our cutters get to work. It seems an impossibility for a sentry not to hear the noise we make, but not a shot or challenge comes from the trench facing us. A Verey light goes up a little to our right, then one almost in front of us, making us stiffen where we are and wait breathlessly. They must see us, and I expect every second to hear the bark of a machine-gun and see the sparks as the bullets tear into the wire, but the Verey light fades away, and not a sound comes from in front. The lane is cut in the wire at last and we file through it, leaving a man this side to ensure that there will be no time lost looking for the gap on the return journey, and the remainder of us drop down into the trench. A strange feeling this, jumping into an enemy trench, keyed up for anything and finding nothing. It is weird. That light was fired almost in front of us, so there must be somebody about, or is it a trap? There's no time now for thinking about that, we've got a job of work to do and it must be done on time.

As arranged, one party turns left and the other right.

My duty takes me to the left to help look after the dug-outs, and with the sergeant leading, then Webby, myself, and a comrade bringing up the rear, we make a start on the fifty yards of trench we have to cover. There are three dug-outs with two entrances each to bomb, and four of us to it in a matter of minutes. We know our jobs thoroughly, and everything is done like clockwork. The sergeant points to the first dug-out and doubles to the second entrance. Webster tears the cover down. There is a light at the bottom of the steps proving the occupants are at home, but we have no time for prisoners. My first bomb explodes and the light goes out. At the same time we hear a muffled report, and something smacks into the side of the trench opposite our legs. Other two bombs follow in quick succession, then another for luck, and we leave the fourth man, who has special bombs for demolishing purposes, to finish the good work, then on to the other entrance where the same process is gone through, and repeated again at the second dug-out. We reach the third just in time to meet a batch of Jerries emerging. The sergeant drops two of them, and Webster, who is our bayonet man, pins a third somewhere about the shoulder. The poor fellow gives a blood-curdling yell as he sinks slowly to the ground. As one of the other wounded men tries to crawl past me, I tramp clumsily over him—hardly aware that I am doing so; his screams mean nothing to me. Another lies on his back at the dug-out entrance wounded but quite conscious. His face shows up pure white in the darkness, his expression one of horrified terror. Webster fires down the dug-out, and I let go a bomb, but the wounded man is in my way and it hits the side exploding half-way down the steps. I have thrown down another three bombs before our fourth man arrives on the scene and I double to the next entrance, where the sergeant and Webby are mixed up in another scrap.

An officer lies dead in the trench, and I am just in time to see the butt of Webster's rifle smash into the face of a Jerry emerging from the entrance, and fling in a bomb over his body as he drops. A shout of warning makes me step quickly to the side of the entrance just as a figure comes rushing out firing a revolver and yelling at the top of his voice. I leave him to the others and throw down bombs in quick succession, being conscious while I am doing so of Webster trying to shake a body off his bayonet in much the same way as one would dislodge a piece of toast from a fork. Queer the comparisons one thinks of at these moments.

Our fourth man arrives to do his bit, and our attention is drawn to the sergeant who is lying at the trench bottom bleeding at the shoulder and side. He yells to us to leave him and get back—good old sergeant. Leave you? We'd fight the whole Jerry army first. We've no time to look at wounds or for gentleness, so hoist him on to Webster's shoulders and commence our journey back, but first I grab the sergeant's rifle, then bring up the rear. Keeping my eyes on the trench along which we have come, I imagine I see a figure trailing us and press the trigger, but only a click greets my ears, the magazine being empty. I fling it down with a curse and pull out my revolver, only to find that the figure has disappeared, if it ever existed. Over three crawling figures I trample, then over a fourth who tries to grab my legs as I pass. More in fear than callousness my finger closes on the revolver trigger, and I hurry after the others without looking to see what damage I have inflicted on an already wounded man.

In front Webster is carrying the sergeant with one arm and dragging his rifle along with the other, so I try to relieve him of it, but he refuses to part with it, and just then a loud explosion brings back to my mind the torpedo bomb, and the other party whose existence I had forgotten about. At the same time I become aware that there is quite a din going on around us, but I have been too centred on my own actions to realise its significance. It certainly is flattering to be the cause of such a dust-up. In the excitement we have some difficulty in locating the exact spot at which we entered the trench, then more difficulty in hoisting up the wounded sergeant, discovering in the attempt that it's one thing dropping into a deep trench and quite another getting out again with a wounded man.

I stay down below and wait for the other party, while Webster, with the aid of the fourth man, gets the sergeant through the wire. They soon arrive, and I report the casualty to the officer, otherwise all correct. Then over we all go, the officer coming last. He even waits on the parapet until we are all through—he's a brick.

A machine-gun commences traversing, but it hasn't found the right spot, and we go across at the double, ignoring the few shells which drop near us and the unpleasant hiss of shrapnel bullets around us, thinking only of the few yards between ourselves and safety. We are going home from a little hell, and that's certainly worthy of a sprint.

Back at battalion headquarters, after another tot of rum, I look at my wrist-watch—1.50 a.m. exactly. Thirty-five minutes since we left our trenches, and we've been home close on fifteen minutes, I should think; quite a successful raid. Our luck has been in this time. Three dug-outs completely destroyed by our party, and one dug-out and a communication trench busted in by the other. Little enough, but it may make all the difference when our battalion goes over to-morrow. And our casualties—one wounded, the sergeant, and if he only knew it perhaps he is the luckiest of the lot, for to-morrow starts another attack. A new method of offensive, something in the nature of a surprise; at least, we hope so. No preliminary bombardment, no destructive creeping barrage, just tanks, hundreds of them. We've seen them parked in the woods and plantations, behind hedges, everywhere tanks and still more tanks, with cavalry waiting further back ready to gallop through the gaps.

Well, let's hope it comes up to expectations. The sergeant won't be there to see it, that's his good fortune, and for myself, well—"I'll put my life and trust in God and he will carry me through." It worked to-night all right. Talk about moral support. It's been as good as another dose of courage. I just knew that everything would go well with me. As for faith, well, I have plenty now in that old padre's doctrine, and no doubt I'll require it all.

Chapter Twenty-One

NEW STYLE OFFENSIVE

November 20th, 1917, CAMBRAI SECTOR. Another battle started but we are only onlookers for the present.

This is the best way to fight, from the rear, applauding the others.

Started to rain; it always does, once we get going.

On the move again.

THE show has been on for four hours now, and everything seems to be going well. For once, too, we are playing the role of interested spectators, our successful little raid last night having earned us the privilege of being part of a divisional reserve. We move forward with the staff about four miles behind the front line, and then only when things are fairly secure. This is something like a war.

We were promised something new in the way of attacks, and we have got it. Five minutes to go and not a sound on the whole front. Nothing peculiar in that, of course, but on the stroke of zero, instead of the deafening crash of a big-scale barrage, just the clanging and purring of tank motors, a little counter-battery and drum fire and the spasmodic burst of machine-guns, that's all. There was more real noise during the raid.

We wait for the Boche barrage to fall but in vain, thank Heaven. The purring of motors grows fainter as the advancing tanks increase the distance between themselves and our position. A field battery commences a little drum fire on its own, along with a more prolonged rattle of machine-guns, then silence.

Dawn gives way to morning, and morning to noon. Messages keep coming in, all telling of success.

"The first and second lines have been taken and an attack is now in progress on the reserve line."

"Reserve line captured, advancing over open country towards second line of defence."

News of this village captured, and that strong point overrun. Success such as we had hardly dreamed of.

Names of places miles within the enemy lines are reported as in our hands.

A few prisoners dribble back, the firing almost dies away in the distance and we get ready to move forward to our advance position. On we go in the wake of our advancing battalions and meet our first walking wounded. Elated with success, they are as happy as only walking wounded can be, and as eagerly as we ask them for news, so they give it. We've evidently advanced miles, and, in their opinion, have Jerry on the run, with nothing between us and Berlin but a few isolated posts.

Seems like the end of the war to me; it's a proper break through at last. And then, most glorious sight of all, the cavalry. How we cheer them as they trot past. This is the first time I have seen mounted cavalrymen so near the front and in full war-paint, tin hat, spare bandoliers of ammunition round their horses' necks, swords and rifles, everything complete. The creak of leather and the jingle of harness sound, to my ears, almost like the bells of peace. They canter over a rise in the ground and are lost to view, and I have an uncomfortable feeling that I won't be in at the death after all. If this advance continues, with cavalry streaming through, the war will be over within a fortnight. It's a great feeling chasing the Boche, even at a distance.

Now that we've crossed the trenches, open country lies before us, and though a slight ridge cuts off our view of what is actually directly ahead of us, to right and left we can see small parties like ourselves advancing, a squadron of cavalry in extended order, wounded limping back, a party of prisoners being shepherded to the rear, and the usual guns and ammunition columns moving forward at the gallop.

As for dead, I've only seen half a dozen of our fellows and about the same number of Jerries, although there's no knowing what those deep trenches we've just crossed may conceal.

But what a battlefield! I've never seen anything like it before. No heaps of dead, no streams of wounded, no battered trenches. It's something entirely new in my experience; no wonder the birds are singing—I feel like singing myself. What a heady wine victory can be.

The firing in front increases, and towards late afternoon the machine-guns bark away continuously; still nothing but a succession of victorious reports keep coming in. We now have patrols in the very outskirts of the fortified village of Masnieres which we can just see in the distance. As darkness approaches, however, the wounded become more numerous until there is quite a steady trickle of them passing our temporary headquarters.

Later we hear again the pleasant sound of jingling harness, but are rather shocked to find it is a party of cavalry returning. We shout to them, and realise by their answers that things haven't gone too well with them; there are too many riderless horses for it to be otherwise. Well, the cavalry are back, and they've evidently had their wings clipped; so that's that. The war isn't over after all.

Shortly after midnight our battalion reports they are digging in and asks for reinforcements. That means us, and with a guide we get on our way.

Finding an unknown spot in pitch darkness is difficult under any conditions, but more so in open country, when you've got to judge the distance of your advance, then find the exact spot you're looking for without delay, otherwise it's liable to mean "finis," as soldiers, both friend and foe, are nervy creatures the first night of an attack and are liable to shoot first and challenge after.

Our guide, as we start off, is quite confident, but after covering the first three miles or so he begins to get a bit windy and commences making excuses—a bad sign. He doesn't recognise a clump of trees, then there should be a track about here, but it has disappeared; in other words he is lost, and so are we. There's only one thing to do; go forward until we come to something that will help us place our position. We listen to the firing, but one minute it's in front, the next it seems to come from behind. This makes some of our party a little anxious, and they want to go back the way we have come, which suits our guide, who suggests he might be able to pick up the route again if we retrace our steps.

For half an hour we roam around, but we might as well be in the middle of a desert for all the visible signs of human life there is, then suddenly we bang right up against the same clump of trees, that, according to our guide, shouldn't be there. Guides never will admit they are lost, it is always the landscape that has moved. However, there's no good arguing about it, we can only do one thing—go straight ahead until we meet something definite, otherwise we may dodge about here all night. A few of our party are for staying where we are until daylight, but Webby takes charge, and under his leadership we start moving cautiously forward. A quarter of an hour goes by, and we see the black outline of a house which our guide thinks he recognises. There is a village between our lines, he explains. We have a post at one end and Jerry at the other. This looks like our post to him, and he suggests going forward, but Webby decides to investigate first. Accordingly I accompany him through the hedge that surrounds the garden and across an overripe cabbage patch, finally lying down in the centre of some prickly currant bushes to get our bearings. We can't hear a sound or see anything except the outline of the cottage, but my heart starts thumping, and I am glad when Webster commences crawling again towards the front of the house. Anything is better than that waiting in the silent darkness.

Round the wall we skirt and are brought to a sudden halt by the sound of a tin can dropping on hard ground. Coming without any warning the noise almost makes me turn and bolt, but, after remaining in a crouching position for a few more minutes, nothing else happens, so we go forward a foot at a time until my hands come in contact with loose earth just at the end of the gable. I touch Webby, who is a little to my right and about two yards from the wall of the house. He comes over and we trace with our hands in the darkness a mound of newly turned earth which seems to continue right out to the roadway. Suddenly it dawns on me it is a parapet. I move another foot forward and find myself looking down into a narrow shallow trench. We hear a mumble of voices now, which seems to come from inside the house, and when our eyes become accustomed to the darkness of the trench shadows we can make out, at the far end which juts into the roadway, two motionless sentries beside a gun emplacement.

We retrace our steps as silently as possible and rejoin the others, who are just beginning to get nervy and are on the point of coming after us. In a whisper we explain to them the position. Somehow or other we have got behind the Jerry lines, but if, as our guide says, their most advanced post is in the first house of the village, then this must be it, and once past that we are laughing, providing our own boys don't let their trigger-fingers get the better of their judgment.

In single file we creep along by the hedge, keeping clear of the garden, but there is no sign of a sentry and nobody challenges us. Once past the house we get on our feet and break into a run, until, at the other end of the village, a few strands of barbed wire hold us up. We notice the outline of a parapet beyond, but before we get a chance to hail the sentries a challenge rings out and half a dozen voices answer it, none too clearly, I think, so I get down on my hands and knees. If he is a nervous sentry anything may happen, and I feel safer near the ground. A few hurried orders are given in the trench ahead, and we are told to advance with our hands up, a command which we obey with some smartness. I think we are all rather anxious to get behind the cover of that parapet.

In the trench we report to a sergeant, then recite it all over again to an officer, who is greatly interested in the machine-gun post at the other end of the village, and gets Webster to draw a rough sketch of its position on his message-pad. Greatly excited he disappears, but returns shortly afterwards with a corporal and a runner. I overhear the sergeant suggesting to him that he should take one of our crowd as a guide, so, as innocently as possible, I edge away until there are half a dozen men between me and the officer's party. Personally I've had sufficient excitement for one night. My precaution, however, proves unnecessary, as the officer is too eager to secure all the glory of a captured machine-gun for himself, and, with his party of two, climbs out of the trench and disappears in the darkness. Word is passed down the trench that a fighting patrol is out. We form a covering party and wait. Ten minutes drag by, fifteen, twenty, then the silence is broken by a long drawn-out wail, which sends shivers down my back, followed by a single shot. A few minutes later a Verey light is fired from further-along the trench, giving us a fitful view of a thousand mysterious shadows and a paved shell-torn road that leads right on into an impenetrable gloom; then silence.

Another officer arrives and has a long confab with the sergeant. Webster's sketch is once more studied with the aid of a torch shielded by the officer's trench coat, then over the sergeant goes, accompanied by a private, and word is passed down that another patrol is going out. We have another anxious wait of twenty minutes or so, and our ears and eyes begin to play tricks with us. Every rustle and shadow amongst the undergrowth in front become moving figures. Twice somebody shouts out a challenge which is not replied to, a nervous finger puts too much pressure on a trigger, and the report has us all itching to blaze away, but when the dawn breaks we are still awaiting the return of the patrols.

After stand-down, and over our breakfast of bully and biscuits, we get all the news of yesterday's happenings. Everything went well until our fellows got the length of this village late in the evening. Jerry, by that time, seemed to have brought up fresh troops, who, with an abundance of machine-guns, peppered everything that moved. Twice they had tried to storm the village and managed to clear all the houses but the two at the far end. Against them they could make no progress, so commenced to dig them-selves in, sending back for reinforcements; and here we are.

At nine o'clock orders arrive for another attack on the village to be made by three parties, one going right up the main street, the other two on each flank at the rear of the houses. I thank my guardian angel that I am in one of the parties that go on the flank. Webster mentions the machine-gun trained on the street from the far end to a sergeant, who, in turn, reports it to the officer in charge of the party concerned. He consults his watch, then turns to the sergeant:

"It's too late now. Up the main street we've been ordered to go, sergeant, and up the main street we are going, machine-guns or no machine-guns."

"Blasted fool," I mutter under my breath, and once

again thank my lucky star I'm not one of his company.

Some trench mortars and a field battery lob over a few shells in the direction of the posts we are going to attack and keep it up for ten minutes, then stop abruptly. The whistles blow and we are up and over.

No shells are fired from either side, but never before have I heard such a concentrated clattering of machine-guns as bursts forth the moment we leave our trench. Men start falling from the very parapet, and I am glad to plunge into the undergrowth of the first garden and wriggle my way towards a rubbish heap, which affords me some cover. Bullets simply whizz and buzz around me like a swarm of bees. Garden palings are splintered by unseen hands, hedges are whittled down to within a few inches off the ground, bullets whack into the brickwork of the houses and create a small cloud of red dust right along their length. I can't help thinking that if we did have Jerry on the run yesterday, he has certainly changed his mind about it to-day.

There's nothing else for it but to wriggle forward. Standing up means suicide. A few of our fellows do make a dash for the gable of the second cottage, but only a third of their number reach it safely; the others roll over and over on the ground, or twist themselves like contortionists in their agony. The remainder lie as they have fallen, but I still keep crawling, it is safer. Forward I go, inch by inch. There's no sign of the fire diminishing; if anything it seems to increase. What is going on across the road I cannot tell, but there is a perfect hullabaloo of noise. As I reach the end of the third house I notice the fellows who got safely to the gable-end are hacking their way through from house to house. They have a couple of picks, and remove a sufficient number of bricks to allow them to crawl into the house, then they come out at the other end by the same method, keeping in Jerry's blind spot all the time. It is a safe method, but there is the gauntlet of those twenty yards to cross before I'd get to the safety of the wall. No, I'll stick where I am.

Three fellows and a corporal just ahead of me worm their way through a hedge, and I follow their example, getting my head and shoulders through the network of twigs just

In time to see the last man of the party I am following roll gently over on his back and lie still, as a spray of bullets spouts the earth up parallel to the hedge and just three yards in front of it. Some still smack into the body of the man lying on his back in front of me, as the hidden gunners traverse along a regular dead line. No creature could hope to cross it alive, at least I'm not going to attempt it unless forced to, so I squirm backwards to the other side of the hedge again and take pot shots at the loopholes in the house in which the Jerries have their guns. It is much larger than the others and stands by itself fully seventy-five yards away. Built at a right angle to the rest of the village, it gives a splendid field of fire both down the main street and to the rear of the cottages. A house similarly situated on the other side of the street commands the village from that direction. Separating these two houses from the last cottage in each row is a strip of waste ground, fifty yards broad, devoid of cover.

We have advanced about one hundred and fifty yards in as many minutes and are still no nearer the capture of our objective. Along the hedge we line ourselves out and commence to dig in, then scrape a trench of sorts connecting us with the second last house on our side. Late afternoon, and with the arrival of the major, we are issued with fresh bandoliers of ammunition and organised for another rush.

The rattle of machine-guns still goes on. I've never heard such continuous and uninterrupted fire before. If only a battery of our artillery or trench mortars would get busy, how simple it would make things. Half a dozen rounds well placed and these Jerry posts would go up in dust, but the artillery, like the cavalry, seem to have gone home and left us to it. And those hundreds of tanks we saw yesterday: where are they? One tank and we'd just walk over these nests of gunners, but even one tank isn't to be had. The job is ours, that's evident, and we'll be made to barge into it until those houses are either ours or there isn't a man left standing.

Just a couple of dilapidated houses belonging, no doubt, to the village padre and doctor, without beauty or value, two red-gabled husks, and yet our very lives are centred upon them, they are our world. We've tried to reach them and failed. We've seen our comrades alive one second and dead the next, blood gushing from wounds or slowly trickling a life away, while those of us who are left are physically still alive, but inwardly dead. All hope seems gone, yet the sky is just as blue and as peaceful-looking as ever it was at home. The wind wafts towards me a stench of stable manure from a dung heap somewhere in front, and it smells good to me. How much I want to live, and how near is death.

A little dazed I watch our Lewis gunners arrive and commence peppering away at the loopholed gable of the Jerry post, and become interested in a middle-aged fellow who rises on his knees to fix a drum of ammunition on a gun. His tin hat flies from his head and a little blue mark appears on his brow above the nose as a spot of blood trickles down. His head slumps to the ground and leaves him in a praying position. The back of his skull has disappeared, and the inside comes creeping out and hangs over one ear like a pigtail. Someone takes his place and fixes the drum, and the gun goes on firing until the shrill blasts from half a dozen whistles make us tear ourselves away from the safety of the little holes we have dug, stumble through the hedge and trot onwards. Vaguely I notice figures falling beside me, then someone passes me at a regular gallop, head down and yelling like a maniac. He veers to the left and there is a crash as his tin hat comes into contact with the brick wall of a cottage, then down he flops. The figures around me become scarcer, until I observe there are only two men and an officer still going forward. One of the men turns right round and commences to sag very slowly. I am past him before he reaches the ground. A few seconds later and the other fellow doubles up as if he had a sore tummy, runs a yard or two in a stumbling manner, then falls on his head and turns a complete somersault. The officer still carries on, neither looking to right nor left. I admire him but have no desire to emulate his magnificent example.

We are only twenty-five yards from the house now, and I can see the white faces of the Jerries behind their loopholes as bullets whip into the ground near my feet, sending up little fountains of earth. Intentionally I stumble and fall down behind the sanctuary of a small rubble heap. Cautiously I look around me. The attack has withered away, and when I look in front again even the officer is down. He lies huddled up barely six yards from the Jerry post. A brave man, but then he is dead.

My attention is drawn to a fellow behind me who scrambles to his feet, and, evidently blind, commences groping his way about.

A voice shouts out: "Get down, for Christ's sake," but too late. The gunners get him before he has gone two paces.

Another jumps up, cursing and shouting, flings his rifle on the ground and starts stripping himself. His equipment comes off, followed by his tunic, and as he tears at his cardigan his shouting becomes a croaking noise in his throat, which ceases abruptly as he drops.

As the darkness approaches, the wounded commence to crawl back to our lines, but every movement is visible to the Jerry snipers and brings forth a burst of directed fire, so I lie behind the safety of my rubble heap until it is completely dark, then make the journey back to the shallow trench behind the hedge. Only a matter of fifty yards or so, but what a strip of hell it has been.

A sergeant-major, with the help of a revolver, is collecting all the stragglers, and we are mustered behind the walls of one of the cottages, then taken back to our original trench at the end of the village. A field battery conjured up from somewhere starts shelling the Jerry posts, and the whizz of these shells as they fly overhead is a welcome sound. If only we'd had a bit more of their assistance this morning things might have been different.

I walk a little way along the trench enquiring after Webby and get various reports from men who saw him fall, others who are sure he is killed, and I am just beginning to think he really has gone west when he suddenly scuttles into the trench trailing three water-bottles in one hand and as many iron rations in the other. We've had nothing to eat or drink since early morning, but hunger never troubles me on these occasions. Not so Webby, he can line his inside on any and every occasion, and while I envy him his appetite, I content myself with a long swig of cold tea from one of the bottles. The lump of bully beef Webster presses on me sticks in my throat. Round and round my mouth it goes, and eventually, in disgust, I spit it out.

For a few minutes we swop experiences. Webster's party, which advanced up the back of the cottages on the other side of the street, fared no better than ourselves and, like us, lost heavily, but the real sufferers were those who attempted to storm up the street. They just hadn't a chance. As soon as their noses appeared above the parapet they were doomed. Their bodies lie in a narrow strip just in front of the trench, the farthest not thirty yards away.

Our chat is interrupted by the arrival of a company from another battalion to reinforce us. N.C.O.s hustle us about and form us into two parties. The artillery starts drum fire, and our machine and Lewis gunners join in. Dazed and dreading the ordeal, I follow the man in front of me over the trench and through the holes in the cottage gables until we are as far as the trench behind the hedge. There is a halt here to allow the rear men to close up. Watches are consulted, and taking a chance with shells that may drop short, we are formed up in front of the trench.

How thankful I am for the darkness. It can be most confusing at times, but it can also be very friendly and comforting. Nervously I wait for the guns to lift, wondering if I should lie still when the others go forward and pretend I'm wounded, or do my duty and throw my life away. Duty, what do I care about duty? What do I care about anything but this life of mine? Cowardice, disgrace, mean nothing if only I can lie here in safety. Then under my breath I commence to pray. I pray to God to give me strength to do my duty, and that I may come back safe and whole. Duty! What a strange word, and yet I feel my prayer has been answered. I've never known that appeal to God fail me yet. I cannot say I am not now afraid of what lies before me, but I am calm about it, that's the only way I can describe it, calm and contented as if I'd put my trust in somebody and knew he wouldn't fail me.

As the guns stop we get on our feet and scramble through the hedge, jumping and stumbling over the victims of the morning's fight. Twice I fall full length over their still forms, pick myself up again and move on. Only one solitary machine-gun opens up on us from the Boche position. Our artillery seems to have done their job well. Only thirty yards to go now. The Jerry gun starts traversing along our front, and in the darkness I notice a few figures fall, but the others still go forward. Twenty yards and I can see the spurts of fire from the gun behind the wall. Ten yards, then we are there. A few bombs explode and there is a good deal of shouting, but in the darkness I can see little. Round the house I follow a sergeant, who mounts a Lewis gun on some sandbags, but there are no targets to shoot at. Victory is ours.

The work of consolidating goes on through the night. A listening post is pushed out and sentries are placed, while the rest of us dig and fill sandbags until we are soaked in sweat. Machine-guns from both sides splutter away throughout the hours of darkness, but no shells fall on our new positions. Even our own gunners seem to have retired for the night and left it to the infantry to settle the scrap in their own way.

We are still digging when another battalion arrives to relieve us. In they file, cursing and complaining, as joyfully we hand over and turn our backs on the Jerry lines. Another respite, and I am still alive to welcome it.

Chapter Twenty-Two

TWENTY-FOUR HOURS' LEAVE

November 29th, 1917, PERONNE—SOMME. Peronne isn't exactly a holiday resort but it has its attractions.

Saw a concert party, "The Verey Lights," quite a good show. Other attractions were—Ivette and Nanette. I'll remember them all right.

THERE'S nothing like a bath for putting the finishing touches to one's happiness. We've been out on rest for a full day, have applied for and been granted twenty-four hours off duty, and now we've discovered a bathing pool in the grounds of the chateau near our camp. Everything of value has disappeared from the house, and Jerry, in his retreat a few days ago, has done his best to make a proper ruin of things, but he has left us this pool, and what more could we wish for. Marble sides with a tiled bottom, just the very thing we've been looking for since coming out here, the pool we dreamed of during the hot summer months, and now it is gifted to us by brother Fritz in November. However, we are going to have a dip if we have to thaw afterwards. In we plunge, and despite all our splashing about, in ten minutes we've had enough. A good rub down leaves us all aglow, with the feeling it is great to be alive and clean, and going on a short holiday.

We've arranged with the signal sergeant for the loan of a couple of bicycles for ourselves. The other two fellows, who with Webster and myself are now the survivors of the last raiding party and share this holiday, are going in a different direction to us and intend to lorry hop.

From a map the signallers possess we get an idea of the route to Peronne and reckon it to be about twenty miles, so taking things easy, we should manage it in an hour and a half.

We have the roads all to ourselves, mile after mile, with not a soul to be seen. It is on a journey like this that one gets an idea of the real desolation of an old battle-ground—rusty wire, old trenches, shell-holes, transport lines and watering places, openings to old dug-outs by the side of the road, some already caved in, but not a house or a wooden shack left standing. As for living creatures, there is none. I haven't even noticed a bird since we started.

The roads, however, due no doubt to the lack of traffic once the armies had finished with them, are in fairly good condition, and we pedal along feeling we have the world to ourselves.

It is only when we near the town that we see any sign of life, and that is mainly clad in khaki. The town hasn't been so very badly knocked about, and there are still a few houses left undamaged, but as we cycle up the main thoroughfare we are rather disappointed at the lack of excitement it offers. Many of the inhabitants have returned, and their efforts to get their old homes in order again are pathetically inadequate. Shell-holed walls and gables have been repaired with sacking and old sandbags scrounged from the battlefields, while, in one case, a lady's undergarment and a gent's shirt do their part to repair the ravages of war. Tarpaulin sheets take the place of roofs, but that is the fullest attempt at any rebuilding.

The streets have been nicely cleaned up. All rubble and masonry have been cleared from the pavements, while hanging walls and gables have been demolished and the bricks carefully laid in a heap on the site of the ruin. It is a town that has had its wounds carefully cleaned and dressed.

As a place of interest for sightseers it is a washout and doesn't even possess a mine crater or a leaning virgin at which we can stop and wonder, while for amusement it only boasts a Y.M.C.A. hut, a canteen and a concert party.

A little disheartened, we enter the Y.M.C.A. to leave our bicycles, and make discreet enquiries if they can put us up for the night. Very kindly they offer us the use of their sleeping-quarters attached to the hut, suggesting at the same time that two of their members should find accommodation elsewhere for the night and give us their beds. Such inconvenience we won't allow, emphasising the fact that we'll be more than content to sleep on the floor, providing they don't mind us sharing their room.

Inwardly we know that we could find shelter at any of the billets in the town, but Y.M.C.A.s usually have a ham-and-egg breakfast, and are happy hunting-grounds for scroungers such as we.

All our arrangements having turned out according to plan, we thank our hosts as we leave for a stroll round. However, there is little to interest us, and after going the length of the station we about-turn and come back to the square. It is a ghost of what it must have been in the days of peace. No busy market, no jostling happy crowd, only an occasional slouching refugee with shoulders bent and hands deep in his trouser pockets who casts a scowling glance in our direction as if we were the despoilers of his city instead of its liberators.

Even the army seems to have gone to earth at this time

of morning, the only sign of its presence being the heavy transport lorries which stream past in twos and threes, and, of course, the inevitable military policeman who eyes us a little suspiciously as we lounge about.

Across the road I notice a little fruit shop which looks rather clean and tidy, so we go over and inspect it. The window has long since gone the way of all glass in the town, but the goods are attractively displayed on tables. We look inside and observe a youngish ma'm'selle behind the counter who is chatting away to a Frenchman, but smiles pleasantly to us as we linger at the entrance.

As the Frenchy takes his leave we decide to go in and purchase some fruit, and find ma'm'selle can speak excellent English. She is a talkative piece of goods, and having nothing else to do, we quite enjoy listening to her. Times are very hard. She had a beautiful shop before the war, patronised by the *élite* of the town, but look at it now— a broken-down hovel.

Her husband worked a small market garden and things were very bright in those days, then came *la guerre*. The army took her husband, and madam became a refugee going to live with relations. When she returned she found her house roofless and dilapidated and her well-fitted shop gone, every piece of wood that could be burned stripped off, only the shell being left. *La guerre, messieurs, la guerre.*

We sympathise with her, at which she regains her former brightness, then in exchange we tell her a little of our own history—but just a little.

As midday approaches we prepare to take our leave, but madam refuses to let us go, insisting that we stay for dinner, and as an inducement informs us that she makes the most delicious eggs and chips. Such a bait is too tempting for our gastric tendencies, but we still have sufficient grace left to demur before finally surrendering to madam's persuasive powers, and we graciously accept before she has time to change her mind. Following our hostess into the living-room behind the shop, we experience much the same feeling as if we were entering some sacred chamber.

It is all very cosy. The fire has just the right heat for a November day, a red glow with flickering flames on top;

the arm-chairs, though worn, are easy to sit in, the rug in front of the hearth a luxury we are almost afraid to touch with our heavy army boots. There is a couch near the window, a chest of drawers and a wardrobe, a table and a few chairs, while behind a coloured lace curtain I get a glimpse of a bed. Everything is nice and clean and has a feminine touch which the lacy gadgets enhance. To us down from the front, the room seems a little heaven and madam is fast becoming an angel.

While preparing the meal she chatters away, then as the bell rings at the shop door, out she pops, carefully closing the curtained glass door of the back parlour behind her. Madam has a reputation to look after.

"And how's this for a gift from heaven;" Webster enquires.

"Suits me," I reply as I stretch my legs in sheer comfort, "but what's she going to charge for it all?"

"You make me laugh, Jock, it's a gift from heaven I tell you"—and Webster, with a wink, starts humming softly: "Just a little love, a little kiss," then getting up from his chair, and with his hands in his trouser pockets, has a look around the room.

"Nice little shack, isn't it?"

"Bonzo," I reply. "Pity it isn't a little nearer the line, then we could drop in often. That would make the war worth while."

The bell rings again as the shop door closes and madam returns. She busies herself round the pots and pans on the fire, while Webster and I, under her instructions and with a good deal of joking, set the table. We feel quite at home already.

Dinner is a great success—eggs and chips, some kind of milk pudding, followed by coffee with biscuits and fruit. When it is all over we help to clean up, and despite all our horseplay, manage it without a breakage. By the time we are finished I notice Webster has got the length of giving madam a sly squeeze which she doesn't seem to resent.

Women certainly get me guessing. Here's this one, a nice woman I should think, with a husband at the front, no apparent family, a home of sorts with a business that provides her with the necessities of life, and yet she is ready to encourage the attentions of the first amorous adventurer who comes her way. Women—H'm! I'm beginning to think they are every bit as bad as men.

When everything is spick and span again, we smoke a cigarette along with our hostess, then enquire how much we owe her. As expected and hoped for, the good lady won't accept money. Instead, she extends a pressing invitation to return in the evening for supper, explaining that to-day she goes to a neighbouring village for vegetables, but will be home at eight o'clock, and will expect us. We promise faithfully to return, and take our leave.

Our walk takes us past the stalls and small shops, and it surprises us the amount of army stuff the Frenchies have to sell. Tins of bully beef and Maconachie rations are displayed openly along with army socks and boots. It is obvious that someone at the dumps must be making a small fortune by flogging army rations and kits, and it is little wonder we fellows in front have to go short occasionally.

Some of the shops do a more legitimate trade, however, and are stocked entirely with souvenirs. There is no necessity to go any nearer the firing line if a Jerry helmet is desired. They have everything from helmets with bullet holes in them to shell cases. Others go in for the daintier articles, such as fancy postcards, lace handkerchiefs and pincushions, rings made from shell nose-caps and, of course, the usual indecent postcards.

From one stall I purchase a petrol cigarette-lighter made from a nose-cap with tunic buttons welded on both sides, rather a smart little thing and it seems to work all right. Webster buys a lace handkerchief, a ring and a pair of silk garters with the Allies' flags all round them. He holds them up for inspection:

"Fetching, aren't they?"

"For madam?" I enquire.

"You bet. What's more, I'm going to put them on before the night's over."

"Good luck to you, soldier. You're welcome so far as I am concerned."

"Hell, can't you be romantic for once, Jock?" Webby

retorts as he pockets the goods, and we walk on, eventually landing at the canteen where we part company, Webster going in for a drink while I cross to the Y.M.C.A. hut where we have arranged to meet in half an hour's time for tea.

Inside the hut someone is banging away at the piano, so I get a chair and settle down for my half-hour's wait. The musician certainly can play, and has the entire audience in the hut carried away by the artistic rendering of his repertoire.

We are a sentimental lot. Give us a song about a girl or home, and the whole army tacks on to it and wears it threadbare.

Eventually Webster comes shouldering his way through the throng :

"Ah, here you are, Jock. Who's the Paderewski?" he enquires.

"Some A.S.C. wallah with plenty spare time to practise."

Webster commandeers a vacant chair, and I go over to the counter for the inevitable tea and biscuits, and we wile away the time reading year-old magazines until, having nothing better to do, we go over to the concert hall and content ourselves by criticising the troops as they slowly arrive for the show.

I can't help thinking that some of these fellows have a cushy time of it, with settled hours of work, no discomfort worth speaking about, civilians to mix with, recreation when the day's work is over, music, and all these other things which we never enjoy for months on end. The amusing thing is they are classed as soldiers like ourselves, and although I suppose we couldn't carry on without them, still that doesn't alter my opinion that for some it can be quite a pleasant war.

As the hum of expectant voices heralds the lighting of the amateurish footlights, I try to locate the most comfortable spot on the wooden form and get ready to applaud. We are so music-starved that we are prepared to encore everything, and it is not surprising that our own divisional party think our battalion the finest audience on earth.

The opening chorus commences, the curtain rises and the war disappears into the realm of forgotten things behind a cloak of sentimental songs, ragtime melodies, sketches and comedian's cross-talk.

For two brief hours our hearts respond joyfully to the well-known songs and age-old jokes, lifting us above the cares and worries of war-time soldiers and installing in their place a light-hearted gaiety which is only suppressed when we file out into the night air and the life which has claimed us.

"Well, it's nine o'clock, Webby, what do we do now?" I enquire.

"Do now? Hell, we've got an appointment, haven't we? We're going round to the back door of madam's fruit shop."

"No, I don't think I'll bother, Webby," I make haste to reply. "I'd only be in the way, anyhow."

"Way be damned. You can come and see what she has for supper. Don't worry, I'll give you the nod when it's time to make yourself scarce. Come on, be a sport."

And with that Webby links his arm in mine as down the street we go and through the alley to the back of the shop. Madam opens the door evidently overjoyed to see us again, and we get rather a surprise on entering to find another girl there, who madam introduces as Nanette, a friend, whose husband is also at the war, then with a knowing look and a wink in my direction adds :

"He hasn't been home to see her for fourteen months. Poor Nanette, it is a long time for a lady to wait monsieur, is it not?"

Her meaning is so obvious that I can only stammer some foolish reply to cover my embarrassment, but in the general laugh that follows I manage to recover a little of my composure. Ladies, however, are not my strong point, and after the first formalities of introduction are over and we are seated round the fire, I have very little to say, leaving all the talking to Webster who, I can see, is thoroughly in his element.

Supper comes as a welcome relief to me from the strain of trying to appear at ease, and as I look at the well-set table I can't help thinking that although rationing is in force in France, there is not much evidence of it here. The fare, though plain, is daintily served, and to we who have become accustomed to eating out of tins with the aid of a jack-knife and our fingers, a table with a white cloth, plates and knives, seems the height of extravagant luxury.

Ivette, as we have discovered to be the name of our hostess, is obviously experienced in the culinary art, and her pork chops, apple sauce and pickled onions are items of a menu we have been strangers to for months. Likewise her home-baked scones and cakes, and her delicious coffee compose a meal we can only classify as a banquet. It is all very enjoyable, and we linger over it, discovering in the process that Nanette, like our hostess, can speak fluent English, only she has an embarrassing habit of making a sally in French to Ivette, after which there is a burst of excited laughter as they make eyes at both of us.

Personally I can never be sure if they are laughing to me or at me. However, for the sake of the supper I overlook this disturbing practice, and secretly envy Webster his easy self-assurance.

We chat away on every subject under the sun : the war, the Germans, our country and finally girls. From then onwards the conversation goes from bad to worse until, in my anxiety to change the subject, I foolishly admit I know nothing about love.

Nanette pretends to be shocked at this confession :

"La, la," she exclaims, "later I must show you how French girls love," which remark provokes a general round of laughter, and I feel more comfortable when we rise from the table and help to clear away the dishes.

That accomplished, Webby and I are persuaded to go behind a screen while the ladies change into something lighter and cooler.

"It is so warm," Ivette explains, "and we cannot open the shuttered windows because of the light restrictions."

Behind the screen Webby clasps his hands, looks up to the ceiling as if in prayer and recites :

"For what we are about to receive, Amen."

"Look here, Webby," I whisper, "I'm getting out of this, I've had enough."

"Don't be a bloody fool," he whispers back, "they're all right."

Then in answer to a call from the girls :

"Coming, *ma cherie*."

Out we get from behind the screen and notice they are both arrayed in dressing-gowns which with girdles gathered tightly round their waists, accentuate the curves of their bodies, and expose a good length of silk stockings and brightly coloured garters with each step they take as they bring over a bottle of wine and glasses.

I try not to take any notice, but when they sit down on the couch beside us they cross their legs, and there's those cursed garters again drawing my eyes like a magnet. I am ashamed of the stolen glances I take, and think how shocked the girls would be if they knew. It never seems to occur to me that this show might be for our special benefit.

We taste the wine and it seems quite good although I am no connoisseur, then Ivette explains how it had been hidden by her friend in the centre of his farm midden all the time the Germans were in occupation. A year later after the Germans' retreat, he had returned to his farm to find it occupied by a British staff. The amazed, and I expect thirsty, occupants turned out in force to watch this eccentric farmer refugee digging away in the centre of his midden, but their amazement must have turned to sheer envy when they saw him haul out from the filth, case after case of wine, load it on his cart and drive off.

After hearing this I take a greater interest in the liquid. It certainly has a dirty past, but nevertheless I still maintain it seems quite good to me.

While we smoke a cigarette, Ivette brings out an old family album, and we get some fun looking at the photos and comparing them with present-day fashions, but after a little of this sport the girls remark that they are tired and stand up to stretch themselves, apparently oblivious of the fact that their girdles have become loose and they are exposing their bodies. They give a suppressed yawn and an almost imperceptible backward droop to their shoulders at which the gowns slip down to their feet and they stand smiling before us—naked.

It has happened so naturally and quickly that for a second or two I can only stare. Webster gives a pleased laugh and pulls Ivette on to his knees, while Nanette comes a step nearer me. The hot blood rushes to my face, and with one jump I am over the back of the couch, grab my hat and turn the door handle violently. It is bolted, but I manage to withdraw the bolt and get out into the cool fresh air. I hear Webster shouting to me "Don't be a fool, Jock," Ivette's shrill laughter and Nanette jabbering in quick French.

Out in the street I slacken my pace, and begin to wonder just what kind of a fool I am, and if I'm really such a fine fellow as I think.

Back at the Y.M.C.A. hut I am still a little excited and flustered, so light a fag and take a puff or two before knocking at the door. It is opened by one of the assistants who enquires after Webster, and I explain that we met an old pal of his and returned with him to his billet after the show, and that I've left them yarning away. I also mention that as they haven't seen each other for years and have a lot to talk about, I shouldn't be surprised if Webby stays overnight with him. I'm a poor liar for I feel my face flushing as I recite my piece, but I think he believes me, and I am certain his companion does.

My bed is already made up, so I sit smoking and talking with them till early morning. They are both over military age and keen to hear all about conditions at the front, so I make it as truthful as possible.

When we eventually do settle down for the night, my rest is somewhat disturbed by visions of enormous red garters, and I am still seeing redder and bigger than ever when I am awakened by a call of "breakfast ready;" so I get washed and dressed, to the pleasant smell of fried ham and eggs.

Breakfast is almost over before Webster puts in an appearance, and I have some difficulty in conveying to him, while the others are going about their duties in the hut, just where he is supposed to have spent the night.

"What's all the fuss about?" he enquires. "I'm not ashamed to admit I've been doing a little love-making."

"No, but I've told them we met an old pal of yours and you stayed the night with him. You're not going to make me out a liar?"

"Oh well, if that pleases you, Jock, I've been sleeping

with a dear old pal"; then in feigned ecstasy: "And wasn't she a pippin; sorry, I mean he!"

Just at that moment one of the Y.M.C.A. workers pokes his head round the door and tells Webster there's some breakfast left if he wants it.

"That's all right, thank you," Webby replies. "I had breakfast at my pal's place." And he winks over at me.

Then more seriously:

"You were a mug last night, Jock; what the hell did you bolt for?"

"I don't know. I've never gone in for anything like that and whether I'm a mug or not, I'm glad I did beat it. What happened when I left?"

"Now what would you expect, leaving a lady like that? Any woman would be upset having her charms ignored in that manner, but"—and Webster adopts a flippant mood—"I explained you were just an unspoiled little boy and didn't mean to be rude. That pacified her a little and to square things, I took them both to bed."

"You didn't," I remark with some surprise.

"I certainly did, soldier. I never leave a lady in distress."

"You're some star, Webby," I retort.

"You mean I'm some man," he corrects me; "ask the ladies, they'll tell you."

"You make me laugh."

"And you make me weep, Jock; a gift from heaven like that, and you bolt from it. By the way, is there anything doing here? We haven't too much time."

"I don't know," I reply. "I've had no chance for a scrounge round. The hut is through that door."

Webster opens the door:

"Sorry we'll have to be rushing away, dad, wars and women wait for no man. Can we help you in any way before we go? Leave those heavy tea urns to us. Come on, Jock, lend a hand."

And we relieve the elder of the two gentlemen of a metal tea urn, fill it with water and place it on the stove at the back. There's another urn to be filled, so we go round the back of the counter to get it. Incidentally some cigarettes and a tin of something find their way into my great-coat pocket. We fill the urn and leave it by the side of the stove, at the same time enquiring if there is anything else we can do.

"Sweep the floor or tidy up?" I suggest.

"No, that's all, boys. It's very kind of you to have filled these urns; they are rather heavy to handle. We are both obliged to you, I'm sure."

"Not at all, dad," I make haste to reply.

"It's we who are indebted to you for the digs and the breakfast."

"You were welcome, my boys, and if ever you pass through here again, look us up. Walter, the boys are leaving."

Walter comes from somewhere in the back regions and with tears in his eyes, wishes us good luck. Poor old fellow, I feel sorry for him. Last night he told me his two sons were killed out here, the younger one at the capture of this very town.

With a "cheero" we leave them, two thorough gentlemen, and ourselves just a couple of war-made rogues.

As we wheel our bicycles on to the road, Webster enquires under his breath:

"What did you win?"

"Three packets of fags and this," I reply, pulling the tin out of my other pocket. "Sardines."

"Good, I got two packets of fags and a tin of peaches"— and Webster displays his winnings.

"Well, I'm going over to say good-bye to Ivette. Coming?"

"Not me."

"Why not?"—and Webby is quite indignant. "After all, you got a dinner and supper off her."

"Will the other one be there?" I ask.

"No, she was leaving when I came away this morning. Come on, be a man."

We wheel our cycles over to the little fruit shop, stack them outside and walk in.

Ivette comes to the counter all smiles. Webby hands her his tin of peaches, so I trot out the sardines, and murmur some apology for my behaviour last night.

"That ees all right, Jock," Ivette replies. "I understand, you are a charming boy and eef it was not so public"—

and she waves her hand towards the window—"I would kees you." And she smiles bewitchingly. This time I do not blush.

"Well, cheero, Ivette," and as an afterthought, "Give my love to Nanette"; then I go outside and leave Webby to say good-bye in his own way, and as I light a cigarette I notice they have retired into the back room. How long is he going to keep me waiting now? I ask myself irritably. But in five minutes out he comes as perky as ever, and with a "Now for the bloody old war," we mount our machines and commence our journey towards the line.

Chapter Twenty-Three

THE SCRATCH BATTALION

December 1st, GAUCHE WOOD, SOMEWHERE ON THE SOMME. Every dog has his day.

We've had ours and now we are for it.

Rumours of a retreat from Cambrai. We join Fred Karno's Army and I scrounge some posh underwear.

IT must be an hour since we left the little fruit shop and in that time we have covered about fifteen miles, and met only one human being, an old French farmer with his horse and cart. But now we notice on a road running parallel to our own, lorry loads of troops with artillery and transport.

"Looks like a division on the move," Webster suggests.

"Yep," I agree, "and they seem to have the whole blasted Air Force along with them"—as my attention is drawn up aloft by the droning of five formations of planes at different heights, all heading towards the front.

Such sights as countless troops on the move and numerous planes are too common to us for much consideration, and beyond an occasional glance in the direction of the road along which they are streaming, we dismiss them from our thoughts.

From far away in front a cloud of dust can be seen and a car comes tearing along the road towards us, the roar of its engine gradually getting louder as it approaches, until, with a rush of wind, it is on us and past before we realise it. Five minutes later another car approaches from the same direction, and at the same break-neck speed. As it passes we get a glimpse of red-tabbed gentry eyeing us as if we were some new kind of insect, and hear the screech as the brakes are applied. The driver, however, changes his mind, and we hear again the full-throated roar of a power-ful motor going all out.

"What the hell's all this about?" Webster asks.

"Damned if I know. That fellow was going to stop just now, then changed his mind. Perhaps they expect us to salute them."

"Salute them be damned," is Webster's rejoinder.

We cycle along for another two miles, and straight ahead, by the cross-roads, I can just make out a group of horsemen and a car.

"Do you see them, Webby?"

"Sure, looks like cavalry to me. There's a car as well, perhaps a General and his escort. Who cares, anyhow? We've as much right on the bloody road as them."

As we get nearer I recognise the red bands on their arms.

"Mounted police," I tell Webby. "Quite a squad of them, too. Looks like the Y.M.C.A. folk have missed that tin of peaches."

"Yep, I'm getting quite windy. What do we do? Ride them down?"

"Sure," I yell. "Let's get a move on"—and we pedal as hard as we can.

The mounted figures in front spread out and block the road. Our pedalling slackens off until ten yards from them we come to a stop as a sergeant spurs his horse towards us.

Military police always get my goat. It's their officious superior manner that does it, and this fellow seems to have all the guff of his kind.

"Where are you men going?" he barks out, at the same time dismounting and handing over the reins of his horse to a private.

"To rejoin our battalion," I yell back just as sharply.

He had really ignored me and addressed Webster, and I am quite pleased with myself as I notice the quick turn of his head as he eyes me up. He knows now I am alive, anyway. I hear Webster give a chuckle—he understands my pet aversion.

"What battalion?" is the sergeant's next query, and I tell him.

"Where are you from?"

"Peronne," Webster tells him.

"What were you doing there?"

"Having a squint round," I reply as insolently as possible.

"Answer my question," bawls the sergeant.

"I have answered it," I bawl back.

An officer approaches at that moment:

"What's this; anything wrong, sergeant?"

The sergeant salutes:

"This man won't answer my question, sir."

The officer eyes me scornfully:

"Answer the question immediately."

"I have answered it, sir."

"What was it?"

"Having a squint round, sir," I reply as innocently as possible.

"What do you mean by squint round?"

"What I say, sir, having a squint round." Then, as if I had struck a bright idea that might penetrate even their dull brains:

"A look-see, sir"—and I change my tone to suit the daft laddie role I adopt.

The officer shrugs his shoulders while the sergeant barks another question:

"Got a pass?"

"Yes."

He holds out his hand, but I ignore it.

"Hand over your pass, man," the officer commands irritably.

"Very good, sir"—and I pull all the collection of papers out of one pocket and commence rummaging amongst them as if my one desire was to do as I am told. I go over them all unsuccessfully, then put them back into my pocket, button it up and pull out the contents of my other pocket.

"Damn it, man, surely you know where you keep your pass." Then to the sergeant:

"Bring it over to me when he finds it, sergeant; the other man's as well"—and the officer strides back to the car in disgust.

Suddenly I seem to have a brain-wave, and return the papers to my pocket, then unbutton the first pocket again and take out a small leather pocket-book in which I discover the pass, and with a smile hand it over to the sergeant.

Webster, after some delay and just as the sergeant looks as if he is going to foam at the mouth, finds his and hands it over as well. The sergeant scrutinises them carefully, but can find nothing wrong with them, so struts over to the officer.

"And what the bloody hell do you make of all this, Jock?" Webby enquires just above a whisper.

"Looks like a round-up of deserters to me. Hello, here comes walrus again."

The sergeant strides over and hands back our passes, then with a leering smile, bends down and examines the markings on our bicycles, but he is unlucky—they tally with our passport. He evidently has one or two brains, though. I'll give him credit for that.

"Can we go now, sergeant?" I ask. "We've got to report to our company by midday, and we've just got time and no more."

"You'll report when and where you are told," he snaps back, and I feel my temper rising again.

"We've got to report back at our company by twelve o'clock; the colonel gave us definite instructions." I mention "colonel" to give it more effect, but it doesn't work.

"Don't talk back to me," fumes our friend, "or I'll put you under arrest."

"What's wrong now, sergeant?"—and the officer comes over again. "Get these men under way immediately."

"Brown," the sergeant bellows, and a dis-mounted policeman approaches. "Take these men and see that they report to Major Wilson at once."

"We must have a chit for that, sergeant," Webster advises.

"Do as you're told," he commands. "Quick march."

"After our passes are endorsed," I cut in.

The sergeant's face turns purple:

"Quick march, I tell you"—and he spits the words out, but neither of us moves.

Over comes the officer again and it's evident he has lost his temper too, but we are right to a certain extent, and we know it.

"What's the matter now, sergeant? Have these men put under arrest if there's any more nonsense. As much time wasted over two men, it might be a battalion."

"Excuse me, sir, but we must have our passes endorsed if we can't report to our battalion. We don't fancy being shot at dawn for dodging the column."

"That's enough," he cuts in. "Where are your passes?"

We hand them over and he endorses them, then we salute and follow our guide down a lane to our right. Once out of earshot, we bombard him with questions.

"And now where does the execution take place? What the hell's it all about?"

"Don't you guys know?"—and our guide is evidently shocked at our ignorance. "Jerry's broken through."

"Broken through?" We can hardly believe our ears.

"That's tripe," I volunteer. "Hell, we broke through ourselves only four or five days ago."

"Perhaps you did," our guide continues, "but Jerry has the boys on the run this time."

"Whereabouts?" we both enquire in one breath.

"Right in front here, from Bourlon to Vendhulle."

"What happened?"

"An attack in force against the new positions. Dozens of divisions to every one of ours. We've no reserves worth speaking about, so the boys in front just had to fight it out or make a run for it."

"And what happens to us now?" I ask in some surprise.

"Oh, you're a couple of recruits towards the scratch army they are collecting in the village; clerks, lorry-drivers, road-menders and anyone they can lay hands on. You never saw such a crew. Talk about Fred Karno's army,

you'll see it in a minute. Thank God we still have a navy"
—and he laughs at the very thought.

"And what about you guys?" Webby asks. "Why don't
you take a hand?"

Our guide turns a bit rusty:

"We'll do our bit all right, don't you worry. The infantry
aren't the only ones who can fight."

"Sure," Webby agrees. "Sure you boys will show Jerry
a thing or two. We've nothing to worry about, Jock, so
long as the M.P.s are at the back of us. That's the damnable
bit, though, they never get any further than our backs."

"We've got our jobs to do, same as you," our guide
excuses himself.

"That's all right, chummy"—and Webby pacifies him a
little. "We're just unlucky, that's all."

The track runs through a small wood, then over a rise
in the ground, and we get a view of a main road and a
village half a mile away.

We have come from extreme solitude into pandemonium,
which the rise in the ground we have just topped has, up
till now, hidden from our view. Refugees, army lorries, an
odd battery of artillery and troops galore, while in the
village itself, confusion, supreme and absolute.

At the entrance a horse-drawn transport is standing,
and a military policeman is flinging out bandoliers of
ammunition and shouting at the top of his voice: "Now's
your chance to prove you are men," while the mob around
the cart scramble for the bandoliers.

A quartermaster beside another cart is dishing out rifles,
gas-masks and various other items of equipment. A corporal,
looking worried to death, comes up the street yelling:
"Any machine-gunners here, any machine-gunners?"

And yet under this crust of seeming confusion there is
a certain amount of solid orderliness.

All newcomers are taken to a hut at the end of the
village. Name, number and regiment are given, and from
there we visit the various lorries in the street, until we
arrive at the far end as fully equipped as the establishment
can make us. We are then marched to a field and form up
in companies, the finest ragtime army I have ever seen.
Labour companies, road-menders, cooks, signallers, a

detachment of balloonists, a company of engineers composed practically of old men well over military age, and odd details like ourselves roped in from anywhere and everywhere. There are one or two officers and a few N.C.O.s. Some know the words of command, others don't, but they all do their damnedest to make us look like a fighting force.

Suddenly there is a commotion on the road; someone shouts "Jerry's coming." The cry is taken up by a few more, and there is a general stampede from all directions. Officers shout and N.C.O.s roar but can't stem the rush towards the houses of the village. Why they make for that quarter I don't know, unless with the idea of getting under cover. All eyes are on the road, expecting to see a detachment of Jerries come rushing down; instead a couple of transport lorries come into view and stop at the beginning of the village. The drivers are anxiously questioned regarding Boche patrols, but they've seen nothing. Just another scare started by some nervy blighter who has let his imagination run riot.

I look around our parade ground, but there's barely a hundred of us left. Webster, myself, an Australian, two artillerymen and four infantry boys are all that have stood their ground in our company; the remainder are even now returning. The first whiff of wind has separated the unripe seed from the seasoned fruit, and it is strange how we old hands recognise each other and herd together. Experience has taught us that it isn't always the safest plan to run away from an imaginary foe.

Back come the runaways, joking and laughing now that the first shock is over. They treat the affair as if it had been great fun. There's no real windiness about them. Just a lack of discipline—somebody ran towards the houses, and like sheep they followed.

Our N.C.O.s get us into some semblance of parade order and stand us at ease until a major arrives. We are then drawn up to attention while he gives a little speech calculated to put some fire into our veins, following on which we form fours after a style and march away towards the front.

Two miles further on and some motor lorries are drawn up by the side of the road. Into these we pile, then forward once again.

Excitement begins to run high amongst the miscellaneous crowd in our lorry when we pass a few ambulances and a stream of refugees, then a despatch-rider, followed shortly after by a gun team at the gallop, after which we hear the more ominous signs—the dull thunder of guns.

Webster and I don't talk much. We just smoke in silence and listen to the chatter of the others. For myself, I miss the familiar faces of our own crowd. This collection of scratch battalions, from anything in the shape of a man with a trigger finger, be he young or old, looks serious to me, and by that I also mean serious for me. I'm not particularly interested at present in the rest of the army, or the nation, if it comes to that, but in what this means to me, to Webster and the rest of us here. It's evident we are up against it, and, unfortunately for us, we are on the spot and will have to take the brunt of anything that's going. That may mean nothing, and again it may mean everything. But what's the good of worrying? What did that old padre say : "Put your life and trust in God's hands and He will carry you through"? Sure, that's it, I feel better already. The rough edges have disappeared, and I am left without any worry as to the future.

Webster gives me a dig and nods in the direction of a group clustered at the side of the road. There are close on fifty, I should think, all our own fellows without rifles or equipment, and in charge of four military police.

I look at Webby :

"Forgot to stop running, I expect," he murmurs. "Well, we are getting near it now, Jock."

Machine-gun fire sounds very close at hand, and I am not surprised when the lorries come to a halt. We jump down and fall in behind the shelter of an embankment. All the sounds of war are present, but very little traffic on the roads, only regimental transports and wounded.

We are marched up in sections towards a village and take up positions in a shallow trench at the extreme edge. The village has evidently been reoccupied by civilians until recently and hasn't been heavily shelled so far. Goods from the three shops it boasted are littered about on the roadway outside. Some of the doors of the houses are wide open, others are heavily barred and shuttered, odds and ends are scattered all over as if dropped by the civilians in their haste to get away.

It's a very different kind of war to what I have known so far. This is the first village I've been in near the line where the civilians haven't been cleared out years ago. My only thought is : there must be something worth while picking up in this place, and I can hardly wait for darkness before going on the scrounge.

Before doing any souvenir hunting, however, we make a start to strengthen our little length of trench, but are interrupted by a sergeant, who wants to know if we can handle a Lewis gun.

"Just a little," I answer.

"And what about you?" he enquires of Webster.

"I know one when I see it," is Webster's non-committal reply.

"Come on, then, follow me"—and the sergeant gets quite excited. "I've found four guns in this village, and there's a splendid field of fire from the end house there."

We trail after him along the trench and climb out of it opposite a house. Entering the kitchen we see, lying on the bed, two Lewis guns and several drums of ammunition. We cart them upstairs and fix up one gun in the front room. A shell has done all that is necessary as far as getting a clear uninterrupted view of the surrounding country is concerned, but in the back room, where we place the second gun to protect our flank, it is necessary to knock out a few bricks near the window before we can get it properly sighted.

That finished, we stand back and admire our handiwork.

"What's happening in front, sergeant?" I enquire.

"Haven't the foggiest," he replies. "All I know is, anything is liable to happen right here. Nobody seems to know where Jerry is. He may be miles away, and again he may come round that bend in the road any minute, so keep your eyes skinned, you fellows," he advises. "I'm going across the road to fix those other two guns. We'll give Jerry quite a hot time if he does come our way. There's a whole dump of ammunition down the street, so I'll send some drums along to you, and, by the way, try out those guns when you get them properly fixed"—and with these parting instructions he clumps down the stairs.

We toss for guns and I get the one in the front room, so start straight away putting into practice my pet ideas regarding gun posts. A few more bricks are knocked out of the wall to extend my view, and a protection of stone-work, together with anything I can lay hands on, is built in a semicircle round the gun, then camouflaged as much as possible. When completed I survey my handiwork with some pride, and suddenly realise I am sitting in a wicker arm-chair. I look up and there's my reflection in a full-length mirror. I look such a queer object that I burst out laughing, and Webby comes into the room to see what the joke is.

"Sit down," I invite him with a wave in the direction of another chair, "and make yourself at home." I'm just think-ing I'll have to raise that gun a little if I'm going to work it from this position.

"How's this for a war, Webby? Arm-chairs and every home comfort, even a bed over there in case you get tired of scrapping."

Just then there is a commotion down below and I yell out :

"Who's there?"

"Sergeant sent us over," comes the answer.

"Right," I shout down. "Wipe your feet on the mat and come right up."

Six young fellows from a labour battalion come into the room, all grins.

"We've got some ammunition," one of them volunteers.

"Good. Half of it here and the other half in the other room," I tell them, "and make yourselves at home, boys, you're at your auntie's."

Webster suggests taking a look over the house to see what other comforts it can provide, so we go downstairs and commence in the kitchen. We overhaul it thoroughly, but unearth nothing more exciting than a barrel of salt herring. I lift out a couple but they are positively stinking, so, in disgust, we go upstairs again. Even there, however, not a darned thing worth lifting can we find, not a souvenir in the whole place. I pull out drawers in a dressing-chest, but they are all empty bar the bottom one, and it is full of clothes and ladies' underwear. I take them out and hold them up for inspection : combinations, woollen knickers, silk knickers very pleasant to the touch, half a dozen silk chemises, a few dresses, garters, stockings, a bottle of perfume, an empty powder bowl and a puff on the end of a stick, all very exciting, but not of much use to a soldier, and I am busy putting them back again when I suddenly remember I am lousy, as usual, and here is a golden opportunity to secure clean underwear. I've always had a fancy for silk next to my skin, so why not?

Off comes my equipment, tunic and cardigan, while I instruct one of the fellows to keep a lookout for approaching sergeants or officers. The lousy shirt I throw into a corner, and, amidst the laughter of the boys, I get into a pink chemise, giving a strut round the room in front of the mirror, but the colour doesn't suit my complexion so off it comes and I try on a pale green one. It is rather nice but has too much lace about it for my masculine taste, so before discarding it and to please the fellows, I entertain them with a dance in the centre of the room, and am just in the throes of some talented high kicking when from across the road comes a "Coo-ee, Pansy." My kicking comes to an abrupt end, and looking through the hole in the wall I see at one of the windows in the house opposite half a dozen men grinning and waving across.

With a fair imitation of a girl caught in the act of dressing I go over to our own window, from which the glass, of course, has disappeared, and with an exaggerated show of annoyance, pull down the venetian blind, but I forget to fix it and as soon as I loosen my hold it springs up again with a clatter and a bang. Immediately there are more "Coo-ees" and chirpings from across the street, so I try again, and this time make sure that it is secured before leaving. Off comes the green chemise and my fancy runs to a blue one. It seems just right, at least so the boys say, and I step over to the mirror to admire myself. One or two ribbons must be removed though, and I am struggling with the last one when there is another burst from the other side of the street and a voice exclaiming "Blimey, it's a tart." The blind is still down, but I've forgotten the hole in the wall, so, as there is obviously no privacy in this house, I pull the blind away from its fixtures and fling it beside the lousy shirt in disgust. Then for the benefit of the spectators, and to the enjoyment of those in the room, I make a pretence of powdering myself with the puff on the end of the stick, splash on some scent, shove the tail-ends of the chemise where they should be, and to the accompaniment of prolonged boos and some chump with a voice like a foghorn who keeps on yelling "Coo-ee, Pansy," I put on my tunic and equipment.

"That's fine," I tell the others in the room; "there's nothing like silk next the skin. Gee, I feel like a thousand pounds."

"You smell like a bloody skunk," is Webby's rejoinder, amidst general laughter.

Just then the sergeant's arrival puts a stop to our fun, and he gives us our instructions.

We are the garrison of the house, he explains. Webster is to be in charge of one gun, myself the other. That agreed on, he leaves us to sort ourselves out. We make sure the guns are working properly, place the ammunition handy and decide to have four on duty with the guns and four off, Webby and three of the others taking the first spell. That settled, I take off my equipment and with a jump land on the bed. It almost collapses under my weight, but not quite, so I make myself comfortable, while the others of my command grab chairs and prepare to follow my example.

I am almost asleep when the first shell comes screeching over and bursts further up the street. It is followed by another and another in quick succession, until they are dropping regularly in the village and vicinity.

The sergeant comes rushing up to our house, yelling for us to bring down the guns and get into the trench. We don't require to be told twice, so, loaded with the guns and drums of ammunition, we make a dash across the fifty yards that separate the house from the trench. It won't be so snug but it certainly will be safer.

This looks like a preliminary bombardment to an attack, and we wait nervously for what may turn up. Nobody seems to know anything definite, so a patrol is sent out to find who, if anybody, is in front of us, but it has hardly been gone a quarter of an hour when a runner arrives, and we are ordered to advance in open order.

. An eerie job this, plodding forward in the gathering dusk not knowing what you are going to stumble up against. Shells start flying around, and we have our first casualties, but they have only been chance shots and soon fade away.

Onward we go until we come to a trench manned by wounded and stretcher cases, then up a communication trench and into the front line. Weary haggard-looking men enquire who we are, then with a "Thank Heaven somebody has come," file out of the trench, in most cases without even bothering about the formality of handing over. But what does that matter? they've been relieved at last and "Fred Karno's army" has taken over.

Chapter Twenty-Four

WEBBY MISSING

December (date unknown) 1917, Lost. *Webby missing.*

WE have been here four nights and three days and still no sign of a relief, while the transformation in our scratch army goes steadily on in the hard school of experience, making veterans out of recruits and providing beyond a vestige of doubt the old army adage : "They may breed soldiers in England, but they make them out in France."

. Precariously we hang on to our slender line of trenches with only a few strands of wire in front, no dug-out, no cover from the sleety rain that falls incessantly, no reserves, no rations, utterly exhausted, almost sleeping on our feet, our nerves never at rest day or night. I marvel at the strength of human endurance and how we have the guts to stick it out.

· Night after night we repel an attack or raid, while day

after day we labour in mud and sweat to repair the ravages of shell fire, always hoping and praying that to-morrow our relief will come. Feverishly we work during the early hours of darkness to strengthen the trenches and make some semblance of a front against the attack which may come at dawn.

As the bombardment increases, we cower and cringe in the puny shelters we have dug in the side of the trench, our tin hats drawn well over our heads to the side on which the shells are falling, a useless precaution but one from which we derive some feeling of security.

The shelling continues, puffs of shrapnel bursting above us and thudding into the sides of the trench. We are in an inferno of noise, blood and death, and yet some of us still live. Crouched in my funk-hole I pray and call upon my Maker to protect me; life is so sweet and I don't want to die. Each explosion seems like a stab at my heart, nerves all over me are pulsing and throbbing and my breathing laboured as the cordite fumes hang low in the trench.

And then as suddenly as the shelling commenced it stops. Dazed and confused, not knowing what will happen next, we man the parapet, but no field-grey uniforms appear across the open. Why can't they come and get it over? If only the relief would turn up; that is our only hope.

Towards afternoon we attempt to get up some rations. Four of us successfully reach a dump, and with loaded sandbags start the return journey. It is hard going, and as we stop for a breather in a shell-hole, Webster realises we have forgotten the most valuable item of the lot—the rum ration. None of us, however, is very keen to retrace our steps even for a jar of rum, so there is nothing else for it but to toss up. We do so but my luck is entirely out, and with a few curses I start off. I reach the dump safely, and burdened with the rum jar I commence my second journey back. From shell-hole to shell-hole I dodge, clasping the jar as if it was the most precious thing on earth, but it would almost appear as if the Jerry gunners were having a game with me. No matter what direction I take, shells rapidly fall and hem me in. At last, breathless and relieved, I stumble into the shell-hole in which I left the other three; it is empty. Surely I've mistaken it, and yet this should be the one. There's the broken duckboards on one side and the tree stump on the other. A little uncertain, I investigate half a dozen shell-holes round about, but still no sign of the others. I shout again and again without any reply, then return to the hole beside the tree stump. Yes, I'm certain this is the one, but it isn't like Webby to move off this way, he'd wait even if the others didn't. Suddenly I realise the hole is much larger than when we first dropped into it. Yes, there's no doubt about it, I can see where the other shell burst just at the side there.

The rum jar is forgotten as madly I run round in a circle, regardless of falling shells, shouting "Webby, Webby," but there is no answer, not even a scrap of equipment lying about. Back I go to the hole and delve with my fingers into the churned-up earth, but a strip of sand-bag and a tin of bully beef are my only reward. Deeper and deeper I scrape as my numbed senses begin to realise what has happened until, frantic with doubt and utterly exhausted, I can only stare at the battered tin of beef. And as if to mock me in my helplessness, I fancy I hear Webby's voice reciting one of his favourite pieces of trench philosophy :

"The safest place is a shell-hole; you'll never find a shell drop on the same spot twice."

Then again that song of his :

"Old soldiers never die, they only fade away."

I refuse to believe that such a fate could have befallen Webby, it just couldn't, he must have gone on without me. I reach our trench, still hugging the jar of rum, but the others have not returned. They'll come back, I keep on telling myself, or, at the worst, they're only wounded.

The day creeps in and still no sign or word of Webby and the others. When the stretcher bearers arrive at dusk I anxiously enquire if they have seen anything of them, but I seem to have been the only one who saw them after they left the dump. I begin to lose hope, and the words of that cursed song keep recurring to my mind :

"Old soldiers never die, they only fade away."

We live on through a night of feverish anxiety, and as dawn approaches the shelling breaks out afresh. It grows and grows until it reaches a pitch when the air is full of rasping demons, of flashes and flying missiles, the earth just one great upheaval. Then it ceases, and for a second not a sound is heard from the other side. We scramble out of funk-holes and man our positions, peering across the strip of ground that separates us from the Boche, and away to our left we see the waves of field-grey uniforms streaming across no-man's-land.

Once more the storm breaks on our trench, intermingled this time with the sharp clap, clap, clap of machine-guns. We cower down and wait.

Idly I watch the pigeon-man and officer fix messages to the legs of two pigeons, then free them, and up they soar. One second they are there, thirty feet above the ground, the next they have gone, just disappeared. A feather or two floats gently down, and the pigeon-man makes off for another pair of birds. He has only been gone three or four minutes when a lance-corporal pokes his head round the traverse shouting "Duggan's hit, sir."

"Badly?" enquires the officer.

"Dead, sir, a shell got him."

"Had he the birds with him?"

"Don't think so, sir; didn't see them."

"All right, corporal."

Then turning to me :

"Purves, see if you can get those pigeons and bring them here."

"Very good, sir"—and off I go.

There's very little semblance of trench left, and I have to crawl past the spots where the parapet has been blown down, over dead bodies, and past wounded who groan when I knock up against them. I step over Duggan's body, he's dead all right, and further along in a little niche cut out of the trench side I find the wooden cage with the two pigeons. I wait a little as three shells fall in quick succession on the trench just ahead, then make a bolt back to my own section.

One of the birds is taken out. Poor creature, it is cooing away as if it was in some quiet country loft, or at some village race meeting. The message is soon fixed and up the bird goes. I watch it until it is lost to sight, but the lieutenant keeps his glasses trained on it, then as he lowers them :

"It's down, we'll have to send a runner."

I pass the word along for a runner. After some delay the corporal from the next bay comes round again:

"No runners left, sir, the last two haven't returned yet. Shall I send one of my men?"

"No, that's all right, corporal."

Then to me:

"Do you think you could manage it, Purves?"

This is what I had dreaded, but there's nothing else for it.

"I'll do my best, sir."

"Good. You know where battalion is. If you go in a straight line you can't miss the sunken road, it's dead straight ahead from here. Read the message first. Now then"—and he gives me a stirrup lift on to the parados and I scramble over. For the first two hundred yards there are few shell bursts, but the shrapnel and machine-gun bullets whistle and smack into the ground around me, and I begin to feel that they are all sniping at me as I crawl blindly onwards afraid to lift my head as the bullets stream over me. I can't possibly cover much more ground without being hit. Where will I get it? The head, I expect. No, that's fatal, I must keep my head down and I press my face so close to the ground that I breathe in earth. It gets in my nostrils and mouth, but I must keep my head well down.

Hope begins to revive as I leave the area of bullets behind, and lie and listen. Yes, there's only a stray one now and then, so I get on my feet, but a sudden hiss-hiss-hiss past my ear makes me hurriedly flop down again. It takes me minutes to summon up sufficient courage to move on again, then, bent double, I start darting from cover to cover. Somewhere ahead lies battalion headquarters dug-out and a respite from this storm of death; so buffeted and knocked about by concussion I stumble on. The shelling increases around me, dense smoke and hot fumes almost blind me, there is a quivering of the ground under my feet and I realise I am well inside a barrage. I make a dive for a shell-hole from which the smoke and fumes still rise, but before I reach it there is a terrific shock just at my feet as the earth opens up in front. Something knocks my legs from me, there is a flash, hot air chokes me, then there is a terrifying explosion. I am conscious of all these things in a matter of seconds, but the next time my bewildered brain functions, I am lying on my side with a stinging, burning pain in my legs. I try to move them and find that I can, but the effort is painful and I am glad to lie still until finally an overpowering thirst makes me attempt to sit up and get my water-bottle, but everything becomes grey and foggy and I immediately lie down again, hovering on the borderland of sleep and wakefulness. Slowly darkness creeps over my eyes. I am tired—so tired, and as vainly I try to rouse myself, ghostly hands haul me over the brink to forgetfulness.

Chapter Twenty-Five

A BLIGHTY

December 8th, 1917, GOING DOWN THE LINE. *Can hardly believe I'm leaving it all. Yet I'm not completely happy. Have a feeling I'm leaving something worth while behind.*

IF I raise my head a little I can just see from the rear of the ambulance lorry the long winding road unfolding itself like a mysterious grey ribbon, guns, limbers, ammunition columns and parties of infantry, all going the same way "up to the front."

But the day for which I have longed and prayed has arrived. I am going down the line, away from it all, and yet a strange feeling mars my happiness. It is something I cannot define very clearly, something almost beyond my ability to explain. I am leaving this man-made hell. That occasions my joy and also my sorrow, my joy at escaping from the shadow of death so lightly, my sorrow at losing all the things that shadow gave me.

No sunset was ever so entrancingly beautiful as the one the evening before an attack, no dawn so bewitching as the one that came with zero hour.

Scudding clouds and drenching rain, how exhilarating and refreshing when marching to a fire and a roof.

Did hot tea ever taste so much like wine as that first mouthful after hours of fighting? Was there ever a place like home when you might never see it again? What friendship so strong and above the strain of everyday life as that formed in a shell-hole with death hovering around?

These are the things that shadow has given me, and though I may be leaving them behind, I must never forget them.

And those staunch comrades I'll never see again on this earth. Mac, who rests peacefully in a little cemetery on a gentle Picardy slope. Webby, who has no known grave, whose restless spirit must for ever haunt the water-logged flats of Flanders, prowling unseen over rain-soaked ridges and hovering in the valleys at dawn with the morning mist as its shroud, seeking, always seeking, the resting-place that was denied its earthly form. Streaky, Naylor, Taffy, old Bellchamber, and all those others I knew whose very names spell "The Salient" to me.

Whatever is before me and whatever life brings, I must always be a better man for having known these things and lived with such men.

Perhaps I have nothing to be sorry for; death has passed me by as I always had a feeling it would, and a new chapter is opening out before me. I must make it my second "Great Adventure," and like the old grey-haired padre, I'll put my life and trust in God's hands, and He will carry me through.

THE END

War in Tandem editions

The War Dispatches Sir Philip Gibbs 25p
Four-and-a-half years of front-line reporting from the
carnage of the First World War

The Conspirators James Graham Murray 25p
These spies played for the highest stakes – and lost

RAF Biggin Hill Graham Wallace (illus.) 30p
The immortal story of one of the Battle of Britain's most
famous fighter stations

The Battle of Britain (illus.) 25p
Official records from the British and German sides and the
recollections of the pilots themselves. The really
authentic story

Operation Cicero L. C. Moyzisch 25p
The most sensational true spy story to come out of the
Second World War

Wingless Victory Sybil Hepburn 25p
An Englishwoman, trapped in Occupied France, waged a
cloak-and dagger war against the German invaders

The Valley of the Shadow H. Oloff de Wet 25p
Six years a prisoner of Nazi Germany, four years under
sentence of death – *he survived*

They Hosed Them Out John Beede 30p
The short, savage fighting life of the Australian air-
gunners of the R.A.F.'s big bomber squadrons

The Red Baron Joe Lavinia..   ..   ..   ..   25p
One came for a gentlemen's duel, the other – to kill

The Israeli Air Force Story Robert Jackson (illus.)   ..   35p
'It is written by a man who understands what war in the air
is all about' *The Economist*